LOVE BOOK: The Top 50 Most Trusted Experts Reveal Their Secrets for Relationship Success

Published by
Excellent Publications
A division of Excellent Communications, LLC
205 De Anza Blvd, Suite 46
San Mateo, CA 94402
http://www.ExcellentCommunications.com

©2009-2014 Copyright by Scott Braxton, Ph.D., MBA
Second Edition 2014
Cover design by Zenergy Designs

ISBN-10: 0-9842092-0-4
ISBN-13: 978-0-9842092-0-0
Manufactured in the United States

1. Family and Relationships 2. Love and Romance
I. Title.

Table of Contents

INTRODUCTION

Why this Book is an Essential read... For Everyone!

Relationship therapy has developed a long way from the stereotypical angry couple sitting on a leather couch in front of a therapist taking notes; each partner struggling to articulate how they feel about their problems, with very little in the way of solutions. Often, couples leave this type of counseling feeling more aggrieved about their situation than when they began, with emotions of hurt and anger brought up by the criticism hurled at them by their partners.

In the past two decades, there has been a shift in relationship therapy, with a surge in the number of experts offering groundbreaking techniques that really do work. Browse the self-help shelves of any bookstore and you'll be amazed at the amount of relationship books written by experts from a multitude of backgrounds and disciplines.

What this new wave of love experts have in common is self-help therapy that not only focuses on the couple creating solutions, but also the importance of working on oneself to create a perfect relationship with another. What they profess is the need to look inside ourselves, and work on our own self-esteem and personal responsibility within a relationship. Otherwise, love and marriage can simply end up a viscous circle of hurt, blame, shame, and guilt.

We are reaching a tipping point in consciousness with regards to self-empowerment. Everywhere you look, self-help gurus, including relationship experts, are promoting the importance of taking responsibility for our own lives, and looking within to create a better universe around us. With the divorce rate and the number of single parents still rising, people are beginning to realize that moving from one relationship to the next is not a solution; all our life baggage comes with us from one partner to another. Relationship therapy in the twenty-first century is as much about personal growth as it is relationship growth.

1

Why this Book was Written

The reason I decided to write this book is to bring together the combined wisdom of the best relationship experts into one central resource; to enable everyone to empower him or herself to create the most joyous and loving relationship possible.

This book helps you find an expert with a style that suits you, without being bewildered by outlandish claims of fixing a marriage in a matter of days or being charged thousands of dollars for a therapy that has no relevance in today's society. You will also be able to triangulate many different styles that all have the same aim – to foster a safe attachment – to increase happiness, contentment, communication, and connection – to learn how to grow within a relationship and heal the pain from past traumas, and to really express the love you have always wanted to express. The guidance each expert provides focuses on self-development within a marriage or relationship, yet these love philosophies and simple-to-use techniques can also be applied to all types of relationships, from family to work, parenting to friendship.

In the coaching work I do, people kept introducing me to new and amazing teachers: "Have you heard of so-and-so? They are my favorite and you simply must read them!" Reading their books, I was astounded at the simplicity and the clarity of the message. I wondered to myself (and sometimes to my partner), "How could I have not known about this person?!" I realized that an in-depth study of the relationship experts was just what I needed. I created my own survey, similar to a university course in "English Literature."

It would be nearly impossible to create a complete list of all the people who are making a difference to individuals and couples. This book could easily become the top 101 or 1001 experts. With some trepidation, this book was ultimately limited to the top 50 experts.

Who Should Read this Book

There is something in this book for everyone. Each and every one of us has some kind of relationship in our life. You may not be married or have a partner right now, but almost everyone has experienced some kind of relationship or has the desire to be in love. And that's what this book is all about – making those relationships the best they possibly can be.

You may be thinking, "But I'm happily married and never argue with my partner!" That may be the case, but somewhere along the line you will encounter experiences that may put pressure or strain on your relationship. Equipping yourself in advance with the tools required to deal with that stressful time can make the difference between feeling isolated, stressed, and alone or that your partner doesn't understand what you're going through, and maintaining a loving relationship where you work together. You may also find tools that will allow you to expand what you thought possible in a relationship.

You may be in a difficult marriage – at breaking point, and cannot decide whether to call it quits and file for divorce, or stick with it. Perhaps you've just found out that your partner has been unfaithful, but for the sake of the children, you're considering staying together, but have no idea how to forgive them and let go of the pain.

Maybe you may have been together for over 20 years and have started to feel like your relationship is merely a routine with no passion or vitality. Do you need help to break out of bad habits and create once again a beautiful and harmonious relationship that fills you with joy?

Perhaps you may find yourself in a relationship of unbalanced sexual desire. You may be wondering, "What happened to my spouse?" You want to know what you can do to bring back the spark, like when you first met.

3

Perhaps you have just come out of a difficult relationship, or spent years alone and want to know where you've been going wrong. Maybe you feel angry towards your ex and are desperate to find another love match who will prove to be the one for you, and you can finally get what you want – a life-long loving commitment.

Or simply, you may just have an interest in creating the best relationship life can offer. This book gives you access to experts who use techniques that have helped couples create the most loving relationships possible. You may have seen an expert on TV, in the newspaper, or have been recommended someone by a friend, and you want to find out more before you buy their books.

Whatever your interest in relationships, this book provides an easy to read guide to the best of the best – with each chapter offering thought-inspiring information and valuable techniques to start you on the road to relationship heaven.

How to use this Book

There are many different ways to use this book:

Finding the Best Expert for You

Maybe you've spent hours on the internet or in a book store looking for help to improve your relationship but are confused by the huge amount of experts out there. You are worried their technique won't work for you, or perhaps you find some experts too technical or steeped in confusing psychology. This book provides clear and concise information about the best relationship experts, with each chapter offering an accessible and easy to understand introduction to a different expert, their relationship philosophy, and what their work entails. Examples show you their work in action. Quotes will give you a feel for the way they speak and write, and will generally help you decide whether that person is the right expert for you.

A Resource of Ideas and Information

You may wish to discover the collective wisdom of many different relationship experts. Each may have a nugget of information that relates to a different part of your life, offering you collective guidance to create relationship harmony. Imagine sitting in a room with the top 50 relationship experts in the world, and each of them giving you a piece of wisdom for personal empowerment and relationship success. That is exactly what this book can offer you.

A Guide to Knowing More

You may have heard of a particular expert and want an easy to read explanation of what their therapy is all about. This book gives you an insight into the philosophy and mind of each expert with an overview of their work, background, and qualifications; as well as links to their personal websites so that you can find out more for yourself.

Daily Inspiration

The book is a wonderful resource of thought-provoking advice and inspiring quotes from the greatest relationship teachers on the planet. Simply reading a chapter every day offers you gentle reminders and countless tips for relationship joy and harmony that you can put into practice.

How the Experts were Selected

Finding and selecting the top 50 relationship experts was a challenge! There are now so many experts out there, many of whom have published works that are available in bookstores or on-line as eBooks. Of course, the process involves some subjectivity, but what we have done is to choose experts according to the following criteria:

- ♥ **Need** – We looked for recurring themes that cause relationship stress
- ♥ **Popularity** – in terms of internet, book success, media appearances, and Google searches
- ♥ **Recommendation** – by other internationally acclaimed self-help experts and authors
- ♥ **Accessibility** – how applicable, accessible, and effective their methods are for the average member of the public

How the Order of the Experts was Determined

There are many ways to order the experts, such as alphabetically, by specialty, area of focus, etc. Here, we chose the way we organize much of our information: by popularity. Popularity was determined by the number of Google searches for an expert's name. Is this system perfect? No. Some experts have common names, and so this method may overestimate the number of searches.

Although getting advice is not based on popularity, this is a valid method of organizing the experts. If many people are searching for an expert, it is either because they have something good to say, or they have a very large platform from which to say it. Dr. Phil and Tony Robbins may be higher on this list because of their broad audience appeal. However, they got these large audiences because they have something valuable to say.

How the Chapters are Organized

Each chapter is a detailed summary of a relationship expert, and contains the following elements:

Background and Qualifications

This provides a biography of the expert; highlighting qualifications and experience, as well as notable achievements. The information adds credibility to each expert, outlining the grounds upon which they stake their relationship advice.

Relationship Philosophy

Provides an overview of the guiding philosophy each expert has used when establishing his or her therapy techniques and methods. It gives simple explanations of the theory behind the practice.

The Therapy

Provides an explanation of how the relationship philosophy is put into practice, with some advice and tips which can be used on a daily basis to begin work on your relationships.

Examples

Provides examples of the therapist's work.

Quotes

Outlines a sample of quotes that provide daily inspiration and an insight into the thinking and writing style of each expert.

Books and Media

Reviews an overview of published titles and TV appearances. All titles are available through personal websites or online through booksellers or in bookstores.

How to Find Out More

Each chapter provides links to the expert's personal webpage, where you will find book excerpts, case studies, articles, advice, and sometimes video links; as well as how to get in touch with the expert directly.

 LOVE BOOK

What about Oprah?

Many people have asked, "What about Oprah?" Oprah has done so much for the self-help community and for relationships, that it almost seems absurd to not list Oprah among the Top 50 Relationship Experts.

Oprah has been described as "The Patron Saint of Self-Improvement." She has provided an opportunity for thousands of self-help gurus to deliver their message to millions of people. Many of the people on this list have either gotten their start on the *Oprah Show*, or have made at least one appearance. For these people, being on the *Oprah Show* was an e-ticket to fame.

She was born Oprah Gail Winfrey on January 29, 1954, in poverty. She is now a media mogul and philanthropist. The Oprah Winfrey Show has earned many Emmy Awards, and is the highest ranked talk show in the history of television.

Her website, *www.oprah.com* helps people in areas as diverse as spirit, health, style, relationships, home, food, money, and the world. She hosts a magazine called "O," has numerous TV, film, and radio involvements, and a book club. Her new Oprah Winfrey Network offers a lifeclass and access to a variety of spiritual leaders and wisdom.

Oprah's Angel Network is for people who want to make significant social impact around the globe. She has many philanthropy projects, such as O-Ambassadors: A group of people who empower others with the opportunity to learn, grow, and break out of poverty. The Creating Schools project helps build schools in poor, remote areas of South Africa. The Leadership Academy is a safe place for girls to learn; where they will be inspired to greatness.

Oprah, on behalf of everyone who is struggling to be responsible for their own life and happiness, thank you for raising the consciousness of the planet.

Expert Synopsis, Alphabetical Order

The following list includes 50 of the best relationship experts in the US today and the page number to read more.

84 *Barbara de Angelis* focuses on empowering people to change their own lives, with positive messages about love and relationships. A best-selling author and personal transformation teacher, Barbara has sold over 8 million books worldwide, including *Secrets About Men Every Woman Should Know and Chicken Soup for the Couple's Soul.*

176 *Alison Armstrong* discovered that women tend to emasculate men as a protection mechanism. She teaches that when women relate to men, taking into account their fundamental differences, they can create trust and have truly satisfying relationships. The founder of the PAX programs, Alison presents the *Celebrating Men, Satisfying Women* workshop to share her research of men.

90 *Dr Laura Berman* is a leading expert on female sexual health. She teaches how to reconnect with your mind and body and with your partner, to get the sex life you've always wanted, and that you deserve. Dr. Berman is The Relationship Expert for Oprah.com.

220 *Dr. Jeff Bernstein* teaches that the way we think about our partners can kill trust, erode intimacy, and cripple communication. He has over 20 years experience counseling couples, children, teens, and families. Author of *Why Can't Your Read My Mind: Overcoming the 9 Toxic Thought Patterns that Get in the Way of a Loving Relationship,* Dr. Bernstein aims to break the toxic thinking cycle and replace it with new and more positive thinking habits for solving relationship stresses.

66 ***David Burns*** shows couples how to change their feelings and behavior by adapting the way they think, using the principles of Cognitive Behavior Therapy. He also points out that people will behave towards you in exactly the way you think about them. He explains how to take a criticism and turn it into an opening for deeper discussion.

122 ***Dr. Leo Buscaglia*** known as "Dr. Hug," Leo was known for creating joy in others by being a cheerleader for life. He taught that you create love by showing love to others. At one time, five of his books were on the New York Times Bestsellers List simultaneously. Dr. Buscaglia touched the lives of millions with his insights into how to seek happiness and create loving relationships.

159 ***Dr. Susan Campbell*** sees intimacy as the spiritual path to wholeness, and notes that many couples end up projecting unresolved issues onto their partner. She has noticed that much of communication is with the intent to control others or the outcome. Giving up the need to control opens the possibility to relate by revealing what's true for you, in this moment. She teaches that being honest and real is the quickest, most direct path to wholeness.

343 ***Dr. Gilda Carle*** teaches the importance of projecting Personal Power and of providing a safe environment for people to open up and share their feelings and fears. Gilda teaches that if one has high self-value, one is able to set healthy boundaries. She is the author of best-selling books: *Don't Bet on the Prince! How to Have the Man You Want by Betting on Yourself!* The New York Times described Dr. Gilda as "the busiest TV therapist in the business."

34 ***Dr. Gary Chapman*** focuses on the premise that everyone needs to feel and express love. People express love in different ways, and this can lead to misunderstanding and conflict. The author of *The Five Love Languages,* which has sold 5 million copies worldwide, Dr. Chapman is a minister and a marriage and family expert with over 30 years experience of marriage counseling.

169 *David Deida* teaches people to "enjoy sex as a cosmic portal," to know your purpose and give your gifts fully, and to master the challenges of work and sexual desire. According to David, sexual attraction is based on sexual polarity, and he teaches how to build passion that arcs between the masculine and feminine poles. Deida is the author of several books, including *The Way of the Superior Man.*

215 *Dr. Bill Doherty* teaches couples to be intentional about their marriage. He focuses on the need for couples to acquire the skills needed to make marriage work. Dr. Doherty is author of five books on relationships and parenting, including *Take Back Your Marriage: Sticking Together in a World that Tears Us Apart,* and has made regular appearances on many nationwide shows.

132 *Patricia Evans* is an interpersonal communications specialist on the topic of verbally abusive and controlling marriages. Evans offers workshops and seminars, is an international author, and has appeared on *Oprah* and *CNN.*

111 *Dr. John Gottman* has come up with a way of predicting marriage success based on the study of emotional communication. Along with his wife Julie, John teaches and writes on building a fulfilling marriage and sustaining relationship. He is author of *The Relationship Cure* and *7 Principles for Making Marriage Work.*

41 *Dr. John Gray* focuses on how men and women communicate differently. The author of *Men Are From Mars, Women Are From Venus*, which has sold over 40 million copies worldwide, John is an expert in communications, helping men and women understand, respect, and appreciate their natural differences.

268 *Dr. Willard Harley* helps couples restore the love they had, rather than focusing on resolving conflict. The author of *His Needs, Her Needs* and *I Promise You: Preparing for a Marriage that Will Last a Lifetime,* Harley works alongside his wife as a marriage coach, helping couples restore the feeling of love.

209 *Drs. Gay and Kathlyn Hendricks* assist people in opening to more creativity, love, and vitality. They invite couples to focus on enhancing the common and shared interests, rather than on differences. Gay and Kate are the therapists behind the Hendricks Institute, and co-authors of *Conscious Living*.

184 *Dr. Harville Hendrix* created the Imago Relationship Therapy to help people replace confrontation and criticism with a healing process of better listening. The best selling author of *Getting the Love You Want: A Guide for Couples,* Hendrix is a clinical counselor who, along with his wife Helen LaKelly Hunt, developed the concept of conscious partnership. One of his many appearances on *Oprah* was included in her top 20 shows of all time.

355 *Drs. Lana Holstein and David Taylor* have been frequent guests on *Oprah* and *CBS Early Show.* Lana is an expert in sex problems and author of *How to Have Magnificent Sex: The 7 Dimensions of a Vital Sexual Connection.* Drs. Holstein and Taylor host the four-day retreat, *Partners, Pleasure, and Passion,* based on the book which they co-authored, *Your Long Erotic Weekend: Four Days of Passion for a Lifetime of Magnificent Sex.*

75 *Dr. Sue Johnson* is the pioneer of Emotionally Focused Therapy (EFT); helping couples create safe emotional bonds with their partner. Dr. Johnson is the director of the Ottawa Couple and Family Institute in Canada and trains counselors in EFT worldwide. She is the author of *Hold Me Tight*, a book for the public, based on the 7 steps of EFT.

51 ***Byron Katie*** created a simple yet powerful method of self-inquiry into the cause of all suffering. By following the four questions of The Work, one is led to a place of freedom, peacefulness, and joy. She has introduced this method to millions of people across the world. Her best-selling books have been translated into thirty-three languages.

317 ***Ellen Kreidman*** has helped men and women put the fun in romance, and the excitement back in relationships. A *New York Times* bestseller, Kreidman has appeared on *CNN, Montel, Oprah,* and regularly in the *New York Times* with her innovative approach to couple's counseling. Kreidman claims her method, *Light his fire, Light her fire* is much quicker than marriage counseling.

230 ***Dr. Harriet Lerner*** is best known for her work on the positive aspects of Anger. Lerner specializes in the psychology of women and family relationships; helping people understand how relationships operate; why they go badly; the part we play in the pain we feel; and how to have the courage to navigate relationships in clear and truthful ways. She is the author of a series of books, including *The Dance of Anger, The Dance of Intimacy, The Dance of Deception*, and *The Dance of Fear.*

97 ***Dr. Pat Love*** helps people discover the connection they felt when they first met. She is known for warmth and humor as she teaches about the fundamental differences between men and women. For more than twenty-five years, she has contributed to relationship education and personal development through her books, articles, training programs, speaking, and media appearances. She has appeared numerous times on *Oprah, The TODAY Show*, and *CNN.*

329 ***Dr. Howard Markman*** is a leading researcher on the prediction and prevention of marital distress. He believes that people wait far too long to gain the skills required to have a healthy marriage. Through the Prevention and

Relationship Enhancement Program (PREP), he offers education to use before problems arise. His books include the bestseller *Fighting for Your Marriage* and *12 Hours to a Great Marriage*. He also offers couples retreats based on his research and has appeared on *Oprah*, *The TODAY Show*, and *20/20*.

293 *Dr. Barry McCarthy* helps couples in no-sex or low-sex marriages improve their sex lives. He provides individual, couple, and sex therapy for adults. Dr. McCarthy is a tenured professor at American University, has a clinical practice, and teaches workshops. He is the author of *Rekindling Desire, Coping with Erectile Dysfunction* and *Getting it Right This Time*.

21 *Dr. Phil McGraw* uses a "get real" strategy to counsel people. Dr. Phil says, "What you don't acknowledge, you can't fix." After making his name on *Oprah*, Dr Phil now has his own TV show teaching people to take responsibility for their own thoughts and behaviors and helping guests resolve complex relationship problems.

348 *Olivia Mellan* believes that money is an extremely emotionally loaded topic. It is tied up with our deepest emotional needs such as love, power, happiness, freedom, self-worth, and security. With over 25 years of experience, Olivia is a trained psychotherapist and money coach. She teaches about the different money personality types, and how to maximize the good qualities and minimize (or change) the shortcomings of each type.

201 *M. Gary Neuman* believes the most common relationship problems are caused by emotional infidelity, because people fail to put enough focus and attention on their marriage. Emotional connection is so important that its lack is the number one reason men have affairs. He teaches the 10 secrets to a great marriage; starting with commitment and co-dependence.

237 *Kara Oh* teaches people to dismantle the barriers to intimacy they have built in response to childhood wounding. Author of *Men Made Easy,* Kara Oh helps men and women create satisfying long-lasting relationships. She has appeared in numerous women's magazines, and has been a guest on hundreds of TV and radio shows.

147 *Susan Page* offers strategies that one partner, acting alone, can use to create a harmonious marriage. Rather than resolving conflict, couples instead should focus on feeling happy together in Spiritual Partnership. Author of *How One of You Can Bring the Two of You Together*, Page has made appearances on *Oprah*, *CNN*, and *Good Morning America*.

225 *Drs. Les and Leslie Parrott* help people become better soul mates by "saving a marriage before it starts." Best selling authors, the Parrotts founded the Center for Relationship Development at the Seattle Pacific University and have pioneered the marriage-mentoring program.

196 *Dr. Margaret Paul* is an expert on marriage and relationships, and co-creator of *Inner Bonding*, a 6-step transformational, spiritual healing process for couples. Inner Bonding focuses on taking responsibility for your feelings, listening to and learning from them, and taking loving action that comes from your Higher Guidance. Her book, *Do I have to Give Up Me to Be Loved by You?* sold over a million copies. Her clients include actress Lindsay Wagner and singer Alanis Morissette.

243 *Drs. Peter Pearson and Ellyn Bader* authors of *Tell Me No Lies,* Bader and Pearson run the Coming From Your Heart Program, which helps couples resolve their difficulties, face the truth, and build a loving marriage. They have over 20 years experience working with couples, and have appeared on *The TODAY Show* and *CBS Early Morning News*.

281 *Terrance Real* helps people focus on what they do want in their relationship. Author of *I Don't Want to Talk About it, How Can I get Through to You?* and *The New Rules of Marriage,* Terry has been a practicing family therapist for more than twenty years. He teaches women to replace accusation with understanding, and men how to become emotionally mature, and step up to the marriage plate. His work has been featured on several programs, including *Oprah* and *Good Morning America.*

361 *Dr. Jonathan Rich* believes that money is always a volatile topic for couples, especially in a difficult financial climate. He teaches that everyone has a particular financial personality that influences our choice of lifestyle, risk tolerance, and willingness to accept help. Dr. Rich helps couples resolve money disputes through understanding, communication, negotiation, and joint financial goals, to create a more secure financial future.

260 *Dr. David Richo* offers practical and spiritual exercises for couples and families who want to have mature and loving relationships. He is a psychologist and author of *When the Past is Present: Healing the Emotional Wounds that Sabotage our Relationships* and *How to be an Adult in Relationship: The Five Keys to Mindful Loving.*

26 *Tony Robbins* is a recognized authority on the psychology of leadership, negotiations, organizational turnaround, and peak performance. He designed *The Ultimate Relationship Program* to give people the tools and strategies needed to create sustainable excitement and lasting fulfillment in their relationships.

189 *Dr. Marshall Rosenberg* believes that needs are behind all communication. The core of conflict and emotional pain are needs that are not being met. The author of *Nonviolent Communication; A Language of Compassion,* Dr. Rosenberg founded the Center for Nonviolent Communication to teach the communication skills people require to get their needs met, to actually hear their partner's underlying desire for connection, and to live peacefully.

287 **Dr. Gail Saltz** is a psychiatrist, best-selling author, and regular sex and relationship contributor on *The TODAY Show* and *Oprah*. In her book, *Becoming Real,* Saltz claims the key to having fulfilling relationships is first being comfortable with yourself. Her therapy involves understanding and rewriting the stories from your childhood to free yourself from your past.

59 **Dr. Laura Schlessinger** helps women see that men need direct communication, respect, appreciation, sexual intimacy, and nurturing, and that in return, they will respond with devotion, compassion, and love. Men have an underlying desire to protect and cherish their wives, if only women would allow them to. She teaches the 10 stupid things couples do to mess up their relationships. Dr. Laura gives straight-talking, often controversial, advice on the radio to over 8 million listeners weekly.

338 **Drs. Charles and Elizabeth Schmitz** teach the 7 core values to have a loving relationship. Doing these simple things every day shows your partner how much you love, value, and respect them. Known as The Marriage Doctors, the Schmitz are authors of *Golden Anniversaries: The 7 Secrets of Successful Marriage,* and have over 25 years experience helping couples.

252 **Dr. David Schnarch** believes that marital problems are an essential part of individual and relationship growth. He is a licensed clinical psychologist and author of numerous books and articles on intimacy, sexuality, and relationships. The Crucible Approach® is widely regarded as the most sophisticated integration of sexuality, intimacy, spirituality, personal development, and marital therapy developed to date.

152 ***Dr. Gary Smalley*** outlines five promises that couples can make to increase their marriage security and satisfaction. The author of *The Language of Love and Change Your Heart, Change Your Life,* Dr. Smalley has spent over 35 years teaching and counseling couples and families in the Christian path.

103 ***Dr. Robin Smith*** believes that self-knowledge is the fundamental key to success in any marriage. You have to discover who you are, and work on your own issues and baggage in order to have a truly fulfilling relationship. It is possible to be love struck after 25 years, if the core of the relationship is strong and healthy. Dr. Robin has a call-in radio program 5 days per week on *Oprah and Friends*.

323 ***Dr. Janis Abrahms Spring*** is an expert on issues of trust, intimacy, and forgiveness. Janis is author of the award-winning, *After the Affair, How Can I Forgive You?* and her latest, *Life with Pop: Lessons on Caring for an Aging Parent*. Janis is a Diplomat in Clinical Psychology, has been in private practice for more than 3 decades, and is a popular media guest and speaker at venues such as the *Smithsonian Institute, Smith College, NPR,* and *Good Morning America*.

311 ***Dr. Steven Stosny*** believes that compassion is essential for a good relationship. He helps people overcome issues of anger with the Power Love Formula to provide moments of connection. He is the founder of Compassion*Power*, and has written many books and articles on anger and relationships. He has been featured in most major print and broadcast media, including several guest appearances on *Oprah*.

127 ***Michael Webb*** is known as "The Worlds Most Romantic Man". Webb specializes in helping couples relight their romance and feel more intimate. He has appeared on over 500 radio and TV shows including *Oprah, Fox News, NBC*

News, and is author of *1000 Questions for Couples* and *The Romantic's Guide.*

278 *Michele Weiner-Davis* is the author of the Divorce Busting series. Weiner-Davis runs various centers to help marriages in crisis and prevent what she terms as unnecessary divorce. She has made countless TV appearances, including *Oprah, 20/20, The TODAY Show,* and *CNN.*

302 *Dr. John Welwood* believes that a relationship can be a transformative path by working with emotional conflict from the past and challenges about the future. The Author of 8 relationship books, including *Journey of the Heart,* Welwood is a clinical psychologist and psychotherapist who combines Western psychology with Eastern spiritual wisdom.

46 *Dr. Ruth Westheimer* is the famous psychosexual therapist who first made her name in the early 80's. Known for her frank discussions of sex and masturbation, Dr. Ruth has become a household name. She focuses on the importance of "sexual literacy" to help couples create a thriving and conscious sex life.

139 *Dr. Jeffrey Young* believes that many disruptive patterns of thinking and behavior were laid down in childhood. These habits, or "schemas," can affect our current relationships in dramatic ways, because they form the basis of our sense of self, and it can be frightening to let them go. The first step is recognizing when one of the 18 schemas is running you, and how it makes you behave.

The Experts by Popularity

1. Dr. Phil McGraw

"Get Real!"

Background and Qualifications

Born in 1950 in Oklahoma, Dr. Phil is a relationship and life strategist who has been married for 31 years and has two sons.

He made his name on *Oprah* in the early 90's, and is now host of the nationally syndicated series *Dr. Phil*, an intervention style show that helps couples, families, and individuals with life issues – from relationships to addictions.

Dr. Phil has a BA from Mid Western State University, and an MA and PhD in clinical psychology from North Texas State University. He opened his first practice in 1979 with his father. In 1989, he founded Courtroom Sciences Inc., designed to assist the legal profession with mock trials, behavioral analysis, jury selection, and mediation. It was this business that was to change his destiny, as he was hired by Oprah Winfrey to help her case against Texan beef farmers, who claimed she'd defamed their industry during one of her shows. Oprah was so impressed by Dr. Phil, that she gave him a regular slot on her show to help couples with their relationships.

Relationship Philosophy

Dr. Phil's brand of therapy is focused around what he terms, "get real counseling." He takes a no-nonsense approach: telling clients exactly like it is, to help them take responsibility for their own behavior, in order to create more positivity in their lives. He works through a series of steps with couples and individuals to strip through their emotional clutter and get to the root cause of their issues.

The Therapy

Dr. Phil's style provides simple to use techniques and exercises that any couple can employ to help improve their relationships.

21

His books are easy to read, containing workbooks that couples can complete alone or individually, which are explained simply, with effective solutions that can be easily employed. His basic concepts are:

- ♥ **The power of friendship:** Dr. Phil encourages couples to work on building a solid friendship between them, based on knowing and trusting, with the aim of meeting each other's needs.

- ♥ **Set specific relationship goals:** Each person within a couple finds a quiet moment each day and comes up with a specific goal to improve their relationship. It could be as simple as calling your spouse everyday just to tell them, "I love you," or working on better listening techniques to make your partner feel more appreciated. Dr. Phil believes this is one of the keys to relationship success.

- ♥ **Getting back to basics:** Work together on defining what makes a successful relationship and take responsibility for living up to those definitions. Focusing on these fundamental issues will make all the difference in the long run.

- ♥ **Take responsibility for your role:** Dr. Phil is very clear that you can't control the way your spouse acts but you can control how you react to their behavior and decide whether that takes a negative course or not.

- ♥ **Don't argue in front of the kids:** Dr. Phil also works hard with couples who have children to stop them arguing in front of the children, which he terms as "nothing short of abuse."

Examples
A Family in Crisis

Dr. Phil worked with married couple Chris and Stacy over several episodes of his show. This family in crisis was struggling to get over adultery, being threatened with bankruptcy, and facing parenting problems. They were on the brink of divorce and presented Dr. Phil with a whole host of challenging problems.

Stacy admitted to cheating on Chris three times during their five and a half year marriage, and had even conceived her baby during the last affair. She ended up giving her son up for adoption. Things looked hopeless for this couple and they went to Dr. Phil in one last attempt to save their marriage.

Straight away, Dr. Phil offered his tough-talking, get real approach; preparing them for a difficult journey where they would both need to be completely honest about their emotions and take ownership of their problems. To Stacy he said, "You are conning yourself. You're conning him. You're conning your family, but you ain't conning me!" Stacy was encouraged to grow up and get real about her role as a mother, wife, and individual; rather than turning away from her partner.

However, Chris also had to take responsibility for his part in the relationship. "Step up and both command and demand respect. Lead this family with dignity!" Dr. Phil advised. Chris needed to set a standard for his relationship; that Stacy treat him with dignity and respect. It was as though Chris had taken so many knocks throughout the relationship that he'd stopped being a man as well as an individual.

Dr. Phil also worked with Chris to stop him blaming himself for Stacy having an affair – "I'm not saying you're a perfect husband, because you're not. But you don't own her decision to have an affair."

Using challenging homework tasks, Dr. Phil helped Chris and Stacy feel more empowered in their relationship and face up to their emotions and problems. Despite still having a long journey ahead of them, they began to take responsibility for who they were in their relationship and work towards achieving relationship success.

Sex Wars

Newlyweds Mark and Rachelle were having problems in their sex life because Mark was working 85 to 90 hours per week. Rachelle was left feeling neglected and worried that Mark could be getting sex elsewhere. Mark on the other hand, felt so much pressure from Rachelle for sex after a tough week at work that making love no longer felt like fun – it became like a job. Both were sick of arguing about sex just 7 months into their marriage.

Dr. Phil asks Mark, "If you're at a point where you succeed in business but lose your wife and damage her in the process, is that OK? A relationship is like a garden – if you water and feed it, it will grow into a beautiful garden. If you only go out there every few weeks to look it over for a few moments, what do you think it's going to look like in a few months? It's going to be a weed patch. It will disappear."

After the show, Mark and Rachelle realized they needed to pay more attention to their relationship. It was the small things that started to change, which overall made a significant difference. Both took a morning off a week so they could wake up in each other's arms, Mark left love notes around the house, and now says, "There isn't a day that's going to go by where I don't do one little thing to show her how I feel."

Dr. Phil McGraw Quotes

- *You don't fix things by fixing your partner!*
- *You get what you give. When you give better, you get better!*
- *Forget whether you're right or wrong. The question is whether what you're doing is working or not working!*
- *The success of a relationship is a function of the extent to which it meets the needs of two people.*

Books and Media

Dr. Phil has sold 24 million copies of his books in 39 different languages across the globe, and has had three New York Times best-sellers. His books are very practical and simple to read, often including workbooks to put his words into practice. He has also dedicated several books to weight loss and family matters.

His best-known relationship books include:

- *Life Strategies: Doing What Works, Doing What Matters*
- *The Life Strategies Workbook: Exercises and Self-Tests to Help You Change Your Life*
- *Self Matters: Creating Your Life from the Inside Out*
- *Relationship Rescue: A seven-step strategy for Reconnecting with Your partner*
- *The Relationship Rescue Workbook: Exercises and Self-Tests to Help You Reconnect with Your Partner*
- His latest book, *Love Smart: Find The One You Want, Fix The One You Got* is a step by step plan for finding not just any relationship, but one that is committed, joyous, and loved filled.
- Dr. Phil's show was an immediate success, becoming the second highest rating daytime show behind *Oprah.* As part of his show, he also set up the *Dr. Phil House,* where couples are observed 24/7 to monitor their dysfunctional behavior, with surprise visits from Dr. Phil to intervene.

How to Find Out More

- Go to his show's website: *www.drphil.com*

2. Tony Robbins

"The way we communicate with ourselves and others ultimately determines the quality of our lives."

Background and Qualifications

Acknowledged as the "father of the life coaching industry," Tony Robbins has been a motivational speaker for over 3 decades. Best known for his teachings on the psychology of leadership, peak performance, and negotiation, he has spoken to over 1 million people across the world in 75 countries. His most famous work is the audio program, *Personal Power*, which is the number one selling audio coaching system of all time (over 35 million copies sold). Tony also created the *Ultimate Relationship Program*, a 10-day program that helps anyone to create a passionate, and truly loving relationship.

His desire to help others began in childhood. He grew up in a difficult household and was always looking for ways to resolve his issues. During his teens, he began to study Neuro-Linguistic Programming (NLP) and trained under John Grinder, one of the founders of NLP. He began to use the techniques to help family and friends resolve their issues and once he began to see results, he developed a positive addiction to helping people transform their lives.

Tony is married to Sage, his second wife, who helps deliver the *Ultimate Relationship Program*. He describes Sage as his "ultimate prize" and aims to help others achieve the true joy of having a relationship filled with both love and passion. Tony is also a father of four children.

Relationship Philosophy

Robbins finds it remarkable that people spend so much time on developing their career and financial well-being, but often neglect their emotional development and working on their relationship. Robbins believes that human motivation is driven by the desire to fulfill six basic human needs. They are the primal forces that shape all of our choices. If the first 4 needs cannot be met in a healthy way, people resort to any method to get them met. The last 2 needs are the needs of the spirit.

6 Human Needs

1) Certainty/Comfort
2) Uncertainty/Variety
3) Significance
4) Love/Connection
5) Growth
6) Contribution

Many couples may comment on how they never argue, but Robbins believes that arguing and disagreement are usually essential elements in a passionate relationship. Without the passion for disagreement, a relationship can become dead and nothing more than a friendship. Robbins wants people to realize that love and passion are what give life meaning. For a relationship to be truly successful, both are essential and should coexist alongside each other. Furthermore, true passion does not have to die over time. If you work on your relationship, then passion can grow and grow. Couples who never argue may have lost interest in each other.

5 Main Stressors

Relationships can be threatened by five main stressors that can cause a break up and destroy love. These are:

27

1) **Loss of attraction**: this has little to do with how you look physically and more to do with the "spark" between a couple.

2) **Frustration and annoyance**: when you no longer feel attracted to your partner, little things they do start to annoy you. Your "behavior filter" changes and the things that never used to annoy you, now become highly irritating. What can happen from here are the four R's: resistance, resentment, rejection, and repression.

3) **Loss of physical passion**: anger and rejection can so easily get in the way of a physical relationship. Often, when a partner does not want to have sex, the other person can feel rejected and angry, yet it may actually have nothing to do with them. It may be problems at work or financial worry, so it is vital to talk about these issues. Also, some people also resort to using sex as a tool, denying their partner a physical relationship as a punishment or to get what they want from them. But the problem with this is that punishing a partner in this way only destroys passion.

4) **Loss of commitment**: this is where a person really begins to feel their partner is no longer there for them, that they're not important to them anymore. They may not be physically cheating, but emotionally they are no longer present and may be seeking emotional support from elsewhere.

5) **Incompatibility**: when you begin to think you're just not suited to each other, this is "relationship death." Very often, a person begins to build the story that they never should have been together, and once a "story" has been created, that person constantly looks for evidence that it's true.

Robbins teaches that it is possible to reverse all five of these stressors by looking at what's truly going on in the relationship.

The Therapy

The *Ultimate Relationship Program* contains DVD's, CD's, Daily Discipline Cards, and an Action Book. The ultimate goal of the program is to create a relationship where love and passion become a daily experience. Robbins bases his work on helping people get their 6 basic needs met in a healthy way. He also examines the forces that inspire pure excitement, joy, and passion between two people, and helps couples to create sustainable and lasting fulfillment in their relationships. This is done using a number of techniques: developing trust, learning to practice the art of giving (which balances your partner's needs, your needs, and the outside pressures of day to day life), breaking down communication barriers, truly expressing yourself with heartfelt honesty and intimacy, and aligning with your partner so that you're truly supportive of each other.

When working with a client, Robbins utilizes the 7 Master Steps to Lasting Change.

The 7 Master Steps to Lasting Change
- ♥ Understand Your World
- ♥ Obtain Leverage – why is change important
- ♥ Interrupt Habitual Patterns
- ♥ Define the Problem in Solvable Terms
- ♥ Create New Options
- ♥ Condition the Change – mentally rehearse the change
- ♥ Relate to a Higher Purpose

Most importantly, Robbins emphasizes the need for commitment to change. It's a difficult process to break down and release the stories we create in our minds about our partners and ourselves, but it's only once we give up these stories that we can have the a wonderful relationship with ourselves and the most important people in our lives.

29

Examples
Need for Certainty

Paul stood up in an audience of 4000 people and said he was scared that if he left his wife, he would lose his identity, his self-worth, her love, and love of himself. Paul was initially attracted to how loving and giving his wife was. Now, he thinks she over-gives to everyone else but him. Tony speaks with his wife, Jenn, because she is the dominant one in the relationship. Tony must understand and change what is holding her back from her husband. He asks Jenn what her top human needs are, and she replies that she needs certainty first and love/connection second. Jenn is not able to feel love, or anything else, until she is certain. She rates herself as a "2" on a scale of 1 to 10 in certainty, and admits that she needs a level "7" to feel comfortable. When she needs certainty, she turns to her children, and ignores her husband. When Jenn is able to access her feelings of love, even without certainly, she radiates, and her husband spontaneously pulls her close in an act of love and protection.

Tony asks Jenn how she tests her husband. At first, she is reluctant to say, but admits that she pulls away and gets defensive to see what Paul will do. She will also question and undermine what Paul says. When she does that, Paul pulls away too, and a crazy eight pattern ensues, where one partner feels sad, lonely, hurt, abandoned, and depressed, and the other partner becomes angry and hostile or cold and unresponsive. When we blame the other for how we feel, we stay stuck in this pattern. The way out is to change physiology, focus on something you can control, then change mood, and take oneself out of the destructive cycle.

When people do not get their needs met in their primary relationship, they will find another way to get them met outside the relationship. For Jenn, she got certainty from her family and children. Paul needed significance – to feel important – and he got that need met at work and from the fantasy of leaving Jenn.

For their marriage to work, each must find a way to meet the other's needs.

To really drive home the message, Tony asks Jenn what Paul has been giving her that she can't get from her family or her children. She replies, "Love and connection and certainty." However, she is really getting those from her family. "Um, I don't know..." is her answer. Tony says "How many of you can see where the problem is now? If it takes you that long to figure out what he can give you, it reinforces his deepest fear: that he isn't the most important thing in your life. All he knows is that you continually tell him he is not enough. He will search out someplace where he is enough."

Tony walked her through the 6 human needs to see at what level Jenn was satisfying each of Paul's needs. Her answers ranged from 2 to 4 on a 10-point scale. For the first time, she could understand why Paul would want to leave her. Just hearing Jenn understand has turned Paul around. He is willing to give her the certainty she craves. Tony asks Paul to come up with specific actions that he will take to demonstrate his love.

Pattern Interrupt

We have probably all been in arguments that seem to take on a life of their own. Perhaps we have even forgotten the reason behind the argument, yet we will continue, intent on making our point and "winning" the argument. You may have already found that you cannot really win, because when you do, you don't feel victorious, and the other person is left feeling diminished. These types of fights can be the most destructive elements of a marriage.

Tony notes that people fall into arguing patterns because they don't know what else to do. He suggests that interrupting the pattern of a senseless argument is much more effective than sitting down to a long, sensitive, and tormented dialogue about the destructive effects of arguing (i.e. blaming *them* and *their*

31

behavior). How do you interrupt a pattern? Do something out of the ordinary that induces confusion, then create the desired emotional state. You could take a walk, start dancing, or use a silly code word that you both agreed on up front.

Tony and his ex-wife Becky used the phrase from Saturday Night Live: "I hate it when that happens," as a way to interrupt an argument that either of them feels has become destructive. It breaks the negative state and causes them to laugh and let go of the argument. If there is a real issue that needs to be discussed, they can talk about it later, when negative emotions are not clouding the issue.

Tony Robbins Quotes

- *You can't punish your partner without punishing yourself.*

- *Some of the biggest challenges in relationships come from the fact that most people enter a relationship in order to get something; they're trying to find someone who's going to make them feel good. In reality, the only way a relationship will last, is if you see your relationship as a place that you go to give, and not a place that you go to take.*

- *The only thing that's keeping you from getting what you want is the story you keep telling yourself.*

- *Beliefs have the power to create and the power to destroy. Human beings have the awesome ability to take any experience of their lives and create a meaning that dis-empowers them, or one that can literally save their life.*

- *If you don't feel like you're growing, you're dying.*

Books and Media

Tony Robbins' media credits are too numerous to mention. His work has been featured in major publications worldwide and he has been interviewed on most major talk shows.

- The *Ultimate Relationship Program* includes 6 DVDs, which feature real-life couples going through relationship problems and the interventions by Robbins, as well as 6 accompanying audio CDs and an Action Workbook with strategies and assignments. There is a professional edition of the program for therapists.

o *Tony Robbins' Inner Strength Films Series 2: Relationship Storms: Man Enough to Stay the Course, Back From the Edge: Creating Everlasting Love, Finding Your True Passion: The Power of Honesty in Action*

Robbins has many other audio programs as well as several books in the realm of personal empowerment. Titles include:

📖 *Awaken the Giant Within*

📖 *Unlimited Power: The New Science of Personal Achievement*

📖 *Relationship Breakthrough: How to Create Outstanding Relationships in Every Area of Your Life*

How to Find Out More

💻 For more information, go to *www.tonyrobbins.com* and *www.ultimaterelationshipblog.com* where you will find video messages from Tony and Sage Robbins.

3. Dr. Gary Chapman

"The language of love"

Background and Qualifications

Dr. Gary Chapman is a marriage and family life expert with thirty years of biblical marriage counseling with thousands of couples.

He holds BA and MA degrees in anthropology from Wheaton College and Wake Forest University, plus an MRE and PhD from Southwestern Baptist Theological Seminary. He has also completed postgraduate work at the University of North Carolina.

Dr. Chapman wrote his first book in 1979, *Towards a Growing Marriage,* which began as an informal resource he gave to couples he was counseling.

For the past 37 years, he has been a pastor in Winston-Salem, North Carolina, and has been married for 47 years, has two children, and two grandchildren.

Relationship Philosophy

The focus for Dr. Chapman's work stems around the concept that everyone needs to feel loved. According to Dr. Chapman, the only way to achieve making your partner feel loved is to make sure you speak their love language.

Love can be expressed in different ways by givers and receivers, and it is this misunderstanding of love and the way it is communicated that can lead to arguments and conflict; even divorce. Usually, we speak to our lover only in the love language we most want. However, once we understand the five languages of love and are willing to learn our spouse's primary love language, then we can become an effective communicator of love and have a more fulfilling relationship.

The Therapy

Dr. Chapman guides couples to understand their unique language of love and enables them to learn to speak and understand their partner's love language. There are five love languages, and each person tends to have a natural affinity for one over the others.

The 5 Love Languages

♥ The Language of **Quality Time**: a person feels closest to their partner when they receive focused attention. It's about focusing all your energy on your mate, through quality conversation, shared experiences or activities, and active listening.

♥ The Language of **Words of Affirmation**: a person feels most valued when told how they're appreciated for their special way. Simple statements such as, "You look great in that suit, or "I love your cooking – you must be the greatest chef in the world!" are appreciated. Words of Affirmation can also be communicated through encouragement, such as reinforcing a difficult decision or acknowledging a person's unique perspective on an important topic.

♥ The Language of **Receiving Gifts**: a tangible expression of love, which demonstrates to you that your partner cares enough to show it. People who speak this language often feel that a lack of gifts represent a lack of love from their partner.

♥ The Language of **Acts of Service**: a person feels most loved when a partner helps them carry out their responsibilities and duties. It's important to understand which acts of service your partner appreciates the most and carry them out in a spirit of love rather than obligation.

♥ The Language of **Physical Touch**: a person feels most loved when their partner makes contact and embraces them. This can be making love, a back massage, or a simple touch on the cheek or hand on the shoulder – especially during a conflict situation. Those who speak this

language feel security and love from being touched by their partner.

Dr. Chapman says his wife's love language is acts of service, so even though he hates doing it, he shows her how much he loves her by always vacuuming the floor. It may sound like a simple gesture, but these small signs build up to prevent resentment and ensure a fulfilling relationship.

Examples
Drifting

Dr. Chapman believes that if any couple just drifts along in their marriage, they will always drift apart. Couples never drift together. Marriages therefore, require a lot of hard work.

He recalls an engaged woman he once started chatting with at an airport. After discussing his work in marriage counseling and seminars, she was shocked that people require help to work on their marriage. "Isn't love enough?" she exclaimed. Dr. Chapman knew instantly that she had never been married before. "Anyone who's been married, whether successfully or not, knows it requires work."

Dr. Chapman believes that being in love during the early part of a relationship is always fun and easy, but it's coming off the love high that requires work and forging a new way of communication. "Communication is key... it's as important to a relationship as breathing is to the body."

The Early Stages of Marriage

Dr. Chapman draws on his own marriage experience to stress the difficulties newlyweds may face. Just 6 months after marriage, he was miserable, and so was his wife. That's because they hadn't yet learned the skills to be good spouses.

A good marriage requires learning, fostering love, communicating, building up your spouse, money management skills, and sexual intimacy. Although we come to marriage with these raw materials, there's no such thing as a ready-made marriage. It requires work to build a wonderful and joyous marriage from those building blocks.

Discovering Love Languages

It was discovering each other's love language that truly benefited the Chapman marriage. Dr. Chapman learned that his wife's love language is acts of service, although he didn't know this in the early days of marriage. He used to blame her for their poor marriage, having the attitude that if she would just listened to him, they'd have a good marriage! "Of course she wouldn't listen... our marriage got worse and worse, until I realized my attitude towards my wife was wrong. It hit me like a ton of bricks!"

He had expected his wife to meet his needs, without meeting hers. His marriage changed when he began to ask her the following three questions:

- ♥ What can I do to help you?
- ♥ How can I make your life easier?
- ♥ How can I be a better husband to you?

The answers came as he let her teach him how to serve her. In doing so, her attitude towards him changed too, and she began asking the same questions of him.

Still, to this day, in order to speak his wife's love language, Dr. Chapman washes the dishes, vacuums, and takes out the garbage as acts of service. Recently, his wife noticed how dirty the window blinds were. So one morning, Dr. Chapman got up and vacuumed them. When she asked what he was doing, he simply replied: "Honey, I'm making love!" A big smile shot

across her face and she said, "You have got to be the greatest husband in the world!" which spoke his love language: words of affirmation.

Money Can't Buy Happiness

Dr. Chapman also teaches couples about the importance of resolving money conflicts within a marriage. It's important to learn how to manage money within your relationship; otherwise, this issue can become a source of misery and frustration. Learning how to communicate about money can help improve your marriage. The first step in doing this, is to realize that when you say, "I do" the concept of "yours" and "mine" disappears, and everything becomes "ours." This extends to debts as well as assets.

Some of the happiest couples Dr. Chapman claims to have met are those who are financially just above the poverty line. Money certainly does not buy happiness, but you have to develop honest, fair, and loving strategies for handling your savings, investments, possessions, and debts, in order to work as a team and build a stronger relationship.

Dr. Gary Chapman Quotes

- We each come to marriage with a different personality and history...with different expectations, different ways of approaching things, and different opinions about what matters in life. We need not agree on everything, but we must find a way to handle our differences so that they do not become divisive.
- Love is a choice. And either partner can start the process today.
- Forgiveness is not a feeling; it is a commitment.
- I am amazed by how many individuals mess up every new day with yesterday.

🗩 *If you are telling yourselves, "We'll be happier when we get more money," you are deceiving yourselves.*

Books and Media

📖 Since 1979 Dr. Chapman has written more than 20 books, with his MUST HAVE book, *The Five Love Languages: How to Express Heartfelt Commitment to Your Mate* has sold over 5 million copies in 38 languages worldwide. His other titles include:

📖 *The Five Languages of Apology: How to Experience Healing in All Your Relationships* (with Jennifer Thomas)

📖 *Love as a Way of Life: 7 Keys to Transforming Every Aspect of Your Life*

📖 *Home Improvements: The Chapman Guide to Negotiating Change with Your Spouse*

📖 *God Speaks Your Love Language* (The Love Language of God)

📖 *The Four Seasons of Marriage*

📖 *The Five Love Languages of Teenagers*

📖 *The Five Love Languages of Children*

📖 *The Five Love Languages of Singles*

📖 *Profit Sharing: The Chapman Guide to Making Money an Asset in Your Marriage*

📖 *The Family You've Always Wanted: Five Ways You Can Make It Happen*

📖 *Desperate Marriages (Loving Solutions)*

📖 *The Five Love Languages: Men's Edition*

📖 *Now You're Speaking my Language: Honest Communication and Deeper Intimacy for a Stronger Marriage*

📖 *Anger: Handling a Powerful Emotion in a Healthy Way*

- *Everybody Wins: The Chapman Guide to Solving Conflicts Without Arguing*

- *Love Talks for Couples: 101 Questions to Stimulate Interaction with Your Spouse*

- *The Marriage You've Always Wanted* (Toward a Growing Marriage)

- His latest books are *Love As a Way of Life: A 90-Day Adventure That Makes Love a Daily Habit* and *Love as a Way of Life: Seven Keys to Transforming Every Aspect of Your Life.* The seven characteristics of a loving person are not just an add-on to the five love languages; they are the foundation for every language of love. What if a significant number of people in our society developed an attitude of love, so that love actually became a "way of life?"

- Dr. Chapman also hosts his own daily radio program, *A Love Language Minute (formerly Growing Marriage),* which is broadcast on 100 stations across the US.

How to Find Out More

- Go to Dr. Gary Chapman's website, *www.garychapman.org* or *www.fivelovelanguages.com.*

4. Dr. John Gray

"Martians and Venusians speak entirely different languages."

Background and Qualifications

Dr. John Gray PhD has over thirty years experience as a family therapist and has made his name famous worldwide through his book, *Men Are from Mars, Women Are from Venus.*

Gray originates from Texas and is married with three children. He is a certified family therapist, having run his own practice for 15 years, and leading personal growth seminars for thirty years.

Relationship Philosophy

Gray's relationship philosophy focuses on the differences between men and women, the way they communicate, deal with emotions, and act in relationships. He claims they even have different brains; with women having more neural receptors than men, which is the main reason women can deal with a lot of things at once and men have to manage things in a more sequential order.

According to Gray, "Martians" and "Venusians" speak different languages when it comes to relationships. For example, she may ask, "What is wrong?" He might simply say, "Nothing, it's OK," which simply means, "I need to withdraw into myself and be alone in my cave!" For women who don't understand the language barriers of Martians and Venusians, this can be seen as a rejection or bring up a fear that her partner no longer loves her, causing unnecessary resentment and conflict.

Or a woman might talk about her problems and her partner may think she is complaining. But for a woman, talking about her problems is a form of sharing – a positive experience, whereas for men it can be seen as a negative – something he is

41

responsible for and must fix. It is these fundamental differences that cause conflict in relationships.

Gray believes it is also during the stresses of modern life in particular that Mars and Venus can collide, because of the different ways they cope with stress. Once again, by understanding these differences, couples can prevent arguments from even happening.

The Therapy

Through lectures and seminars, Gray teaches men and women how to communicate better and achieve relationship harmony by acknowledging the differences between them. There is a compromise required in every relationship, but he teaches that this compromise shouldn't be at the expense of oneself and who you truly are.

The original book, *Men are from Mars, Women are from Venus,* guides you through improving your relationship one day at a time. One of Gray's top tips to reignite the flame of passion is to set a romance diary to help improve communication and connectivity by setting a challenge one day at a time. For example, Martians should ask how their partner's day was and really listen to her answers – asking several questions to show interest. When she needs reassurance, offer it willingly and without judgment. Give her a hug when he gets home before anything else, and write her a love letter and send it in the post.

Venusians can show their men love by letting him know about something he did that week that she appreciated, and thank him for it. Venusians should also never forget that if he pulls away after being close, it doesn't mean he doesn't love her, but that he's doing the very best for both of them, and that he's with her because he loves her. To stir up his passion, a Venusian could send him an SMS text to tell him what she's wearing under her outfit and that she craves his touch!

All these romance techniques focus on the way each gender gives and receives love and optimizes the chance for intimacy.

Examples

Yes, I am from Mars! My wife is from Venus!

Dr. Gray injects humor and fun into his lectures and seminars, bringing stories about his own relationship to illustrate his points. It's obvious when watching the audience when those "eureka moments" occur – when Gray says something so strikingly obvious yet they'd never come to that realization in their own relationship.

For example, while discussing the differences in what makes men and women happy, a huge reaction comes from the audience as many have that moment of realization. Gray explains: "Whenever a woman is happy it brings a man up. Whenever a man is happy, it does little for a woman! Women don't brag about making their husbands happy, they brag about how he made them happy."

For example, "He noticed I got my hair cut!" This is something a man can do for his wife that will make her feel truly happy and special – noticing things. Gray tells how he used to wonder why his wife always told him on a Monday she would be getting her hair cut on Thursday. Men don't go out and tell people they're going to get their haircut! But he came to the realization that it was to prepare him to notice on Thursday that she'd had her hair cut without her having to prompt him.

Why Focus on Differences – How About Similarities?

Many of Dr. Gray's critics question the importance of focusing on differences between the sexes. Wouldn't it be better to embrace similarities in order to create peace? Gray's response to this question is that of course we should embrace our similarities, but if we don't recognize the way we are different – physically how we're made and hardwired – when problems

arise because of these differences, we can end up judging or blaming our partners and being torn apart by conflict. All it takes is an understanding that our partner is hardwired to be the perfect support in our life. He quotes Seinfeld by saying, "If partners were made to be just like us, it would be completely boring – they would finish all our jokes!"

Dr. John Gray Quotes

- *We mistakenly assume that if our partners love us, they'll react and behave in certain ways – the ways we react and behave when we love someone.*

- *Men are motivated and empowered when they feel needed. Women are motivated and empowered when they feel cherished.*

- *A woman under stress is not immediately concerned with finding solutions to her problems, but rather seeks relief by expressing herself, and being understood.*

- *We need to constantly educate ourselves about what our partner might really be needing and what they are really saying when they are speaking to us. If we don't speak their language, many misunderstandings develop.*

Books and Media

Gray has written 16 books and sold over 40 million copies in over 43 languages.

- His first book was published in 1992 with the title, *Men are from Mars, Women are from Venus.* It was this book that really put Dr. Gray on the self-help map. 15 million copies of this book alone have been sold, and in the words of *USA Today,* "This is the number one relationship book of all time!"

- *Why Mars and Venus Collide: Improving Relationships by Understanding How Men and Women Cope Differently with Stress*

- *Mars and Venus Together Forever*
- *Mars and Venus on a Date*
- *Mars and Venus in the Bedroom*
- *The Mars and Venus Diet and Exercise Solution: Create the Brain Chemistry of Health, Happiness, and Lasting Romance*
- *Venus on Fire, Mars on Ice: Hormonal Balance - The Key to Life, Love and Energy*
- *Mars And Venus In Touch - Enhancing The Passion With Great Communication*
- *Men, Women, and Relationships: Making Peace with the Opposite Sex*
- *What Your Mother Couldn't Tell You and Your Father Didn't Know: Advanced Relationship Skills for Better Communication and Lasting Intimacy*
- John Gray has appeared on countless TV programs throughout the world, including *Oprah, Good Morning America, The TODAY Show, The View, Time,* and *Larry King Live.*

How to Find Out More

- For more information on Dr. John Gray, go to his website, *www.marsvenus.com*

5. Dr. Ruth Westheimer

"Keep active sexually until the age of 99!"

Background and Qualifications

A psychosexual therapist, Dr. Ruth is one of the world's most famous sex therapists, renowned for her open and frank discussions of sex.

She was born in Germany in 1928, and from the age of 10, she grew up in a children's home in Switzerland. The home became an orphanage for German Jewish children to escape the Holocaust, and unfortunately, Dr. Ruth lost her entire family at Auschwitz.

She came to the US in 1956, and received her Masters Degree in Sociology and went onto receive a Doctorate of Education in the interdisciplinary study of the family from Colombia University Teacher's College. She studied and then lectured in human sexuality under Dr. Helen Singer Kaplan, at New York Hospital Cornell University Medical Center for seven years, and is now an adjunct professor at NYU.

Despite being 80, she still runs a private practice in New York and lectures across the country. She has been married three times and has two children. Her third marriage lasted 34 years until her beloved husband died.

Relationship Philosophy

Dr. Ruth focuses on the importance of "sexual literacy" for couples to have a fulfilling emotional and physical relationship. She claims far too many couples don't understand the physical changes they may go through in life that will affect their libido and sex life, or enough about their bodies to have truly great sex.

She combines a medical knowledge of sexual dysfunction with advice on the psychological and emotional aspect of sex; from trust to insecurities and sex drive inequality. Sex therapy is one of the most valuable exercises for any couple having problems with their love life, according to Dr. Ruth. This enables a couple to talk about, deal with, and find the root cause of their sex problems – which often has nothing to do with sex, but with emotional insecurity – before anxiety and tension can build up – threatening the relationship altogether.

Dr. Ruth also believes in the importance of maintaining a sex life during pregnancy, otherwise resentment can set in and blame can be placed on the baby.

The Therapy

Dr. Ruth claims one of the best ways to work on your sex life is through sex homework. You have to make a conscious decision not to let your sex life die out and work together to improve your lovemaking.

Women also need to take control of their orgasms, learning how to do it themselves, and then teach their men how to bring them to orgasm. If we don't tell our partner what our needs are, then how can they give us pleasure?

Dr. Ruth also works with more elderly clients to help them keep their love life alive into their sixties and seventies.

Examples

The Pressure to Orgasm

As part of her question and answer problem page on her website, Dr. Ruth offers advice to a 40 year old wife who is worried because she can't orgasm unless she is on top of her husband. Even then, it doesn't happen every time and often she ends up faking it. After 15 years of marriage she's desperate for help.

Dr. Ruth wants this woman to stop putting so much pressure on herself. She needs to understand that most women can't orgasm when their partner is on top, and many can't orgasm at all.

She also advises against faking an orgasm and instead suggests just enjoying sex anyway. She should simply tell her husband she doesn't mind, because according to Dr. Ruth, "It's better to fake that you don't mind than that you've had an orgasm. Then at least when you do have one, you can both enjoy the experience."

The amount of pressure this wife is putting on herself to have an orgasm could also be the reason why she is not having one. Dr. Ruth offers practical advice: "It might help you to give yourself orgasm by masturbating. You might learn exactly what sensations you require and then you could teach your husband."

Relationship Norms

A 21-year-old woman asks for advice from Dr. Ruth. She's been dating her boyfriend for a few months; they have a great sex life but he doesn't like sleeping in the same bed as her. She wants to know if this sleeping arrangement is "normal."

Dr. Ruth responds emphatically by saying how much she dislikes the word "normal," because normal isn't relevant in most situations. Clearly, the vast majority of couples sleep in the same bed. However, Dr. Ruth reveals that her and her late husband couldn't sleep in the same bed, let alone the same room, because he snored so loudly. Her advice is to weigh up all the factors in the entire relationship, and if there are more positive factors that outweigh the negative, then it's worth continuing.

She also advises against counting on him changing, because "many people get married believing that after the marriage, their spouse will change and they're sorely disappointed when that doesn't happen." However, if this develops into a relationship that's heading for marriage, Dr. Ruth suggests it might be worth doing some digging to make sure there's no secret he's hiding behind his sleeping patterns, which could have a negative impact on their relationship.

Dr. Ruth Quotes

- *The most important ingredient for good sex is knowing each other.*
- *I just want people to know that they need to be touched.*
- *In my private practice, the advice I give most often to women is that they have to be able to bring themselves to orgasm before they can expect to do so with a partner.*
- *Don't criticize in the sack. Discuss constructively later.*
- *Do tell your partner how you feel and what your needs are, but choose your words carefully and express them at the right time. Be sure what you are saying is what you want him or her to hear.*

Books and Media

- Dr. Ruth became famous on her radio program, *Sexually Speaking*, which began in September 1980 as a 15-minute taped show. Just a year later, it became a live show, nationwide, answering call-in questions from listeners.
- Her first TV show was local to New York and the *Dr. Ruth Show* went national on Lifetime. She became famous for her brand of therapy, which combined humor with practical and straight-talking advice for any couple wishing to improve their sex life.
- She has made three videos, her first was *Terrific Sex* and two more followed for Playboy.

She has written over 30 books including:

- *Dr. Ruth's Sex After 50*
- *Dr. Ruth's Top Ten Secrets for Great Sex: How to Enjoy it, Share it, and Love it Each and Every Time*

 LOVE BOOK

- 📖 *52 Lessons on Communicating Love*
- 📖 *Dr. Ruth's 30 Days to Sexual Intimacy*
- 📖 *Dr. Ruth's Encyclopedia of Sex*
- 📖 *Dr. Ruth's Guide to Erotic and Sensuous Pleasure*
- 📖 *Guide for Married Lovers*
- 📖 *Sex for Dummies*

How to Find Out More

- 💻 For more information on Dr. Ruth Westheimer, go to her website *http://www.drruth.com*

6. Byron Katie

"When you argue with reality, you lose – but only 100% of the time!"

Background and Qualifications

Katie was a mother of three and a successful businesswoman when she became severely depressed in her mid-thirties. For 10 years, she was agoraphobic, paranoid, and suicidal; she slept with a loaded revolver under her pillow. During the last two years, she could rarely leave her bedroom. Then, one morning in 1986, she had a life-changing experience, which she refers to as, "waking up to reality." She realized that all her suffering came not from the world around her, but from her *thoughts* about the world. "When I believed my thoughts, I suffered; but when I questioned my thoughts, I didn't suffer. And I saw that this was true for every human being." Instantly, all her problems were gone – replaced by a radiance that has never left her.

This experience gave her the process of self-inquiry that she calls The Work. She had no knowledge of religion or psychology, and just a semester of college education. All her insights came from within.

Katie has one job: to teach people how to end their own suffering. When Katie appears, lives change. As she guides people through The Work, they find again and again that their stressful beliefs – about life, other people, or themselves - radically shift. Through this process, anyone can learn to identify and question the thoughts that cause their suffering. Katie not only teaches that all the problems in the world originate in our thinking, she gives people the tools to open their minds and set themselves free.

Over the past twenty-two years, she has worked with millions of people at free public events, in prisons, hospitals, churches,

51

corporations, universities, and schools. Participants at her weekend workshops and her nine-day "School for The Work" report profound experiences and lasting transformations.

Relationship Philosophy

Katie's work is a powerful method of self-inquiry that helps people to observe their problems from a different perspective by identifying and questioning their stressful thoughts. It shows them, beyond a doubt, that the problem is never their partner; it is always themselves, and that this is very good news. You can't change the other person, no matter how hard you try, or how loving your intentions are. But there is one person you *can* change: yourself.

The truth is that nothing outside you can ever give you what you're looking for.

There's no mistake about the person you're with; he or she is the perfect teacher for you, whether or not the relationship works out, and once you enter inquiry, you come to see that clearly. There's never a mistake in the universe. So, if your partner is angry: good; if there are things about him that you consider flaws: good; because these flaws are your own. You're projecting them, and you can write them down, inquire, and set yourself free. People go to India to find a guru, but you don't have to. You're living with one! Your partner will give you everything you need for your own freedom.

The Therapy

Katie's books are extremely accessible and provide simple exercises and case studies that you can work through alone. The work is a way of identifying and questioning the thoughts that cause fear, suffering, frustration, and loneliness. The Work allows your mind to return to its true, peaceful, and loving nature.

The Work

"The Work" is a three-step process. The <u>first step</u> is called "Judge Your Neighbor," where you write down your stressful thoughts about your partner or about any situation in your life. According to Katie, it's essential to write them down to prevent the mind from self-editing. These thoughts could be about someone who is making you angry or sad, someone who has harmed you or disappointed you, or someone who you think ought to change. The thought could be, "My mother doesn't love me," "I'm too fat," or, "My husband should listen to me." When you question these thoughts, you will discover what is really causing your suffering. The Judge Your Neighbor worksheet asks five other questions about the situation.

Judge Your Neighbor Worksheet

1) I'm angry (or upset) at _____, because _____
2) In this situation, how do you want them to change?
3) In this situation, what advice would you give them?
4) In order to be happy, what do you need them to think, say, feel, or do?
5) What do you think of them in this situation – make a list.
6) What is it about this situation you never want to experience again?

The <u>second step</u> of The Work is asking the four questions.

The 4 questions of The Work:

1) Is it (the belief) true?
2) Can you absolutely know that it's true?
3) How do you react – what happens – when you believe that thought?
   - ✓ Does that thought bring peace or stress
   - ✓ What emotions do you have
   - ✓ What physical sensations do you have

- ✓ What images do you see (past, future)
- ✓ How do you treat yourself/others
- ✓ What addictions to you engage in to avoid feeling
- ✓ What's the payoff for holding onto that belief
- ✓ What do you fear would happen if you didn't believe that thought
- ✓ What are you not able to do

4) Who would you be without that thought?

After you have investigated your stressful thought, the <u>third step</u> is to find the turnarounds. This allows you to experience the opposite of what you believed. So, for example, the stressful thought, "He should understand me," can be turned around to, "He *does* understand me," or "He *shouldn't* understand me" to, "*I* should understand *him,*" or to, "I should understand *myself.*"

Turnarounds

1) **The Opposite** – He does understand me
2) **To the Other** – I should understand him
3) **To the Self** – I should understand me

Then you are asked to pause, and look inside to discover at least three specific, genuine examples of how each turnaround is true in your life. The insights that come from truly experiencing these turnarounds are profound.

For the other five question in the Judge Your Neighbor worksheet, turn around the statements to apply to yourself. In other words, look at how you want them to change, or the advice you want to give them. Use the exact sentences, applied to yourself: how do you want to change, what advice do you have for yourself, what do you need to think, say, feel, or do.

For the last question, turn it around from "I never want to experience X again..." to "I'm willing to experience X again." If it is likely to happen again, will you actually experience it, or not? Will it do any good to resist it? The advanced phrase is, "I look forward to experiencing X again." Who will you be the next time this happens? Can you be a little curious? This is about embracing all of life – without fear, and always being open to reality.

The process of identifying and thoroughly questioning one's stressful thoughts can radically transform relationships, reduce depression, stress, and anger, increase energy, and bring about a state of peacefulness and joy. It also helps us discover our motives for carrying out certain actions. Katie uses the following example to explain this:

> When you keep manipulating your partner to get her to love you, everything you do has that motive – even when you take her out to dinner. It's very painful. But when you step into inquiry, your patterns change and you become a total question mark. Your mind becomes free of its motives - totally open to reality. Once you're aware of your motives, you start to become free of them. And you realize that your happiness is in loving her; it has nothing to do with her loving you. And then you can take her out to dinner and you're unlimited. Or you can not take her out to dinner and you're unlimited. You come to love yourself totally, and she doesn't have to participate. So there is no motive when you say, "I love you." Your thinking about what she was thinking about you was your hell.

Without a motive, the suffering disappears, and what's left is gratitude and laughter.

Examples
Open Heart Surgery

During a Byron Katie workshop, a woman in the audience volunteers a situation in her life that is causing stress and pain.

With reference to her partner, she says, "I need him to open his heart to me." Katie asks her, "How do you react when you believe that thought?" The woman says, "I close my own heart, I get upset, and feel like I shouldn't be in the relationship. I emotionally move away from him and put a sad look on my face."

As Katie helps this woman work through the process of inquiry, the woman begins to unravel the myth of, "He should open his heart." As understanding grows, Katie says, "Why should someone open their heart to you? 'Oh, mine is a little shut down right now, but YOU should open YOUR heart! My heart will open when yours does.' The whole planet is waiting for someone to do it first!" The irony of this is delicious, and the woman bursts out laughing. It is obvious to everyone in the audience that her "He should open his heart to me" is absurd, and that one of the turnarounds, "I should open my heart to him," is the only thing that she can do something about, and the only way for her to be happy.

A second statement the woman has written down is, "He shouldn't be so judgmental." She describes an argument she had with her partner before she left for the workshop about the fact she is no longer willing to vacuum their carpet and he can't breathe. Playing the role of the woman, Katie imagines how the situation would be if she responded, "I'm so glad you shared this with me, sweetheart. My goodness, you can't breathe. I really hear that. You're right, I don't vacuum, isn't that strange? What do you think we can do about this? Let's put our heads together and find a solution." Not only could the argument have been diffused, but also the absence of any defense or justification on her part could have helped her partner find a solution that he had been blind to before.

He Should be more Understanding

At another conference, Sophia reads a statement about her husband; "Frank should be more understanding of me." Katie says, "Is that true?" and Sophia says, "Yes." "Can you absolutely know that it's true?" Katie asks. Sophia looks puzzled, is silent for a while, and then says, "No, I can't *absolutely* know that it's true." Katie asks, "How do you react when you feel that he should be more understanding, and he isn't?" "I actually feel physical pain," Sophia says, "in my heart and body, and it's like I can't breathe."

Katie asks her to imagine she's looking at Frank. Katie asks, "Who would you be without that thought?" The woman closes her eyes, and says, "Without that thought, I'd feel free, at peace. I see a kind man who loves me, and is doing the best he can." She has tears in her eyes. "You know what, sweetheart?" Katie says, "You're meeting Frank for the very first time." Then they go on to find examples for the turnarounds. "Frank should *not* be more understanding of me," "I should be more understanding of Frank," and "I should be more understanding of myself."

Byron Katie Quotes

- *Nothing you believe is true. To know this is freedom.*

- *Peace doesn't require two people; it only requires one. It has to be you. The problem begins and ends there.*

- *It takes only one clear person to have a loving relationship.*

- *Nothing can cost you someone you love. The only thing that can cost you your husband is if you believe a thought. That's how you move away from him. That's how the marriage ends.*

- *When you argue with reality, you lose – but only 100% of the time!*

- *Would you rather be right or be free?*

- *An unquestioning mind is the world of suffering.*

- *All the advice you ever gave your partner is for you to hear.*

- *If I think you're my problem, I'm insane.*

- *When I am perfectly clear, 'what is' is what I want.*

- *Forgiveness is realizing that what you thought happened, didn't.*

- *Seeking love keeps you from the awareness that you already have it – that you are it.*

- *Everything happens **for** me, not **to** me.*

Books and Media

Katie has written three bestsellers and appeared on various radio and TV shows, including *Oprah's Soul Series. Time Magazine* recently called her a "spiritual innovator for the new millennium." Eckhart Tolle calls The Work "A blessing for our planet; it acts like a razor-sharp sword that cuts through that illusion and enables you to know for yourself the timeless essence of your being."

- o She offers an Audio CD called *Your Inner Awakening: The Work of Byron Katie: Four Questions That Will Transform Your Life*

Her best-selling books include:

- 📖 *Loving What Is: Four Questions That Can Change Your Life* (written with her husband, Stephen Mitchell)

- 📖 *I Need Your Love – Is That True?* (with Michael Katz)

- 📖 *A Thousand Names for Joy* (with Stephen Mitchell)

- 📖 *Question Your Thinking, Change The World: Quotations from Byron Katie*

- 📖 Her latest book is *Who Would You Be Without Your Story?*

How to Find Out More

- 💻 Go to Byron Katie's website, *www.thework.com*, where you will find her blog, a list of upcoming events, a network of facilitators, a free hotline, audio and video clips, articles, and basic information about Katie and The Work, including free materials to download.

7. Dr. Laura Schlessinger

"The proper care and feeding of relationships"

Background and Qualifications

Dr. Laura Schlessinger has been giving no non-sense, often controversial, advice on the radio for more than 30 years to approximately 8.25 million listeners weekly. Her guidance is infused with a strong sense of ethics, accountability, and personal responsibility.

Dr. Laura, as she is affectionately known, has a PhD in physiology from Columbia's University College of Physicians and Surgeons and has a postdoctoral Certificate in Marriage, Family, and Child Counseling from the University of Southern California. She had a private practice for 12 years, and now dedicates her time to her radio show. She has been married for 24 years and has one son.

Relationship Philosophy

Dr. Laura has become famous for her straight talking approach to relationship advice. She describes a truly intimate relationship as one of the greatest blessings in life, especially if you both strive to continually bless each other's life.

According to Dr. Laura there is a fundamental difference between masculine and feminine energies. When couples blur the gender roles and don't respect these differences, relationship strife can occur. Satisfaction and intimacy can only be achieved when each person respects and appreciates the other's uniqueness.

Men need direct communication, respect, appreciation, sexual intimacy, and nurturing in order to respond with devotion, compassion, and love. They have an underlying desire to protect and cherish their wives. It doesn't matter to a man what

profession his wife chooses as long as she is "his woman" and "a woman" to him. All too often, women want to be seen by their men as the high-powered executive they are at work. According to Dr. Laura, women can learn to achieve a deeply satisfying marriage if they adhere to the fundamental requirements of men and help create the kind of home life that truly makes a man happy. This is not a form of oppression or subservience – it's simply about bringing out the best in each other.

Dr. Laura also believes the most important thing in a woman's life is to be her children's mother. She calls childcare centers "day orphanages," because hired help is never the same as the nurturing love from a parent. Your legacy when you die is not in your résumé or bank account, but rather from the people who tell the wonderful stories about you because you meant so much to them and were actually there. The way you nurture your children and your husband will be your lasting legacy.

With the changing roles of women within society over the past 50 years, this basic concept has been lost and all too often a woman's marriage and children become secondary to her career and success. Women have become out of tune to their husband's needs and often begin to suffer from a hypersensitivity about any action or reaction from him; reactions that are usually more than reasonable due to her behavior. This double standard mentality stems from the modern "self-centeredness" of women.

Dr. Laura also believes that many young women have lost the essence of what it is to be female and says it's no wonder men have little respect for women these days. Instead of embracing modesty, pride, values, and self worth, they have begun to engage in extra-marital sex, parade around in little clothing, have children outside of serious relationships and use abortion as birth control.

The Therapy

Dr. Laura encourages people to first look at their relationship with truth and honesty before they get married. Engagement is the perfect period to evaluate whether the marriage is going to work. Just because you've bought your dress or your shoes doesn't mean the marriage is a done deal.

One of the best ways to keep your marriage alive is with small day-to-day kindnesses and reminders of the love that brought you together in the first place. One small sweet gesture can help the pump of love begin to flow and help you remember how much you love each other. Marriage is much more than what you do on that one day in a long white dress. Finding time for each other is essential to help prevent feelings of estrangement later on.

There are "**10 stupid things**" that couples commonly do to mess up their relationship and these should be avoided at all costs:

♥ **Stupid Withholding:** withholding important information out of fear of rejection – for example, something embarrassing from your past.

♥ **Stupid Egotism:** not thinking about what you can do for the relationship, only what it can do for you.

♥ **Stupid Pettiness:** sweating the small stuff.

♥ **Stupid Power:** always trying to be in control.

♥ **Stupid Priorities:** not making enough time for each other and the relationship.

♥ **Stupid Happiness:** seeking stimulation and assurance from the wrong places in order to feel good.

♥ **Stupid Excuses:** unacceptable for bad behavior.

♥ **Stupid Liaisons:** not letting go of negative attachments to friends or relatives who are damaging the relationship.

- ♥ **Stupid Mismatch:** not knowing when to leave and cut your losses.

- ♥ **Stupid Breakups:** disconnecting for the wrong reasons and giving up too easily.

Examples
The Perfect Life

Carrie was very unhappy in her two-year marriage. She had fantasies of the "perfect life" that were not being met, so she thought it was time to get out. She filed for divorce and moved out. However, their basic friendship kept them talking. They started discussing their thoughts, feelings, fears, and desires without the resentment of their failed expectations. They ultimately found that suffering was something all people have to go through to get to where they want to be. They are now celebrating their ten-year anniversary and have a greater appreciation for all that marriage provides; savoring the good, the bad, and the in between times in a committed relationship.

Men Have Feelings

The approval from a man's wife is an important as oxygen; surviving their wife's lack of approval is emasculation. Dr. Laura's experience with letters and on-air practice shows a world rife with women's crass disdain for the feelings of their husbands. Although men are not generally forthcoming about their feelings – talking about what happened, their emotional state, etc., – they do have feelings. Often, wives simply translate their husband's pain into annoyance and conclude their man is being selfish or insensitive, instead of listening for the inherent desire to connect.

Danette describes this situation with clarity. She recalls talking with a girlfriend and paying complete attention to what she was saying and feeling. Her friend asked her a personal question and then made sure she didn't offend or hurt her feelings by asking. She added, "Nothing you do will ever offend or bother me. But my husband regularly bothers and offends me." It was soon thereafter that Danette realized that her own husband often got on her nerves. When she got into a fight later that week, she started seeing that she was taking advantage of him without even considering his feelings. She would always be considerate of her girlfriend's feelings, because she didn't want to offend or lose her friendship. But she didn't have the same consideration for her husband. "How stupid is that?" she pondered.

Dr. Laura points out that the main source of a husband's bad mood, attitude, negative responses, and disappointing behavior is their wife's attitude toward them and *their* feelings; plain and simple. One male caller put it succinctly: "I have never known a happy man who initiated or was involved in an affair. Affairs start and are fueled by something missing in their marriage. The affairs that I have known about started with a man alone, crying on a park bench or into an 'adult beverage.' A man in tears usually isn't alone long." Men telegraph their unhappiness for years and then just give up. Then the affairs come.

Dr. Laura points out that is it *easy* to have a fantastic marriage and husband. Men are rather easy to please. What attracts a man to a woman is her femininity. Looking like a woman and behaving sweetly and flirtatiously are enormous gifts women can give to their husbands. If a woman presents herself as appealing to her spouse, she will get much more romancing. On the other hand, if she flirts with other men in order to get attention, she will create tremendous stress in her partnership.

Frump Syndrome

When Kelly was dating, she put a lot of effort into looking good. She looked forward to cooking romantic dinners. After marriage, she focused on paying the bills, two careers, and raising the children. After the second child, there was cleaning, playing with the kids, etc. When her husband came home tired, she had a long list of things for him to do, and nothing to do with

romance, intimacy, or other loving activities. She became bitter, hostile, and nagging, and was feeling that she was being cheated out of her life. She was blaming her husband and stopped hugging him, kissing him, showing signs of affection, and even having sex with him.

This is the death sentence for a marriage. As one caller put it, "Sex to a husband is like conversation to a wife. When a wife deprives her husband of sex for days, it is tantamount to his refusing to talk to her for days." Realize what a deleterious impact forced sexual abstinence has on a good man who is determined to remain faithful.

Kelly had contracted the "Frump Syndrome." Only when she was advising a good friend of hers did she realize that she was using her husband as a scapegoat. She was blaming him, and not noticing what she wasn't giving him. She is on the road to recovery by realizing how lucky she is. Things completely switch when she gives the most important thing she can give to her husband: herself. Taking care of the intimate, tender, loving, sensual, and sexual aspects of a marriage should never be set aside or outsourced!

Dr. Laura Schlessinger Quotes

- *The first and most obvious issue in approaching the glory and angst of marriage is to understand the fundamentals of the two people involved: one is a woman, the other is a man. And that's no small thing!*
- *There isn't a day that goes by when I don't ask at least one woman caller on my radio program if she expects to stay married considering her hostile, dismissive, or undermining attitude and actions towards her husband.*
- *The notion of love as a gift, as a verb, as an attitude, as a commitment, is a revelation to some. Unfortunately, love is usually looked at as a feeling that comes over you and makes you happy.*

Books and Media

- Dr. Laura is the best-selling author of 11 adult books and 4 kids' books, including her MUST GET book, *The Proper Care and Feeding of Husbands.*

- *10 Stupid Things Couples Do to Mess Up Their Relationships*

- *10 Stupid Things Women Do to Mess Up Their Lives*

- *The Proper Care and Feeding of Marriage*

- *How Could You Do That? The Abdication of Character, Courage, and Conscience*

- *10 Stupid Things Men Do to Mess Up Their Lives*

- *Stupid Things Parents Do to Mess Up Their Kids: Don't Have Them If You Won't Raise Them*

- Her latest book is *In Praise of Stay-At-Home Moms*

How to Find Out More

- For more information go to *www.drlaura.com* as well as *www.drlaurablog.com* and *www.youtube.com/drlaura*

8. Dr. David Burns

"You <u>can</u> change the way you feel."

Background and Qualifications

David D. Burns, M.D. has been a pioneer in the development of Cognitive Behavioral Therapy (CBT) and shows couples how to change their feelings and behavior by adapting the way they think.

Dr. Burns is an Adjunct Clinical Professor of Psychiatry and Behavioral Sciences at the Stanford University School of Medicine and has served as Visiting Scholar at Harvard Medical School. He graduated magna cum laude from Amherst College, received his M.D. from Stanford University School of Medicine, and completed his psychiatry residency at the University of Pennsylvania, School of Medicine.

His self-help books, *Feeling Good* and *The Feeling Good Handbook,* have sold more than 5 million copies and he has just published his guidebook for relationship help, *Feeling Good Together: The Secret to Making Troubled Relationships Work.*

Relationship Philosophy

Dr. Burns believes that feeling bad, unhappy, depressed, or anxious are NOT things that are beyond our control. They may be influenced by other people, a lack of success, hormones, body chemistry, childhood trauma, or the state of the world, but they are not controlled by them. This is because we can control the way we feel and behave by learning to change our thoughts and the messages we send ourselves.

The premise of CBT is that you will have constructive or destructive behaviors, and supportive our unsupportive emotions, based on your thoughts, attitudes, beliefs and meanings you ascribe to certain events (whether imagined or real events). In reality, the order is more like 1. You imagine failing at an interview, 2. You believe "I'm such a loser, there's no way I'm getting this job," 3. You experience anxiety (emotion) and butterflies in your stomach and tightness in your throat (physical sensation), and you are closed (behavior) during your interview.

There's no point being a victim of your own misery. Everyone has the power to change how he or she feels and behaves. Dr. Burns teaches people how to use the principles of CBT to help change the way they think, feel and behave, and subsequently bring about a dramatic change in their relationships.

Dr. Burns' brand of CBT is called cognitive interpersonal therapy. He describes how, when we are having problems in a relationship, it's a natural instinct to blame the other person and become upset because of the way we think about events that have happened. But this way of thinking can only make things worse in a troubled relationship. Dr. Burns shows couples how to take control of their relationships by taking control of and changing their thought processes.

10 Steps to Self-Esteem

- ♥ The Price of Happiness
- ♥ You FEEL the Way You THINK
- ♥ You Can CHANGE the Way You FEEL
- ♥ How to Break Out of a Bad Mood
- ♥ The Acceptance Paradox
- ♥ Getting Down to Root Causes
- ♥ Self-Esteem – What is it? How Do I Get It?
- ♥ The Perfectionist's Script for Self-Defeat
- ♥ A Prescription for Procrastinators
- ♥ Practice, Practice, Practice!

The Therapy

The way to better relationships is to stop pointing our fingers at everyone else and start looking at ourselves. Dr. Burns uses this underlying principle of CBT to help people with everyday problems such as nervousness, phobias, stress, low self-esteem, and guilt. He teaches people how to remove these mental obstacles that are keeping them from relationship success.

The first step is to realize that anger and interpersonal conflict ultimately result from a "mental con" – you're telling yourself things that aren't entirely true when you're fighting with someone. Yet, the distorted thoughts end up as self-fulfilling prophecies. For example, if you tell yourself your partner is a jerk, you'll treat him like one. He'll then get angry and start acting like a jerk in response. You'll then tell yourself you were right all along and that he really is a jerk.

The alternative is to change the way you think, which can then change the way you feel and behave. By thinking about people and yourself in a more positive and realistic way, it's far easier to resolve conflict and develop rewarding relationships.

Negative forces such as over-generalizing, discounting the positive, jumping to conclusions, mentally filtering out positive things, dwelling on the negative, labeling, and blame can all be destructive forces. These "mental cons," or Cognitive Distortions, get in the way of truly satisfying relationships.

Cognitive Distortions

1) **All-or-nothing thinking** – Seeing things as black or white
2) **Overgeneralization** – Always - and Never - thinking
3) **Mental filter** – Only looking at the negative
4) **Disqualifying the positive** – Reject positive experiences

5) **Jumping to conclusions** – This includes mind-reading; believing you know what other people are thinking and the fortune teller error; convinced that your prediction of a dire future is an already-established fact.

6) **Catastrophizing or Minimizing** – Exaggerate the importance of negative experiences or reducing your achievements

7) **Emotional Reasoning** – "I feel bad, therefore it must be true"

8) **Should statements** using guilt to whip and punish yourself

9) **Labeling** – "I'm a loser;" Using emotionally loaded language

10) **Personalization** – Making it all about you

Dr. Burns provides practical tools to get over these mental barriers and change the way we think about our partners. For example, if your partner criticizes you, turn the criticism on its head using positive reframing. So, if he accuses you of being a control freak you could say, "You're right. I may have a tendency to be overly controlling," and use it as an opening for discussion. You could go on to say, "We seem to be having a conflict right now, but as awful as it feels, I'm thinking this could be an opportunity for us to explore a deeper relationship. I love you. Tell me more about how you're experiencing this." That way, you're taking the blame away from your partner and opening the relationship up to more intimacy.

This type of effective communication dissolves tension almost immediately. Suddenly, partners are on the same team. These techniques are not gimmicks, but rather powerful ways to connect to another person, and speak from your heart.

The 5 Secrets of Effective Communication

1) **Disarming Technique** - Find some truth in what the other person is saying.

2) **Empathy** - Put yourself in the other person's shoes. See the world through the other's eyes.

3) **Inquiry** - Ask gentle, probing questions, and let the other person answer from a thoughtful place.

4) **"I feel" statements** - Focus on yourself, and bring your partner into your world.

5) **Stroking** - Find something genuinely positive to say to the other person. This conveys an attitude of respect.

Examples
Resistance

Eileen was an intensely unhappy woman. During sessions, she often complained about all the people in her life who had let her down. She was deeply mired in her anxiety and depression. Dr. Burns suggested a paradoxical "cost-benefit analysis." What are all the advantages of being depressed and anxious, and all the disadvantages of getting better? Eileen could come up with many advantages of remaining stuck and disadvantages of recovery. Dr. Burns agreed that her depression was clearly a good thing and he would miss arguing with her if she recovered. That simple acceptance of her resistance gave her nothing left to resist, so Eileen could actually do the needed work between sessions.

Most people desperately want to change their lives, but are afraid to. There are always hidden benefits for the status quo, and one has to pay a price if one wants to change their life.

Daily Mood Log

Marsha is a psychologist and also suffers from worry about her 26 year old daughter's ability to take care of herself. She first writes about the event in detail, then fills out a Daily Mood Log; a device used to identify and rate negative feelings and thoughts. There are nine different categories of emotions, with synonyms from which to choose. One circles the emotion that most fits, and rates it 0-100%.

Negative Emotions

- Sad, blue, depressed, down, unhappy
- Anxious, worried, panicky, nervous, frightened
- Guilty, remorseful, bad, ashamed
- Inferior, worthless, inadequate, defective, incompetent
- Lonely, unloved, unwanted, rejected, alone, abandoned
- Embarrassed, foolish, humiliated, self-conscious
- Hopeless, discouraged, pessimistic, despairing
- Frustrated, stuck, thwarted, defeated
- Angry, resentful, annoyed, irritated, upset, furious
- Other Emotions?

For Marsha, she was sad (100%), anxious (100%), guilty, ashamed, inadequate, incompetent, lonely, embarrassed, discouraged, stuck (200%), irritated, and overwhelmed (200%). Clearly, some of these emotions were off the charts.

The third step is to evaluate the negative thoughts that dominate these emotions. Her main negative thoughts were, "I shouldn't be so silly and stupid," "I should be able to let go," and "I am so over-controlling." She has two problems that many people exhibit: she tells her self what she should and shouldn't do, and then she beats herself up because of it. The fourth step is to identify the distortions involved in the negative thought, and give examples. Once the though is seen as a distortion, it is easier to let it go.

The fifth step is very important. Marsha needs to evaluate why she is resisting letting go of her anxiety and self-criticisms. She is holding on to these for some important reason; it is imperative that the reasons are uncovered so she can let them go, and make the change she wants to. Some of the reasons include:

this is what a loving mother should do, perhaps guilt and self-criticism will force her to solve the problem, the constant worrying may keep her from dealing with other issues she has been ignoring, such as loneliness in her marriage.

One of the things that made it particularly difficult for Marsha was the fact that she already had a daughter who died, and she blamed herself. "If she had just been there and taken better care of her, she wouldn't have died," she thought. She wanted to make sure that didn't happen again. She went back through the emotions, thoughts, and distortions. Dr. Burns describes several critical ways to eliminate these negative thoughts completely in his book, *When Panic Attacks,* including. "What would you say to a friend in a similar situation?" The new, positive thoughts are written next to the negative thoughts in the sixth step, and the brain now sees these thoughts as real, and lets one see the negative thoughts as the lie.

It came as a complete shock to Marsha that she was being overprotective as a strategy to avoid losing another daughter. This changed her view of herself from a compulsive neurotic to a loving mother.

In summary, the steps are:
1) Find the trigger event
2) Identify the negative emotion
3) Determine the belief or thought that enabled that emotion
4) Illuminate the distortion
5) Uncover why you hold onto negative stories
6) Write an alternative belief
7) Imagine the effect of the alternative thought or belief

Dr. David Burns Quotes

- *Make life an exhilarating experience.*

- *If you say, "I just can't help the way I feel," you'll make yourself a victim of your misery and you'll be fooling yourself because you can change the way you feel.*

- *The messages you give yourself have an enormous impact on your emotions.*

- *If you want to feel better, you must realize that your thoughts and attitudes – not external events – create your feelings.*

- *You can learn to change the way you think, feel, and behave in the here and now.*

Books and Media

- Dr. Burns' latest book is *Felling good together: the Secret to Making Troubled Relationships Work*

- He is also the author of several self-help books on mood and relationship problems. His best-selling books, *Feeling Good: The New Mood Therapy*, and *The Feeling Good Handbook,* have sold over 5 million copies in the United States, and many more worldwide. In a national survey of American mental health professionals, Dr. Burns' *Feeling Good* was the top-rated book on a list of 1,000 self-help books for patients suffering from depression. American and Canadian mental health professionals "prescribe" *Feeling Good* for their patients more often than any other self-help book.

Dr. Burns is also the author of:

- *When Panic Attacks*
- *10 Days to Self-Esteem*
- *Intimate Connections*

- More than 100 articles about Dr. Burn's work have appeared in magazines such as *Reader's Digest, Psychology Today,* and *Ladies' Home Journal.*

- He has also been interviewed by numerous radio and television personalities such as Oprah, Mike Wallace, Charlie Rose, Maury Povich, Phil Donahue, and many others.

How to Find Out More

- For more information, go to *www.feelinggood.com*

9. Dr. Sue Johnson

"The power of emotionally focused couple's therapy"

Background and Qualifications

Dr. Sue Johnson is based in Ottawa, Canada, with her husband and two children. She grew up in a pub in the UK, which is where she says she learned and became intrigued about relationships. She watched all the drama of couples and analyzed the signals that humans send each other.

Dr. Johnson is now Director of the Ottawa Couple and Family Institute and International Center for Excellence in Emotionally Focused Therapy (EFT). She is also Professor of Clinical Psychology at the University of Ottawa and Research Professor at the Alliant University in San Diego, California. She has received numerous awards for her work, including the Outstanding Contribution to the Field of Couple and Family Therapy from the American Association for Marriage and Family Therapy, and the Research in Family Therapy Award from the American Family Therapy Academy.

She now leads groups for post-deployment couples, as well as training therapists in Emotionally Focused Therapy for couples throughout the world.

Relationship Philosophy

Dr. Johnson is one of the pioneers of Emotionally Focused Couple's Therapy (EFCT), which has a clinically-proven 70 to 75% success rate with long-lasting results. Through her work she aims to show couples how to create a safe emotional bond with a partner that can last a lifetime.

The basic premise of Emotionally Focused Couples Therapy does not center on learning how to argue more effectively, analyzing early childhood, making grand romantic gestures, or finding new sexual positions. It focuses on creating and strengthening emotional bonds between couples, which create secure attachment and an ability to turn to a partner for nurturing, soothing, and protection. It helps to identify and transform the key moments that foster an adult loving relationship.

Emotionally Focused Couples Therapy is based on extensively researched theory of adult love – Attachment Theory. According to this theory, rigid patterns and ineffective actions, so common to couples in distress, actually stem from separation anxiety, which undermines a couple's sense of safety and security. This triggers fears of engulfment or abandonment, rejection, and isolation. People play out common patterns of anger and fear with anxious pursuit or rigid avoidance. These responses become stuck in an ever-worsening pattern, creating increasingly greater insecurity and crushing despair.

The EFCT approach seeks foremost to strengthen a couple's bond by focusing on the often unknown needs for attachment, safety and security with the partner, and increasing emotional disclosures in a net of loving acceptance and responsiveness.

In the past, emotions have been considered as a complication arising during interactions: dangerous and to be avoided or gotten over. Sue helps us realize the critical role emotions play in communication and the power emotions bring to change.

As we become more and more dependant on our intimate partner for support and connection, healthy attachment is even more critical. A strong bond, where partners can share attachment needs and fears, and offer mutual comfort and support, is associated with self-esteem, ability to deal with ambiguity and anxiety, and self-actualized growth.

The Therapy

According to Dr. Johnson there are 7 conversations that capture the defining moments in a loving relationship. It's important how we shape these moments to create a secure and lasting bond.

The 7 Conversations of EFCT

♥ **Recognize demon dialogues:** identify those dialogues that are negative and destructive. That way we can really get to the root of the problem and discover what each person is really trying to say, rather than dealing with words said during conflict that bear little relevance to what is really going on.

♥ **Finding the raw spots:** it's important to look beyond the immediate, impulsive reactions and find out what is really important, what truly upsets a partner, and how they react to certain situations.

♥ **Revisiting a rocky moment:** by going over a difficult time in a relationship, this enables couples to create a platform for de-escalating conflict in the future.

♥ **Hold me tight:** this is the heart of the program, which moves partners to become more accessible to each other, emotionally responsible, and deeply engaged.

♥ **Forgiving injuries:** injuries never disappear but need to become integrated into the couple's conversations as a demonstration of renewal and connection.

♥ **Bonding through sex and touch:** emotional connections are achieved through great sex and touch, and great sex and touch is achieved through an emotional connection. Both are important for a fulfilling relationship.

♥ **Keeping your love alive:** love is a continual process of losing and finding emotional connection. Couples need to be mindful about maintaining their connection.

Emotionally Focused Couples Therapy is really a process-orientated approach because you focus on the ever-evolving process of how partners co-construct their relational experience. The therapeutic session involves a therapist reflecting the emotional dynamics in terms of the couples' own dance. The therapist also shifts the general to specific, abstract to concrete, obscure to tangible, and global to personal, so that each person can become more in tune with their relational dynamics.

There are three main stages of EFCT. In the first stage, couples learn to identify their interaction style that leads to conflict. The couple gets to reframe their problem in terms of the interaction pattern and their attachment needs. This is really about uncovering the dance you and your partner have created, and to start to listen to the music.

In the second stage the interactions patterns are restructured. This is about changing the music so you can de-escalate the tension. Each person is guided to acknowledge and reveal their emotions triggered by their unmet needs for attachment in such a way that the other is moved by their vulnerability and actively responds to their desire for comfort. The resulting security acts as an antidote to the habitual patterns of disconnection.

The third stage is consolidation, where a couple can reprocess past issues in terms of the fears and hurt triggered by unmet attachment needs, and experience the relationship anew as a safe haven and a secure base. Here, you are able to deepen your engagement with your partner and develop deep bonds.

There is an additional stage of integration for advanced EFCT. This is where at least one person is able to recognize the demon dance as it is beginning to occur, and instead of being reactivated, is willing to express feelings, as well as comfort and soothe themselves and the other. By talking about what was happening, they ultimately become closer as a couple.

Conversations evolve at each phase of EFCT, as couples learn to move from reactive comments; to noticing the enmeshed pattern; to revealing emotions; to making requests; to becoming vulnerable and available to the other. Initial problems, such as:

♥ "You are always belittling me" evolve into...

♥ "Hold on here a second. Something's not right. I think you are criticizing me again", into...

♥ "I feel inadequate, and live in fear of you finding this out and leaving me", to...

♥ "I'm tired of living in fear. I want to feel important to you. I request that you hold back criticism of me until an appropriate time, and that you treat me as if you actually want to be with me," to

♥ "I'm getting tense because I think you are getting cold and demanding, and I'm afraid I did something wrong last night, and the fear this brings up is that I am inadequate and will never get it right."

Examples

It's been a Long Time Since Vietnam

But it seems like yesterday for Doug, who, at 23, led a unit of Army Rangers through peril and back home. He still bears the scars of being a commanding soldier. "Never reveal fear and never be wrong," is his motto. What worked well in battle is tearing his marriage apart.

Doug admits that he "hides, safe in the dark tunnel," because his main fear is that his wife, Pauline, will see who he really is. "You wouldn't love me if you knew what I did there."

During a Hold Me Tight conversation, Doug is able to open up a bit about his "secret shame." As he looks for the telltale signs that no one can love him, Pauline says, "You are a fine and

loving man. You did your best; you did what you had to do, and you have paid for it every day since. And right now, I love you even more because you took a risk like this and opened up to me."

The transforming moment happens during the next conversation. Pauline tells him softly, "I need you to let me in – to come close. I love you and I need you so." Doug doesn't hear this as an invitation, but rather as an indictment. "Well then, you are just too demanding," he retorts. When Pauline turns in despair, Doug stops himself and looks up. "What did you say? I heard you say that I wasn't doing my job; that I was blowing it with you. If you were happy, you wouldn't have to ask for those things."

Doug understands, for the first time, that he was listening to his own fear of rejection, of not being good enough, rather than Pauline's words of love. Finally, Doug opens up completely. "I need you too. I need your reassurance. I want to be there for you." After forty years, Doug is finally home.

Auntie Doris and Uncle Sid

Being able to de-escalate conflict is one of the most important ways couples can stay connected and create a relationship based on emotional safety, as well as avoiding demon dialogues. In her book, *Hold Me Tight,* Dr. Johnson recounts a Christmas story from her childhood.

She remembers her Auntie Doris was in the kitchen pouring rum over the Christmas pudding, at the same time arguing with her husband, Uncle Sid, who was quite drunk by this time. Doris turns to Sid and says, "We is getting into a doozy here. One of them dead-end doozy fights we does. You are half cut and I sure as hell don't feel like no shining Christmas fairy. Are we going to fight it out? I'll swing like always and you'll duck if you can. Both feel bad then. Do we need to do it? Or can we just start over?" Uncle Sid nods and mutters, "No doozy, no ducking... lovely pudding, Doris!" He pats her on the behind and goes into the living room.

Although this seems like a joking situation, and has a quaint, happy ending, you probably know people who will let a situation like this devolve into a full-blown fight. Dr. Johnson recalls the conversation and years later realizes that in their interaction they deflated the conflict by recognizing a negative pattern, declaring a ceasefire, and re-establishing a warmer connection. This is a skill that disconnected couples can learn to achieve emotional balance and create a platform for repairing rifts within their relationship. Find the humor in the fact that, as a human, you are almost automatically drawn into a fight; then celebrate the fact that you have the skills to do something different.

The Three Kinds of Sex

Dr. Johnson believes there are three kinds of sex, which can define the emotional safety and intimacy levels in a relationship. The first is sealed-off sex, which works fine for a one-night stand, but if it is the norm between a couple, the relationship is in trouble. It is characterized by the need to reduce sexual tension, achieve orgasm, and feel sexually virile. The relationship with the other person is secondary and can make a partner feel used and emotionally alone.

Dr. Johnson uses the example of Bill and Kerrie. Kerrie says, "When we make love, I feel like I could be anyone. It just reinforces for me the sense that I don't really matter to him." Bill replies by saying, "Well we haven't been getting along, so I try to get close by coming onto you." As Dr. Johnson explains, this

81

lack of sexual connection reveals the need to reconnect emotionally outside the bedroom.

The second kind of sex she describes as solace sex, which happens when we're not quite sure if our partner is really there for us, so we end up pleasing them to win their approval. If our partner isn't in the mood to make love, often we end up feeling unloved and get into arguments about why they're not feeling sexy. It's important in this case to talk to a partner about these anxieties, and the underlying desire for connection and to matter.

The final kind of sex is when emotional openness, tender touch, responsiveness, and erotic exploration all come together. Sex is fulfilling and satisfying because of the safe emotional bond that allows us to relax into sexual feelings. This kind sex, which Dr. Johnson terms synchrony sex, deepens our bond with our lover. "The thrill in this kind of sex is like dancing the tango with a trusted partner... this is the way sex was supposed to be."

Dr. Sue Johnson Quotes

- *To reconnect, lovers have to be able to de-escalate the conflict and actively create basic emotional safety. They need to be able to work in concert to curtail their negative dialogues, and to defuse their fundamental insecurities.*

- *If we are connected, my feelings will naturally affect yours. But seeing the impact we have on our loved ones can be very difficult when we are caught up in our emotions, especially if fear is narrowing the lens.*

- *We need to recognize how our usual way of dealing with our emotions pulls our partner off balance and turns on deeper attachment fears.*

- *Voicing your deepest emotions, sometimes sadness and shame, but most often attachment fears, may be the most difficult step for you, but it is also the most rewarding. It lets your partner see what's really at stake with you when you argue. So often we miss the attachment needs and fears that lie hidden in recurring battles about everyday issues.*

Books and Media

📖 Dr. Sue Johnson's MUST READ book for couples, entitled: *Hold Me Tight: Seven Conversations for a Lifetime of Love.* This is a life-transforming book.

○ *Hold Me Tight: Seven Conversations for a Lifetime of Love (Audio CD)*

○ A DVD of 3 couples going through the conversations in *Hold Me Tight* is also available at *www.iceeft.com*

Dr. Johnson has also written several professional books for therapists:

📖 *Becoming an Emotionally Focused Couple Therapist: The Workbook*

📖 *The Emotionally Focused Therapist Training Set: The Emotionally Focused Casebook*

📖 *Attachment Processes in Couple and Family Therapy*

📖 *The Practice of Emotionally Focused Couple Therapy: Creating Connection*

📖 *Emotionally Focused Couple Therapy with Trauma Survivors*

How to Find Out More

🖥 For more information, go to Dr. Sue Johnson's website: *www.holdmetight.net*

10. Dr. Barbara de Angelis

"Happiness is not an acquisition."

Background and Qualifications

Despite being married and divorced several times herself, Barbara de Angelis is one of the world's leading relationship experts. With a PhD, over 25 years experience as a relationship coach, through both private sessions and workshops, and 12 years as founder and Executive Director of the LA Personal Growth Center, Dr. Barbara de Angelis was one of the founding self-help experts of the late 1980s.

Dr. Barbara de Angelis often talks of her failed marriages and past relationships as the experiences that have pushed her to find the answers for relationship success. She claims it was for her own emotional survival that she had to become an expert at change and transformation; "Painful experience turned me into a transformational specialist." She has been there, done that, and certainly got the t-shirt when it comes to knowing what doesn't work and how it feels to be in a loveless marriage. She talks from real experience.

Relationship Philosophy

Dr. de Angelis focuses on empowering people to change their own lives, with positive messages about love and relationships. She puts the emphasis on the individual to become more aware of him or herself, how they behave within a relationship, and to take responsibility for their role. For example, if they've been divorced, they need to examine the problems that they caused themselves, not what their ex- did or didn't do.

According to Dr. de Angelis, happiness is not an acquisition: "I'll be happy when..." Often people expect happiness to suddenly arrive when a particular event happens or someone in their life makes a change. Dr. de Angelis tries to bring people to an understanding that it's about the way you live your life every day. It's the real moments and how we feel inside of ourselves that make us happy, not what's going on outside. Happiness is a skill that we need to work at, which we can only feel when we experience moments fully in the present. Such real moments could be enjoying sex, smelling the grass after a rainfall, or even comforting words to a partner during hard times.

She believes that true happiness comes from within ourselves, and that we cannot rely on others to make us happy. If we do look to others for joy, we often end up resenting them when they can't make us happy. Relationships are about growth and working not only within a partnership, but also on ourselves to enrich our lives, and in turn our relationships.

The Therapy

Dr. de Angelis has developed a wide range of programs for couples, singles, and parents that help create fulfilling relationships. By researching thousands of responses from her questionnaires, she highlights the different ways men and women communicate. For example, women put love first and often misunderstand a man's vagueness, emotional withdrawal, and lying to avoid unpleasantness. Understanding the different communication techniques is a way to avoid confrontation, according to Dr. de Angelis.

What Women Want Men to Know About Us

- ♥ Women put love first
- ♥ Women are creators
- ♥ Women have a sacred relationship with time
- ♥ Women need to feel safe
- ♥ Women need to feel connected
- ♥ Women need to feel valued

The 6 Biggest Mistakes Women Make with Men

✓ Acting like mothers and treating men like children
✓ Sacrifice who they are
✓ Fall in love with a man's potential
✓ Cover up their excellence and competence
✓ Give up their power
✓ Act like little girls to get what they want from men

In her book, "Secrets about Men Every Woman Should Know," Dr. DeAngelis solves the three biggest mysteries about men: why they hate to be wrong, why they hate it when their women get upset or emotional, and why men seem to care less about love and relationships than women do.

Examples
Taking Responsibility for who you Choose to Spend Time With

On the problem page on her website, there is a question from a woman who has recently left a dysfunctional relationship in which her husband lied, cheated, and used her for money. It took her 8 years to pluck up the courage to leave, and she is scared of dating again because she doesn't feel like she can trust men.

Dr. de Angelis points out very clearly that it's not men whom she needs to learn to trust again, but rather, herself. The truth is, she's the one who chose her ex-, allowed him to mistreat her, and never stood up for herself. Therefore, she is the one who needs to heal and learn to never give her power away to anyone again.

She became lost in a vicious cycle, whereby she was disrespected by her partner and was left feeling little respect or love for herself. "Love didn't hurt you – you hurt you by mistaking the dysfunctional relationship you had for love. Those painful events didn't just happen – they were allowed to happen by giving your power away."

This may seem harsh, but imagine how wonderful this woman's life will become as she begins to take more responsibility for herself and her decisions?

Does Passion Decline with Years of Marriage?

A woman asks Dr. de Angelis for advice on her sexless marriage. She's been married to her husband for 18 years and they are now more like best friends than lovers, rarely have sex, and she wonders if it's normal for all couples to feel this way after years of marriage?

Dr. de Angelis responds with a resounding NO! "Don't buy into the popular but misinformed attitude that losing romantic attraction to your partner is an inevitable part of marriage. That's like saying becoming unhealthy and having a heart attack is an inevitable part of growing older. Are heart attacks common? Yes... but now we know they are preventable if you take good care of your body. In the same way, just because it's common for many couples to lose the passion in their relationship over time, doesn't mean it is natural."

She advises the woman that relationships don't just lose their chemistry overnight; it takes years of neglect, not making the marriage number one, not communicating needs, or resolving hidden resentment. If both partners decide to do what it takes to rekindle the passion and learn more skills to make their relationship better, they can have a partnership that grows in love and passion year after year. She advises the first step is sitting down with her partner and telling him how much she misses the physical and emotional closeness, without blaming him or making him feel criticized. She should explain that they both deserve more and should recommit to learning to love again. If she also inspires him with how amazing things could

become once those old habits are overcome, he may actually help lead the changes they both are wanting.

Dr. Barbara de Angelis Quotes

- *You never lose by loving. You always lose by holding back.*
- *The more anger towards the past you carry in your heart, the less capable you are of loving in the present.*
- *The problem is not that you need love, but that you depend on others to create love in your life.*
- *Difficult times always create opportunities for you to experience more love in your life.*
- *If you aren't good at loving yourself, you will have a difficult time loving anyone, since you'll resent the time and energy you give another person that you aren't even giving to yourself.*
- *Love is a choice you make from moment to moment.*
- *Remember your partner is a mirror, reflecting all the parts of yourself you may not want to see.*
- *Marriage is not a noun; it's a verb. It isn't something you get; it's something you do. It's the way you love your partner every day.*

Books and Media

Dr. Barbara de Angelis has written 14 bestsellers, sold 7 million books, and has been published in 20 languages.

- Her first bestseller was *How to Make Love All the Time: Make Love Last a Lifetime.*

Other titles include:

- *Are You the One for Me?*
- *Secrets About Life Every Woman Should Know: Ten Principles for Total Emotional and Spiritual Fulfillment*

- *Secrets about Men Every Woman Should Know*
- *What Women Want Men to Know*
- *Real Moments: Discover the Secret for True Happiness*
- *The Real Rules: How to Find the Right Man for the Real You*
- *Chicken Soup for the Couple's Soul*
- *Chicken Soup for the Romantic Soul*
- *Confidence*
- *Passion*
- Her latest Book, is *How Did I Get Here? Finding Your Way to Renewed Hope and Happiness When Life and Love Take Unexpected Turns*
- Dr. Barbara de Angelis also wrote and produced a highly successful infomercial, *Making Love Work,* which was broadcast nationwide.
- Her TV appearances have been numerous, including *Oprah, The TODAY Show, The View,* as well as being the *NewsNight* relationship expert on *CNN* for two years.

How to Find Out More

- For more information about her work and extensive list of books, visit Dr. de Angelis' website: *www.barbaradeangelis.com*

11. Dr. Laura Berman

"Better sex and intimacy at any age"

Background and Qualifications

Dr. Laura Berman is dubbed America's leading expert in female sexual health. She has worked as a sex educator and therapist for 20 years, obtaining her master's degree in clinical social work and a doctorate in health education and therapy at New York University. She has also completed a fellowship in sexual therapy at the Department of Psychiatry at New York University Medical Center.

Dr. Berman is now assistant clinical professor of psychiatry and obstetrics/gynecology at The Feinberg School of Medicine at Northwestern University. She also runs the Berman Center, a specialized healthcare focused on women's and couple's sexual health. It offers couples and individual therapy and retreats.

Relationship Philosophy

According to Dr. Berman, there's a lot more to improving your sex life than buying sexy underwear or learning a new sexual position. It's about reconnecting with your mind, body, and your partner to get the sex life you've always wanted and that you deserve.

She stresses the importance of coming to terms with the fact that sexuality is an innate and healthy part of being alive and human. It's as natural as breathing. Unless we're comfortable with our sexuality, we cannot have a great sex life or love life. When it comes to taking charge of our sexuality, we need to take the leap, be brave, and not let the fear of change or the unknown hold us back. It's important to challenge any view that confines our sexuality, and instead, to allow ourselves to fully understand our sexual desires and needs.

Dr. Berman believes that sex affects every aspect of our relationships with our partner, not just in the bedroom. That's because a woman in touch with her sexuality feels confident, attractive, strong, and self-sufficient. Sex can make you feel healthier, happier, and improve the bond with your partner.

However, there are many obstacles that can get in the way of great sex. One of these is time – people are so busy with their day-to-day lives that often they don't make enough time for sex, which can become a common source of frustration. Other obstacles to intimacy are stress and difficult times, such as problems at work. Anything that puts us in a poor mood, especially stress, can have a negative impact on our sex life and intimacy.

There are gender issues that become entwined too. For some couples, it's difficult to match how long sex lasts, with men typically reaching orgasm much quicker than women. The different roles of sex and intimacy can also be disruptive – with men needing sex to feel intimate with their partner, but many women needing intimacy to enjoy sex.

The Therapy

Dr. Berman gives advice for all types of sexual problems, which can be medical in nature or stem from the problems outlined above. These include couples conflicts, loss of intimacy, low libido, difficulty reaching orgasm, dryness, low sensation, early ejaculation, erectile dysfunction, and pain during sex.

For Dr. Berman, sex and romance are crucial for intimacy and a truly fulfilling relationship. It's important to keep the passion and physical connection alive by regular touching and kissing. Even talking can increase intimacy. All too often, couples in long term relationships lose the spark between them that they once felt at the beginning of their relationship, but there are many ways to get this back.

First, in order to feel sexy, one has to feel confident. Taking care of your body and learning what feels good for you can increase confidence levels. Then, it's important to get in touch with sexual fantasies and tell or show your partner what turns you on. You can also experiment with new techniques as well as learning to embrace foreplay and fantasy to enhance excitement in your sex life.

Dr. Berman is also a believer in tantric sex. This technique can help couples tap into the well of energy that is our sexuality. Sexual energy can be harnessed to intensify the sexual experience. One version of Tantra teaches men to control the desire to orgasm. Once mastered, this can help to prolong lovemaking, create more intense erotic experiences, and increase feelings of connectedness with each other, yourself, and the universe. It's about letting go of the fears, regrets, and boundaries that hold us back from enjoying an intense and satisfying erotic connection.

Dr. Berman also stresses the importance of looking after our own health, which is vital for a good sex life. Basics, such as a good night's sleep, can work wonders for lovemaking. When we don't feel good, women in particular, we don't want to have sex. Dr. Berman also quotes research that REM sleep is important for good genital blood flow.

Too many women put sex at the bottom of their to-do-list because life is just too busy. It's important to find time to enhance sex and intimacy with your partner by delegating your workload, prioritizing, and learning how to let go of perfection. Disengaging from the busyness of life is essential. Exercise and meditation can help, and it's also important to take some "me time" and reconnect to your single self – the person you once were – and recapture your femininity. Although alcohol in small amounts can help people relax and be more comfortable, too much alcohol is a depressant, and will actually destroy desire, cause sleepiness, and get in the way of a well-functioning mind.

Examples
Trying too Hard in Bed

36-year-old Nicole is jealous, and accusing her partner Kahlen of flirting and not spending enough time with her. While working with Dr. Berman, she reveals that she has no real reason to be jealous; it is just that Kahlen is 10 years younger than her, and she is insecure. "I try to impress him sexually. I just want to be sure he has everything he needs at home." In her attempts to keep him faithful, she acts like a porn star to stop him from fantasizing about anyone else.

Nicole found this situation very frustrating, since she was in charge in other areas of her life. Kahlen was also frustrated, because lovemaking was no longer an intimate time for him; it was more "like being on stage."

Dr. Berman suggested that they make a detailed list of their fantasies and share them with one another. She also helped them connect emotionally. Nicole was thrilled to discover some of Kalhen's fantasies included some very simple and sweet things, such as making love under the stars while camping. Kahlen found that Nicole wanted simple romantic requests, such as love notes and roses, kisses, and cuddles on the couch.

When the pressure to perform was lifted, Nicole was free to really enjoy sex.

Berman Center

Nearly all of the cases seen by Dr. Berman include some combination of medical, emotional, and relationship problems. Another Nicole is a perfect example. She is taking SSRI medication for depression, which often reduces libido, and can cause vaginal dryness and difficulty reaching orgasm. Several years earlier, Nicole had laser surgery for skin cancer of the vulva. The surgery left an emotional impression on Nicole. She seemed to have some negative body issues from her surgery, and that made it more difficult for her during sex. Because of

some of these issues, she and her boyfriend were having some difficulty in the bedroom, and tensions were rising. He felt inferior because he could not bring her to orgasm, and thus, had difficulty getting or maintaining an erection. She started resenting having to work at it to get it hard. They were in a vicious cycle.

The Berman Center performs one of the most complete examinations for women like Nicole. It starts with several questionnaires and a Biopsychosocial Sexual Evaluation to give a full understanding of the problem. They also ask about childhood experiences, family attitudes about sex, and early experiences. Nicole admitted something Dr. Berman often hears: "I don't use a vibrator because I don't want to become dependent on it, or be unable to become aroused or reach orgasm without it."

Next, they provide a full gynecological and urological exam, checking internal and external structures, including the clitoris. Nicole often had bladder infections, which can cause pain and irritation. They check the vaginal pH, use an ultrasound probe to get a complete picture of the clitoral and labial anatomy and blood flow. Next, they give Nicole a vibrator and 3-D glasses for erotic visual stimulation so they can evaluate lubrication and blood flow after 15 minutes of stimulation. Day 2 is repeated with a dose of Viagra one hour before the exam.

They have had tremendous success treating women with Viagra. However, the issues often go much deeper into relationship problems, communication difficulties, or an unskilled or unwilling partner. It is very difficult for women to separate their sexuality from their environment or relationship. Some of the problems are long-standing and they affect every aspect of her self-esteem. Dr. Berman finds that it is important to integrate all aspects of the woman's life when treating sexual dysfunction.

Dr. Laura Berman Quotes

- *By giving in to our most primal sexual desires, and also remaining in control of them, we are able to learn new things about ourselves, increase spiritual awareness, and intensify the sexual experience.*

- *Celebrate sex and you celebrate life!*

- *Whoever you are, whatever your circumstances or age, sex is vital to your emotional well-being, self-esteem, health, and relationships.*

- *Many men can't feel intimate with their partner unless their sex life is satisfying, but many women can't enjoy sex without intimacy. For men, sex feeds intimacy and for women, intimacy feeds sex.*

- *Sex and romance are crucial for long-term intimacy.*

- *The stronger the sexual connection, the stronger the emotional intimacy will be.*

- *Intimacy is the fiber that binds us to the people we love, and is built on time, investment, and honest communication.*

- *Ongoing intense sexual excitement in a loving relationship goes against our biological instincts. This means you have to work at keeping the intimacy and attraction between you.*

Books and Media

- Dr. Laura Berman has appeared on countless TV and radio shows, most notably as a regular contributor on *Oprah* and *The TODAY Show,* as well as appearances on *Fox News, CNN,* and the hit reality TV series, *Sexual Healing,* which followed real-life couples through a week in therapy with her at the Berman Center.

- Dr. Berman also hosts Oprah's Radio show, *Better in Bed,* which is a lively call-in program

- She is a columnist for the *Chicago Sun Times*

- Co-author of the *New York Times* bestseller *For Women Only: A Revolutionary Guide to Reclaiming Your Sex Life,* as well as:
- *Secrets of the Sexually Satisfied Woman: Ten Keys to Unlocking Ultimate Pleasure*
- *The Passion Prescription* – which offers a step-by-step guide to improving your sex life in just 10 weeks.
- *Real Sex for Real Women,* to teach women how to reconnect with themselves and to communicate your sexual needs.
- Dr. Berman's latest book was published in 2011 – *Loving Sex: The book of joy and passion* helps couples overcome barriers to intimacy to have a deep and meaningful experience of sexuality

How to Find Out More

- For more information, go to *www.drlauraberman.com* and *www.bermancenter.com*

12. Dr. Pat Love

"Love is not about better communication."

Background and Qualifications

Dr. Pat Love Ed.D has over 25 years experience of helping people improve their marriages through her books, articles, training programs, therapy, speaking, and media appearances. She is faculty Emeritus of Imago Institute for Relationship Therapy and is a licensed marriage and family therapist. She was also a past president of the International Association for Marriage and Family Counseling.

Relationship Philosophy

Dr. Love teaches that it's the fundamental differences between men and women that make relationships hard. This is why improving communication does not work. She helps couples to rediscover and maintain the connection they felt when they first met. The journey to achieve this is not via better communication. "Relationship talk" does not help and can even drive a couple apart.

Women cannot talk to a man in the same way as you do one of your girlfriends. Most men will back away and withdraw because male emotions can be likened to woman's sexuality; you can't be too direct too quickly. The ways to connect with a man are through touch, activity, sex, and routines.

Relationships also have many natural highs and lows and unfortunately, many couples mistake the lows for the end of love and finish the relationship too quickly. Each relationship goes through a natural progression:

Natural Progression of a Relationship

1) Infatuation
2) Post rapture
3) Discovery
4) Connection

The heady infatuation stage is fuelled by powerful hormones and chemicals in the body, which are definitely not what love is all about. In fact, Dr. Love describes infatuation as the cause of 70% of all divorces.

The Therapy

Dr. Love explains in her books that underneath most couples' fights, there is a biological difference at work. Talking definitely won't solve this because there's no point trying to turn a man into a woman! The key is connection, before any kind of communication with words can begin. This can be through touch, sex, or doing things together, but just talking about the relationship will often have a detrimental effect.

Even during the heat of an argument, it's important to find a way to keep the connection. One way of doing this is to previously agree with your partner on a hand signal that you can use to halt the argument. It's not about ignoring your partner and what they are saying; it's a signal that you love that person more than the issue you are fighting about. It takes courage to be the first one to make the gesture, but it can have the immediate effect of breaking the argument and re-establishing a connection.

Dr. Love believes that far too many women criticize and blame their partners, which puts a man into a position of feeling shame; shame that they're not a better husband or lover. This often causes them to become emotionally stonewalled or more aggressive and critical themselves. Women have to learn to be more positive about their partners and decide that the relationship is more important than the little things that annoy them about their partners.

Dr. Love also uses the SOS technique – which stands for "Skin On Skin." It helps keep love and the connection alive and should be part of your daily routine. It can be holding hands or touching your partner's cheek, but not through their clothes, as you actually need to stimulate their nerves, as well as yours. This creates a message of love more powerful than words.

Examples

Lost Sex Drive

A woman writes in that she has been married for almost five years with their second child on the way. She lost her sex drive during her first pregnancy and hasn't gotten it back. "Is there anything possible to put myself in more of a mood for sex? I don't want him to lose interest in me. I want to satisfy him, and I'm not doing that."

Dr. Love responds that it is natural to lose one's sex drive in the months following pregnancy, so that you can focus on your baby. With a second child, tiredness becomes a critical factor. If the couple could be swept away to a tropical island, with the children well taken care of, her sex drive would naturally pick up. If this isn't feasible, there are other suggestions.

Suggestions for Satisfaction

♥ Some people need to be intentional about their interest in sex. That is, they need to psyche themselves up to put themselves in the mood.

♥ Make time for sex. Since sex is important to a healthy marriage, it must be a priority. Do whatever it takes to put yourself in the mood: read romance novels; take a long bath; spend 15 minutes focused on yourself. Have take-out or sandwiches instead of cooking.

♥ One of the greatest forms of foreplay is for the man to take care of the children, clean up the kitchen, cook, and let her sleep a little bit more.

♥ Keep in mind the question, "What is best for the relationship?" and do it.

Desire Discrepancy

One day, when Dr. Love was taking a taxi to a hotel in Manhattan, the taxi driver started a conversation. Finding out that she had a book on sexuality for couples, called *Hot Monogamy*, he started telling her his story. "I love my wife. We've been married 16 years. I've never fooled around, but the truth is, I'm not always happy with the lovemaking part. I am always the one wanting her; doing the initiating. One day I asked her why she didn't initiate. 'I just don't think about it,' she said. I even tried laying off it for ten days. I don't think she even noticed."

Dr. Love describes "sexual desire" as the first of three overlapping stages. Desire can be sparked by a sexy ad, a glimpse of your partner, or a random thought. If you can entice your partner to follow you to the bedroom, and with sufficient stimulation, you might arrive at the second stage, "arousal." This is where the penis becomes erect and the woman's genitals become engorged and lubricated. If arousal continues to build, you may arrive at the third stage of lovemaking, "orgasm."

Pamela and Dan

Pamela would be content to have sex three or four times a month. She is easily orgasmic, but has very low desire. Like many women, it takes her a long time to become aroused. Her husband Dan, on the other hand, would like sex every night. Soon after lovemaking, he is wondering how soon before they can do it again. He only knows for certain that it won't be soon enough.

Studies of human sexuality have consistently shown that, in general, men think about sex more often, are more easily aroused, want sex more frequently, and desire more partners than women. Dr. Love's suggestion is to have each partner tell the other what it feels like. Dan says to Pamela, "There is rarely a moment when I have no sexual desire. All I need is the slightest bit of encouragement, and there it is. Sex is the only thing worth doing."

Pamela said she used to have thoughts about sex in her twenties. "Now I rarely think about sex. If it weren't for pressure from you, I could go a week without having one sexy thought. You initiate sex when your level of desire builds up; I initiate sex with my level of guilt builds up."

To Dan, this makes no sense. "If you enjoy sex, and always reach orgasm, I don't understand why you don't want to do it more often." And to the male mind, it doesn't make sense. Dr. Love helps couples make sense of desire discrepancies – how to talk about it, and how to create intimacy.

Dr. Pat Love Quotes

- *The right to intimate physical contact is one of the privileges that define and separate a romantic love relationship from other relationships.*
- *Don't break up before the breakthrough!*
- *The number one myth about relationships is that talking helps.*
- *The deepest moments of intimacy occur when you are not talking.*
- *Sexual desire is not love. Sexual desire has as much to do with hormones as with relationship harmony.*
- *A commitment to marriage has to include a commitment to being a decent human being to live with.*

- *Love is ever changing. Throughout the life of a relationship, individuals change and life itself changes. Love has to be flexible enough to accommodate new information, new roles, and new ways of loving one another.*

- *Putting together a modern-day marriage can be likened to assembling an airplane in flight.*

Books and Media

Dr. Patricia Love has written and co-authored many books on love and relationships including:

- *Why Women Talk and Men Walk: How to Improve Your Relationship Without Discussing It*

- *How To Improve Your Marriage Without Talking About It* (with *Steven Stosny*)

- *The Truth About Love: The Highs, The Lows, and How You Can Make It Last Forever*

- *Hot Monogamy: Essential Steps to More Passionate, Intimate Lovemaking*

- *Never Be Lonely Again: The Way Out of Emptiness, Isolation, and a Life Unfulfilled* (with Jon Carlson)

- Dr. Love has also created a DVD education course entitled *Love: What Everyone Needs to Know*

- Dr. Love has appeared many times on *Oprah, The TODAY Show,* and *CNN* and is a regular contributor in *Cosmopolitan, Men's Health, Good Housekeeping, Men's Magazine,* and *Woman's World.*

How to Find Out More

- Go to Dr. Pat Love's website *www.patlove.com* or her blog *www.patlove.wordpress.com*

13. Dr. Robin Smith

"You have to be whole before you can be joined."

Background and Qualifications

Dr. Robin Smith is an ordained minister, keynote speaker, and licensed psychologist famous for her book, *Lies at the Altar: The Truth About Great Marriages*, which became a national number one bestseller.

She earned her PhD in counseling psychology from Temple University and a Masters from the Eastern Baptist Theological Seminary. She served on the advisory board of the Barrister's Association of Philadelphia and was a former member of the Board of Directors of the Albert Einstein Medical Center, Belmont Hospital, and Eagleville Hospital, a drug and alcohol rehabilitation center.

Dr. Robin, as she is affectionately known, is now adjunct professor at Palmer Theological Seminary (formerly Eastern Baptist Theological Seminary) and a regular contributor on Oprah Show. She also has her own call-in radio show, *The Dr. Robin Show,* on *Oprah and Friends* five days per week.

Relationship Philosophy

Long-term relationships can be passionate and exciting and Dr. Robin wants to challenge the misconception that marriage implies a life sentence: dead and boring. You can still be love-struck after 25 years, if the core of the relationship is strong and healthy.

She believes that self-knowledge is the fundamental key to the success of any marriage. If you don't know who you are, it is impossible to build the life of your dreams. There isn't anyone building the path of living in the truth, so we live in fear of the truth. Perhaps they won't love us or they won't want to live with

us. If we live in this fear, we cheat ourselves, and minimize the chance of having a good, strong marriage.

If you're waiting on the sidelines for someone to care about you, love you, or help you, you can never have a truly fulfilling relationship. You have to discover who you are first, and work on your own issues and baggage.

Combined with self-knowledge, truth is also a key ingredient for a great marriage. Without truly looking at yourself and being honest about what you want, you cannot have satisfaction and intimacy. Without it, you'll end up settling for less than your heart desires. Too many couples enter into a marriage and live their relationship with unspoken needs, unasked questions, outrageous expectations, and hidden agendas. These can all cause power struggles, suffering, and a feeling of hopelessness further on down the line. Women in particular often get caught up being the caregiver and give everything to the ones they love without placing enough emphasis on self-care.

Discovering who we are is a process of unlocking a complex mesh of lessons learned from our childhood. We have to acknowledge and understand the messages we learn from our upbringing in order to mature emotionally and to heal unfinished childhood wounds.

When we get married, we bring to the "marriage table" a group of people from our past — former partners and lovers, family members, friends — all of whom impact on how we conduct our relationship; in both positive and negative ways. Some will be saying, "Don't trust him," others may say, "Move forward and forgive," others may say, "Marriage never works." They all bring a different set of influences to the relationship, but all bring baggage that immensely impacts what we do when we get married. It's not simply a case of two people going to the altar to get married. Your baggage is standing there with you.

Most of us are very good at describing what baggage our partner is bringing to the marriage table and where they got it from, but it's much more difficult to unpack our own bags. Without clearing our marriage table, it's difficult to find the resources of love, compassion, and accountability to show up to our marriage like grown-ups.

Dr. Robin labels shame and blame as the "two toxic twins" because they are the most deadly components in a relationship, leading to destruction and hopelessness. Whether we are shaming and blaming ourselves, or our partner, these qualities prevent intimacy, trust, and respect, and become a barrier between you and the person you <u>chose</u> to be with.

The Therapy

According to Dr. Robin, before you even make it to the altar, it's important to examine your relationship and ask yourself if this is the right person for you. All too often people get married without truly examining the person they are with, somehow expecting change after the romance of the wedding day. Yet, it's important to speak the unspoken and truly establish what it is you want. Speak your truths before you get to the altar to make sure you achieve your heart's desires. After all, the person at the altar will be the one at the breakfast table!

Dr. Robin uses her "under new management" approach to help empower individuals to take charge and responsibility for their own life, job, and relationships. Once we truly know ourselves and take responsibility for ourselves, then we can create the life we want. This empowers us to succeed in communication, conflict management, dealing with differences, resilience, and accountability.

A quick tool to gain insight into what kind of person we are is to ask ourselves the question, "What is it like living with me?" If you can answer this question truthfully and honestly, this will

help you to fully appreciate what and who you're bringing to the marriage table and who you need to say goodbye to.

Dr. Robin also encourages people to understand and use the 90/10 theory. If you're struggling over issues that cannot be resolved, and take 90% responsibility for creating them. They are about your stuff, your baggage, and your issues, which you have not resolved. You can only attribute 10% to your partner. Before you focus on your partner and what's wrong with them, spend 90% of your energy on what is wrong with you, without resorting to shame or blame. This "passionate accountability" can help to get a couple out of a rut and the associated downward spiral of destruction.

Top 10 Lies

- ♥ Marriage is an automatic ticket to self-esteem.
- ♥ You have to go along to get along.
- ♥ If the package is beautifully wrapped, its contents will be fabulous.
- ♥ The past is over.
- ♥ Anything is better than being alone.
- ♥ It's important to be right.
- ♥ You can learn to live with compromises that trouble your soul and make you suffer.
- ♥ It's you and me against the world.
- ♥ If you believe in the same God, you'll share the same values.
- ♥ Marriage magically changes people for the better.

Top 10 Truths

- ♥ You have to be whole before you can be joined.
- ♥ In a great marriage, you can ask for what you need without fear of reprisals.
- ♥ The packaging doesn't tell you anything about what's inside

- ♥ The past is driving you to the chapel.
- ♥ Being alone and free is better than being together and controlled.
- ♥ It's more important to relate.
- ♥ Suffering is not love.
- ♥ You can't have a great marriage if you live in a bunker.
- ♥ Values are what you live, not what you believe.
- ♥ The person at the altar will be the person at the breakfast table.

Examples
True to Myself

Dr. Smith knows first hand what it means to live a lie. She was in a long relationship with a man whose addictions ruled life. Although the eventual breakup was painful, it was more difficult to face the truth of why she stayed so long. Why did she lie to herself to remain with this man? She was slowly fading away and recreating herself in an image meant to please him.

He would taunt her for her insecurities and weaknesses. He criticized her regularly. She acquiesced and gave away her power in futile attempts to placate him. It did, only temporarily, and she had to give away even more of herself just to exist. But she really didn't exist; not for him and not for herself. He grew tired of her and erased her from his life.

This almost crushed her spirit, but was also the turning point. She made a decision to stop letting lies dominate her, and made a commitment to walk in truth, no matter how difficult the road or how long the journey. Today, she could only choose a man who had demonstrated trustworthiness and truthfulness as values he actually lives. Through her experience, Dr. Smith invites women to join her in the journey of self-discovery and truth. Once you truly know yourself, you will decide how to spend your life and

with whom to share your emotional, spiritual, financial, physical, and sexual wealth.

Toxic Power of old Wounds

Larry learned he could not rely on others from a very young age. His father was distant and rarely available. His mother was impatient and had a short temper. When he was 5 years old and beaten up by older boys who took his favorite toy, his father just look at him disgustedly; "You have to learn to defend yourself," then went back to reading the paper. From that moment on, Larry knew he had to take care of himself because nobody else would.

He fell in love with Sonja in college. She had an entirely different upbringing with a warm, nurturing mother who loved being with children, and a strong, capable father who always knew exactly what to do. Sonja was attracted to Larry because of his sensitivity. She knew she could trust him to never leave her. After they were married, Larry's sensitivity became a weakness; she wanted a man more like her father – strong, stoic, and resilient. They drifted apart and Sonja left him for an older man who was a replica of her father.

Larry went back to being 5 years old. "It only proved what I always knew; I have to take care of myself because no one else will." Rather than believe that no partner could be trusted, Larry was encouraged to see that he entered the marriage from a place of being wounded. "You chose a partner who you could finally trust to take care of you as your mother and father did not." He could see that his ideal left no room for her to disappoint him without him taking it personally. Of course, Sonja was also wounded and needed a man who was "bigger" than she was to be her problem solver and the leader.

To some extent, we are all wounded because of our childhood. We must learn the difference between our wounded self and our true self: the person who can see beyond fear. Dr. Smith poses these rhetorical questions: "What would you do if you weren't afraid of losing; if you weren't afraid of rejection? Who would you be if your wounds weren't in the driver seat of your life?"

Questions to ask Before you Marry

Dr. Smith's book, *Lies at the Altar,* presents 276 challenging questions to ask your partner before marriage. There are sections about Work, Money, Sex, Parenthood, and Religion, among many others. For instance, questions to ask about Money include: What is your annual income; Should couples have joint or separate bank accounts; do you have significant debt; do you believe in establishing a budget (and do you do it); how important is it to you to make a lot of money? These straight-talking questions leave little doubt and little to the imagination. Imagine if you knew this level of detail about the person you are about to marry?

A better question is why don't people ask these sorts of question of their soon-to-be-mates? If you were merging two companies, you would certainly ask these questions, and many more in the "due diligence" phase. Perhaps we think of asking these questions as "breaking the romance," and are unwilling to find out things that would ruin the relationship. Perhaps we think it rude to ask such pointed questions. However, you will learn about these things sooner or later; you deserve to know exactly what you are getting yourself into.

These questions open new lines of communications and make sure you do not enter a marriage fraught with difficulties. This is also useful for married couples, so they can find where they are stuck. Her book provides the tools to empower your life and your marriage.

Dr. Robin Smith Quotes

- *The person at the altar will be the person at the breakfast table.*

109

- *No one is your friend who demands your silence or denies your right to grow.*
- *If you want to walk on water you have to get out of the boat.*
- *In a great marriage, you can ask for what you need without fear of reprisals.*
- *Make sure that all of your communication is coming from a place of awakened awareness, so that you can be in tune with yourself and the audience you are speaking with.*

Books and Media

- Dr. Robin's first book was *Inspirational Vitamins: A Guide to Personal Empowerment.* It contains a foreword by Stevie Wonder and offers 16 key tools to expand your vision of what it means to be a truly inspirational human being.

- *Lies at the Altar: The Truth About Great Marriages,* was published in 2006 and was a number one bestseller on the lists of The *New York Times*, *Wall Street Journal*, *USA Today, Publisher's Weekly*, and *Entertainment Weekly*.

- Her most recent book is *Hungry: The Truth About Being Full,* takes the reader on a journey of emotional and spiritual starvation, to understand where the hunger truly comes from.

- Dr. Robin has made countless TV appearances, most notably on *Oprah, Larry King Live*, *NBC, ABC News, CBS, MSNBC*, and *Fox News*.

How to Find Out More

- For more information, go to *www.drrobinsmith.com*

14. Dr. John Gottman

"We need to teach couples that they'll never solve most of their problems."

Background and Qualifications

John Gottman, PhD has spent years researching and observing couples to establish what makes a successful and fulfilling relationship. Famous for his work on marital stability and divorce prediction, during research at the University of Washington, his team even came up with a method of predicting with up to 90% accuracy whether a marriage would survive or not. This was achieved through the study of emotions, physiology, and communications by watching couples interact in a research apartment that became known as "The Love Lab."

Dr. Gottman is Professor Emeritus of Psychology at the University of Washington, and he has been awarded 4 National Institute of Mental Health Research Scientist Awards. He is also executive director of the Relationship Research Institute.

Alongside his wife, Dr. Julie Schwartz Gottman, he founded the Gottman Institute, which helps couples work on their marriage as well as training mental health professionals and care providers on his marriage guidance techniques.

Relationship Philosophy

Gottman believes that a successful relationship is far more than just good communication. This conclusion is based on his many years spent studying marriage, observing the habits of those that achieve wedded bless, and those who don't. By comparing the Masters (couples who have happy marriages) to the Disasters (couples who breakup or are terribly unhappy), he has come up with seven principles for making marriage work:

111

7 Principles for Making Marriage Work

1) Maintain awareness of your partner through a Love Map

2) Foster fondness and admiration

3) Turn towards, not away (Emotional Bank Account)

4) Create positive sentiment override

5) Solve solvable conflicts; Cope with perpetual conflicts

6) Make dreams and aspirations come true

7) Create shared meaning through rituals of connection

Referred to as the Sound Marital House theory, this is the conceptual framework of the Gottman Method Couples Therapy. Through the lens of this theory, clinicians not only assess a couple's ability to navigate conflict, they also assess the emotional connection and friendship system as well as the more existential issues of shared meaning, life dreams, and life philosophy. From this perspective, Gottman Method Couples Therapy not only emphasizes conflict management skills, it also addresses social skills training, enhancing emotional connection between partners and existential dilemmas, as addressed by the "Dreams Within Conflict" intervention.

The Dreams Within Conflict is a speaker-listener exercise that can be used to in gridlock situations. It is designed to deepen the understanding of each other's gridlocked position. It is assumed that a deep value or dream is underlying the gridlock, and compassionate questions can be used to help both partners better understand themselves and their divergent positions. Focusing on the dream behind the conflict will dramatically reduce the strain, without having to solve the conflict

A Love Map is the part of your brain where you store important information about your mate you want to remember. A love map can include things like your partner's goals, aspirations, joys, fears, hopes, dreams, frustrations, likes and dislikes, friends, hobbies, and favorite things. The more you know about each others thoughts and feelings, the more likely you will stay connected thought difficulties, challenges, and change.

When the first three of the principles are present (Friendship and intimacy through love maps, fondness and admiration, and turning towards bids for emotional connection), the Positive Sentiment Override is automatically created. This means that you give your partner the benefit of the doubt, and believe he or she has positive intentions by their actions and comments.

According to Gottman, 69% of conflicts never get solved. This means that you inherit a set of insolvable conflicts with your partner, and if you leave the relationship for another, you will get rid of those conflicts, but inherit another set.

At this point, some couples find themselves in Gridlock, with no compromise possible. How a couple handles gridlock is critical for long-term happiness. Gottman found that not all negative behaviors are equally corrosive to the marriage. There are four negative behaviors that do the most damage.

The Four Horseman of the Apocalypse
1) Criticism
2) Defensiveness
3) Contempt
4) Stonewalling

Criticism implies there is something globally wrong with one's partner and uses terms like "you always" or "you never." A complaint, on the other hand, deals with a specific time and issue, but adding blame to a complaint becomes criticism, and is erosive.

Defensiveness is an attempt to protect oneself from a perceived attack. A common tactic is to counter-attack. Another tactic is to ignore your partner's complaint and counter with, "But what

about all the good things I do for you. I never get any appreciation." Another counterattack is, "But you did the same!"

In Gottman's studies, contempt is the biggest predictor of divorce. Imitating your spouse with a mocking tone or body language is particularly humiliating. Correcting their grammar or word usage when they are upset is another way to demonstrate contempt. Whining, eye rolling and increasing sarcasm are part of the contempt cycle. There are also universal facial expressions of contempt, and if you have ever been on the receiving side of that expression, you will know how hurtful it feels.

Stonewalling occurs when one partner withdraws from the interaction. Rather than actively listening, with all the attendant listening cues, a stonewaller turns away as if gone.

Sometimes, stonewalling comes when a person is flooded, that is, experiencing too much emotion, has an elevated heart rate above 100 BPM, and is having difficulty self-soothing. Gottman recommends taking a break when either partner is flooded, as long as both partners are committed to resuming the discussion later at an agreed upon time.

Repair attempts are a critical portion of the healing conflict. It can be almost anything, and takes the form of supporting or soothing one another, expressing appreciation, bringing in humor, or even commenting on the communication itself.

Another choice when dealing with an insolvable conflict is to talk about it and to understand the dream within the conflict. This allows a couple to move from gridlock to dialog on the issue. The first step is to reveal the dream that underlies the conflict. Often, this dream is so buried, the person is not even aware of the dream. The second step is to honor the other's dream. This could take the form of interest, respect, and encouragement, or direct involvement and teamwork. The key is respect.

One of the most important things in a marriage is the way it enables both people to fee that the relationship supports their dreams. Most conflicts are actually about what the issue means, rather than the issue itself. Creating shared meaning and purpose allows the partners to align their values, and feel as if they are building something beyond just the relationship.

The Therapy

Through private sessions as well as his weekend workshops entitled *The Art and Science of Love,* which he conducts alongside his wife, Dr. Gottman teaches couples how to reshape their relationships and create a marriage that will last. He advises couples to seek help early if they detect a problem, because the average couple lives with unhappiness until it's often too late to repair.

He also teaches techniques to argue with your partner without losing control by:

- ♥ **Self-editing** – avoid saying every critical thought when discussing touchy subjects.

- ♥ **Softening your start up** – by bringing up problems gently and without blame to avoid creating a full-blown fight.

- ♥ **Repair and exit the argument** – before it gets out of control. Tactics are changing the topic, using humor, or stroking your partner on the arm and saying, "I understand how difficult this is for you." If an argument gets too heated, take a 20-minute break and agree to discuss it when you're both feeling calmer.

Other skills that are essential in developing and strengthening marital friendship are the ability to accept influence from the other, to compromise, and to accept physiological soothing.

It is also important to build emotional connection with your partner. To connect in an intimate level, you will want to ask specific questions to understand how they feel, deep down.

The Art of Intimate Conversation

- ♥ Put into words what you are feeling
  - o I'm feeling angry, happy, content, accepted, appreciated
- ♥ Ask targeted questions to deepen intimacy
  - o Are you wanting x, y, or z
  - o Are you feeling like you need to do something about that
- ♥ Express empathy and understanding to engage your partner
  - o That makes a lot of sense. I can see why you feel that way. I'd feel the same way in your situation
  - o I wish I'd have known earlier
- ♥ Follow up with statements that deepen connection
  - o That's a really tough position to be in
  - o They are lucky to have you
  - o I am lucky to have you

It is too easy to give advice, telling someone they shouldn't feel a particular way, that they are too sensitive, or that they have misread the situation, and got it all wrong. Any of those strategies will break connection. Gottman points out that understanding must always precede advice, and that advice should only be give when specifically asked for.

Couples build trust and intimacy with being attuned to the other and to themselves. It is the basis for "being there" for the other.

ATTUNE

- ♥ **Awareness** of the emotion
- ♥ **Turning towards** the emotion
- ♥ **Tolerance** of the emotional experience
- ♥ **Understanding** the emotion
- ♥ **Non-defensiveness**, listening to the emotion
- ♥ **Empathy** toward the emotion

From Empathy, you can move to Validation, "It makes sense you would have these feelings and needs because..." Being attuned to your partner means you put more emphasis on understanding your partner's emotion, and give up responsibility for having to fix or change your partner's emotional state, or their reasoning, beliefs or thoughts behind the emotion.

Think about it, trying to fix or change your partner more likely comes from your inability to be with the anxiety their emotion causes in you. These highly charged emotions could lead to flooding, the state where one is unable to remain present and connected. Flooding happens when one feels the shock of feeling attacked, blamed, shamed, or abandoned; when one notices that it is not possible to calm down, so the response is emotional shutdown. It is not possible to listen or communicate when flooded. The only remedy is to take a break and be with yourself and your emotions. That's why it is so important to be attuned to being flooded, so you know when to ask for a time out.

An important factor for relationship success is having high standards for your relationship, and refusing to accept hurtful behavior. Couples can get into the pattern of accepting insults or unreasonable behavior, and becoming immune to it. The less acceptance newlyweds have to hurtful behavior, the happier they tend to be in the long term.

Trust is an essential part of any relationships. Gottman offers these criteria for evaluating the trustworthiness of others.

- ♥ **Honesty** – practices no deceptions, does not lie to you
- ♥ **Transparency** – his or her life is an open book, with no secrets from you
- ♥ **Accountability** – he does what he says he will do and takes responsibility for the outcomes of his actions – doesn't blame
- ♥ **Ethics** – consistent standards of being fair and just
- ♥ **Alliance** – this person can be counted on to be totally on your side, perhaps even against others

Examples

It's all in the First Three Minutes!

Through his research at the University of Washington, Gottman and his team discovered that they could predict whether couples would divorce from the way they interacted in the first three minutes of a discussion about an area of continuing disagreement. 124 couples who had been married less than six months were video taped, with their facial expressions, tone of voice, and speech content examined while they discussed a difficult topic that they disagreed on.

Those who began with a positive display tended to still be married at the end of the six-year study. Those who went on to divorce began these talks with an increased display of negative emotions, words, and gestures. Gottman labels the four types of emotional expression that can be dangerous for a marriage as the "Four Horsemen:" criticism, defensiveness, contempt, and stonewalling.

How you present an issue and how your partner responds to you is absolutely critical. Gottman explains that it's important for women to soften their approach to bringing up a problem, and men have to learn to be more accepting of what she's saying. Furthermore, women initiate discussions about problems around 80% of the time; and in couples headed for divorce, the opening statement is usually in the form of criticism with statements such as, "You're lazy and never do anything around the house," rather than making specific complaints such as, "You didn't take the trash out last night."

All you Ever do is Work!

Sam fell in love easily with Katie. She was attractive, intelligent, and fun. After 10 years of marriage and 3 children, they understand each other quite well. However, they have some serious challenges. "He puts in so many hours at his start up Biotech Company, that he has little energy left for the family," Katie complains. She understands how compelling his work is, but demands that he find a better balance, for the sake of the marriage. After they put the children to bed, he often disappears in the basement office until late in the morning. "What happened to the guy who wrote love letters?"

At the same time, Sam has complaints of his own. All he ever gets from Katie are complaints and criticism. Can't she see how hard he works for the family? Can't she see all the problems he has to deal with at work? "I need more down time," Sam explains.

"When we try to talk about our problems, we get angry quickly," explains Katie. "Sam gets upset with me, so he leaves. It makes me crazy."

Gottman records Katie and Sam for 10 minutes while they rehash their argument. Both wear electrodes to measure physiological signs of stress. The conversation is later analyzed in great detail, like a Monday morning quarterback review. They look for when the conversation drifts from complaints to criticism; from open to defensive; from clarification to blame.

What Gottman finds is a cycle of criticism-defend-counter criticism. Katie's complaint of Sam's work slips into criticism. Sam gets defensive and launches a counterattack against her needs. Katie gets defensive, angry, and more critical, perhaps as a way to crack his armor. The cycle picks up more energy and Sam withdraws. Katie feels alone and frustrated.

The solution is to learn how to complain without making it personal and criticizing. Listen to the other for their needs – what is their longing? Validate the other's needs and express appreciation for each other. "Catch them in the act of getting it right," and let the other know you appreciate them.

Many people have a difficult time hearing appreciation because praise is often coupled with criticism: "I love how you take care of the family, **but** you are always too busy for the family." That **but** negates everything that came before it, and all the listener

is left with is the criticism. Also, some people have an inherent internal conversation of "I'm not lovable. If they really knew who I was, they wouldn't love me," and that blocks any acceptance of appreciation. Gottman advises people to make a mental note and repeat the complement in your mind. Over time, you may learn to accept the fact that you *are* worthy; you *are* truly loved.

Why Marry When you Don't even Like Each Other?

In an interview with *Seattle Weekly*, John Gottman marvels at the amount of people who get married and don't even like each other. They're not having good sex; they don't feel like their partner is that interested in them, but they still get married anyway! Perhaps they hold some desperate hope that marriage will solve their relationship problems?

What Gottman advises is truly evaluating a relationship before a commitment such as marriage is made. First, it's important to discover whether you have a quality friendship – are you interested in each other, do you notice when they need you, are you affectionate and respectful? Do you feel special to this person? Also, it's important to honestly examine whether you are really attracted to and turned on by them?

Although these are tough questions to answer that may require some soul searching and self-honesty, it's essential to examine these feelings before marriage. It's surprising how many couples don't go through this process; it could have saved them an unnecessary trip to the divorce courts just a few years later.

Dr. John Gottman Quotes

- *I liken an affair to the shattering of a Waterford crystal vase. You can glue it back together, but it will never be the same again.*
- *Happy marriages are based on a deep friendship. By this, I mean a mutual respect for and enjoyment of each other's company.*

● *It's a myth that if you solve your problems, you'll automatically be happy. We need to teach couples that they'll never solve most of their problems.*

Books and Media

☐ Gottman has appeared on many TV shows, including *Oprah, Good Morning America,* and *The TODAY Show.*

📖 His book, *The Seven Principles of Making Marriage Work* was a New York Times Bestseller, which outlined the concept that there's more to making a solid marriage than communicating and sharing every feeling and thought.

📖 The book, *The Marriage Clinic,* should be mandatory reading by all therapists.

Other titles include:

📖 *Ten Lessons to Transform your Marriage: America's Love Lab Experts Share Their Strategies for Strengthening Your Relationship*

📖 *Why Marriages Succeed or Fail: and How You Can Make Yours Last*

📖 *The Relationship Cure: A 5 Step Guide for Building Better Connections with Family, Friends, and Lovers* (available also on audio CD)

📖 *The Mathematics of Marriage*

📖 *A Couple's Guide to Communication*

📖 *The Science of Trust: Emotional Attunement for Couples*

📖 *What Makes Love Last?: How to Build Trust and Avoid Betrayal*

📼 *Relationship Exercises – for Effective and Loving Marital Communication Audio Cassette*

How to Find Out More

🖥 For more information, go to the Gottman Institute website, *www.gottman.com*

15. Dr. Leo Buscaglia

"Dr. Hug"

Background and Qualifications

Born in 1924, Dr. Buscaglia was the son of Italian immigrants in Los Angeles. He was raised as a Roman Catholic, and was greatly influenced by Buddhism.

After serving in the US Navy during World War II, Dr. Buscaglia went on to achieve a Bachelors degree in English and Speech and, a Masters and PhD in Language and Speech Pathology. After graduating, Dr. Buscaglia supervised special education and counseling at Pasadena city schools from 1960 – 65, and went on to teach at The University of Southern California School of Education in the 1970s. It was here that one of his students committed suicide, which had a major impact on Dr. Buscaglia, and was the reason he set up his Love 1A class; a course without grades for students to have a forum to consider emotions, the essential things in life, and discover their own magic. He taught the class without salary.

It was this class that formed the basis for his lectures on love, which he took worldwide. Hugging became the trademark of his lectures, where thousands of people would stand patiently waiting to hug him afterwards. He almost never left until he'd met everyone in line.

Relationship Philosophy

Dr. Buscaglia emphasized the value of human touch, especially hugs. He taught people to create love by showing love and finding that emotion from within, stating, "To give love, you must possess love."

He always worked to dispel the myth of "happily ever after;" that love will conquer all, as if it's not a growing or changing thing that requires work. Buscaglia believed that you can't leave love alone and believe it will find a way. You have to nurture it; you have to practice relationships. He often used the analogy of cooking – you can't make a soufflé without instructions or thinking about the ingredients, or it would fall flat. Likewise you have to make a relationship blossom and bloom.

He used to say, "You'd be a fool to continue in a relationship that didn't seem to honor both partners. He was also against relationships that had a conditional aspect to the love, as in "I'll love you if..." That would be conditional love, and who wants that? On the other hand, he believed in not smothering anyone in relationships in a way that would prevent nurturing their growth. "You can't grow in my shadow."

The most vital of human behaviors are love, tenderness, compassion, caring, sharing and relating. Live is empty without these qualities. Since this is so, why do we spend so little time developing these skills? Learning to love requires skills as delicate as a surgeon, a master builder and a gourmet cook

The Therapy

Dr. Buscaglia's beliefs on Love were brought to couples, individuals, and professionals alike through his lectures and seminars, delivered with passion, enthusiasm, and humor. He used a mixture of stories, both real and imaginary, to bring his message of love alive. Many people felt such an awakening of spirit and a realization of how to give love without expecting anything in return, that it changed their life irreversibly.

He helped couples analyze the dynamics of their relationships and fears of commitment, which he believed were established by society's suspicious attitudes towards tenderness, compassion, caring, and sharing by emotionally detached people. His love quiz helps analyze a person's loving strengths and points out ways in which people can learn to show even more love towards one another.

To love, one has to really care about himself. "Everything is filtered through me, and so the greater I am, the more I have to give. The greater knowledge I have, the more I have to give. The greater understanding I have, the greater is my ability to teach others, and to make myself the most fantastic..."

A survey of over 600 people reported that the top qualities that most enhanced continued growth in love were: communication, affection, compassion/forgiveness, honesty and acceptance. Clearly, the desire to be open, to share and relate, and to actively speak and listen are critical for good relating. These qualities must be cultivated if we are to overcome loneliness, and learn to love one another.

Examples
The Gift of Relationships

In one lecture, he passionately discusses the importance of relationships to enable us to grow. The other person in the partnership is a mirror to reflect who you truly are. He questions: "Who in this audience has experienced walking into a room and have everybody light up and say, 'Look! She's here!' As opposed to walking into a room and hearing people say, 'Oh my god! Look who's coming!'"

Buscaglia explains that we should cherish these interactions. Any type of relationship, not just with a partner, is a chance to reflect who we are by looking at people's responses to us. We should evaluate those interactions; "Is it a celebration because you are there, or a bummer?!"

Mama and Papa

Buscaglia used to feel great remorse that so many of his students had no idea about who their Mamas and Papas truly were. They couldn't tell him what made their parents happy, what were their greatest losses were; how they fell in love. He felt that people were missing out on a history of learning, which could be passed down from their parents and grandparents.

Leo Buscaglia always used stories about his own Mama and Papa to bring his lectures alive. One of his favorites was their story of courtship. His parents grew up in tiny villages about two miles apart. Papa had to walk along a dirt path to Mama's village, and the first time he saw her he knew she was the woman he wanted to marry. But when his Mama saw Papa for the first time, she didn't dare think he was right! Both families had to get involved first. Papa went home and talked to his Papa, who talked to his Grandpapa. Papa was eventually allowed to visit Mama's house every Sunday for polenta and they got married with their family's blessing.

His Mama later admitted to Leo that she never really got to look at her husband until they'd been married for two weeks. So how come they lived together for more than 50 wonderful years of marriage? It was because they were open to a journey of discovery and sharing. According to Leo, life was never boring for them. Even after 50 years of marriage, Leo was fascinated by their interactions and how they never grew tired of the learning they brought each other. Everyday, they had to work on their marriage, without buying into the unrealistic belief of happily ever after.

Dr. Leo Buscaglia Quotes

- *Love can relieve you of conflict. If people have to be right, smile and let them be right!*
- *Don't smother each other. No one can grow in shade.*
- *It is when we ask for love less and begin giving it more, that the basis of human love is revealed to us.*
- *Love is a verb. You've got to go out and give it!*
- *I have a very strong feeling that the opposite of love is not hate – it's apathy. It's not giving a damn!*

- *Love is always bestowed as a gift – freely and without explanation. We don't love to be loved; we love to love!*

- *Live love… don't go looking for it!*

- *My love has a condition that if ever my love keeps you from you – from your growing and realizing your personal potential – then I must step aside.*

Books and Media

- Dr. Buscaglia's first book, *Love,* sold over one million copies, offering an examination of human love as one unifying force, as well as identifying the barriers to love and the means of overcoming them.

Five of his books were on the New York Bestsellers list simultaneously. He has written a dozen books selling over 11 million copies worldwide in 20 languages. Titles include:

- *Love: What Life is All About*

- *Living, Loving, and Learning*

- *Loving Each Other: The Challenge of Human Relationships*

- *The Fall of Freddie the Leaf: A Story of Life For All Ages* (a book that helps the healing process after losing a loved one).

- *Born for Love: Reflections on Loving*

How to Find Out More

- Go to Dr. Buscaglia's website: *www.buscaglia.com*

16. Michael Webb

"The World's Most Romantic Man"

Background and Qualifications

Michael Webb claims that in 17 years of marriage to his wife Athena, they have never had a single fight! He has written 16 books to show other couples the secrets of his blissful marriage and how to keep the romance alive. Dubbed the "World's Most Romantic Man" and "Mr. Romance," Webb offers practical tips for any couple wishing to rekindle the sense of love and romance they once felt.

Michael Webb grew up with his Mom and sisters, all of who went through failed marriages, and it was these experiences of how bad marriage could be that made him determined to one day be the best husband ever! His Mom also shared a secret with him that all women desired to be loved and shown often that they are special. Now, in his own marriage, Webb makes sure he lets his wife know how deeply he loves her every day by what he says and does.

His foray into writing began with a simple 8 page newsletter with romantic tips and ideas, and now his website has 20 million annual visitors, and offers everything from creative date ideas, romantic getaways, sex advice, love making tips, to romantic proposals.

Relationship Philosophy

Michael Webb aims to focus on what blissfully happy couples are doing right, rather than where couples are going wrong. He believes that relationships take work, are constantly a challenge, and each partner has to be prepared to really put in the hard work.

One of the main reasons that relationships fail is that couples don't spend time asking the right questions of each other before they marry to really make sure they are compatible. He also believes that men and women express love in different ways and it takes effort, practice, and diligence to really understand their partners, and to give them what they want.

It's about the small things you do everyday to show your partner you love them – the little love notes, the special gifts, the rose left on a pillow, or sensual massage. Yet, many men are not natural romantics and find it difficult to express love verbally and with actions. However, Webb implores both men and women to find their inner romantic; to really show and prove to their mate how much they love them, which is guaranteed to kindle a depth of romance and desire never felt before.

The Therapy

Webb teaches that there are four main ways to reignite passion and fire in a relationship:

- ♥ **Deeply understand your partner:** this is important before marriage and after too, but it's surprising how many couples embark on a lifelong commitment without asking the right questions. Webb lays out a series of important questions about money, careers, the past, sex, religion, and children, which are vital to ensure conflict does not arise. Examples include – where do you want to live? Could you live in a hot climate? Do you want children? Do you have any phobias? Would you mind if my Mom came to live with us if she was unwell? These questions provide an insurance to stay happily married for a lifetime.

- ♥ **Show your love in a UNIQUE way:** it's very easy to say, "I love you" on a daily basis, but putting in time and energy to the "I love you's" can turn a relationship around. Ideas include:

- ○ **Sending your partner a unique gift at work** inside a formal envelope "For the personal attention of Mrs. X. URGENT!"
- ○ **Bringing back childhood memories** by asking your partner's family what they always wanted as a child.
- ○ **Sensual massage with a difference.** Leave a gift box beautifully wrapped with a bottle of massage oil and a card saying, "I know a great masseur" with your name and phone number on it.
- ○ **Leaving a long stemmed rose** on your partner's pillow with a message saying, "Thank you for coming into my life."

- ♥ **Go on dates... and never stop dating:** It's easy to slip into a routine where you lose the spark that made the relationship special in the first place. Dedicate time each week or month for a special date with your partner, whether that's a picnic, a trip to an art gallery, or just laying on a blanket under the stars.

- ♥ **Spark and fuel intimacy:** having a hot love life is one of the most profound ways to keep the romance alive. Surprise your partner with a little gift after lovemaking, try a new position, sensual massage, or just spend time staring into each other's eyes and caressing bare skin before making love.

Examples

How to get my Husband in the Mood

Michael Webb receives a letter from a desperate wife, Sherry. She complains that her husband is rarely in the mood for sex anymore. They used to make love about once a week but now it is every two or three months. It's not that he is against sex; he just says he's tired. She is desperate for help!

Webb replies by explaining there could be a number of different issues going on that might be affecting her husband's libido.

129

His hormone levels might have dropped which would affect his sex drive, and a trip to the doctor could determine this. Secondly, he could be having problems getting an erection and be too embarrassed to discuss it. Webb also suggests that Sherry could be wanting sex at the wrong time and that they should try in the morning during a man's natural sexual peak.

He also advises that after years of marriage, sex could be boring to her husband and that they should try something new. Finally he could be masturbating too much and has "run out of juice" when it's time to become intimate with his wife.

Saving Sex Until After Marriage

Another letter asks for advice on making a first sexual encounter truly enjoyable. The woman explains that she's getting married soon and they've saved sex for marriage. She's nervous about her honeymoon because they have two weeks to do nothing but explore each other. She understands that it may hurt but she's more concerned about the advice she's received that honeymoon sex often isn't that great. She'd like tips on how to make their honeymoon more enjoyable; anything that may be easier or fun if she's sore or things to do when they still feel shy.

Webb responds by first congratulating her on keeping sex for marriage – "what a beautiful gift that you can give each other." He agrees that honeymoon sex can be a let down as you learn to please your partner. It can be frustrating and very nerve wracking, but it will also be fresh and exciting, and can offer the chance for great pleasure. "For some people, it is such a wonderful experience that they barely make it outside the hotel room."

He advises soaking in a hot tub together and having an alcoholic drink to help relax the mind and muscles, which may help reduce the pain that some (but not all) feel with the first penetration. He also recommends she be on top so that she can control the pressure. Extended foreplay can also help. If she finds she's sore, he advises ordering a platter of fresh fruit and having fun with that, then enjoying a nice shower together.

Michael Webb Quotes

- *I believe a lot fewer couples would get divorced if they actually knew each other before they got married!*
- *Is dating only for new relationship? NO!*
- *Keeping your relationship strong is a huge challenge. The biggest problem is that most couples simply don't have the time to be creative and spend hours every week finding new ways to surprise and be romantic.*

Books and Media

Michael Webb has written 16 books to help both men and women with different relationship and marriage problems. 9 have been bestsellers. Titles include:

- *The Romantic's Guides*
- 1000 Questions For Couples
- 50 Secrets of a Blissful Relationship
- 101 Romantic Ideas
- 300 Creative Dates
- 50 More Secrets of a Blissful Relationship
- 500 Lovemaking Tips and Secrets

How to Find Out More

- For more information, go to: *www.theromantic.com* or *www.relationshipcollection.com,* where you will find links to Michael Webb's many other websites.

17. Patricia Evans

"Words DO hurt!"

Background and Qualifications

Patricia Evans is an interpersonal communications specialist, with expertise in verbally abusive and controlling marriages. She has brought the subject of verbal abuse to the forefront of American consciousness through her work as a consultant, trainer, and seminar leader, and through private phone consultations.

Relationship Philosophy

Patricia Evans is a leading expert on verbal abuse and aims to highlight this common form of pain within relationships that can make the victim's life a misery. She also talks about how verbal abuse can sometimes lead to physical abuse, and aims to help couples before this happens. She works with victims to make them realize that it is not their fault; they are not the cause of the abuse, and to give them the confidence to have a successful, loving relationship, either with the same partner, or someone new.

She defines verbal abuse as a "secret form of control" and manipulation that creates a pretend world, invading a victim's inner world, and destroying his or her self-confidence, often making them feel ostracized. Evans believes it is a lie that words cannot hurt, and verbal abuse of any kind can break a spirit, cripple confidence, and even make a person physically ill because of the stress caused. Verbal abuse involves accusing, blaming, judging, criticizing, and intruding on the victim's freedom to act as they choose.

According to Evans, it takes two to build a relationship and that often, verbal abuse may be happening without either the perpetrator or victim even realizing or acknowledging it. Very often the victim is too ashamed to speak up, with close friends and family having no idea what is happening and believing the perpetrator to be the most wonderful partner ever. Yet, verbal abuse is a common problem and painful experience within marriage. Through awareness and understanding, many issues can be resolved and an authentic human bonding established. It is not specific to any one gender; men are abused and controlled as much as women.

Perpetrators often end up driving away the people they are aiming to be closest to in their attempts to control them, and victims are often convinced they're blowing things out of proportion, too embarrassed to seek help.

"You don't know what you're talking about." "You're just being too sensitive." "You are driving me crazy." "Its no wonder I can't sleep, with someone like you around." "If you leave me, no one else will ever want you." These are some of the things people say when they are trying to control people.

The Controller usually has no idea of the hurt she or he is causing. A "spell" seems to come them, as they indulge is oppressive behavior. They are often unaware of their own behavior and unconscious of their motivation. If asked, they would either deny the situation, or dive further into it, claiming the other person was very much in the wrong, and needed to be corrected. This is the way the Controller keeps the other person into a role.

Typically, the Controller has created a Dream Person, and will do nearly anything to get the real person to conform to the

dream. When the person doesn't act according the Dream, the Controller will lash out, unconsciously labeling the other, "You're hopeless." What is left unsaid, is, "You're hopeless because you won't act like I want you to, and be the person I'm pretending you are." To the Controller, trying to control the other is the same as "working on the relationship."

The Therapy

Through therapy and workshops, Evans helps couples to recognize the abuse that is occurring. She also trains therapists how to spot and treat verbal abuse to prevent victims from keeping it hidden, which often happens even during therapy sessions.

Commonly, people in verbally abusive relationships believe that the way they're being treated has something to do with them. Evans helps victims recognize that verbal abuse has nothing to do with them or their qualities, and works with them to set limits and boundaries, listen carefully to their own feelings; with a reminder that the abuser can change him or herself if they choose to, but that the victim cannot change them. The victim can only learn to honor and nurture him - or herself.

If anyone suspects they could be in a verbally abusive relationship, Evans has come up with seven telltale signs.

7 Tell-Tale Signs of Verbal Abuse

- ✓ Your partner appears irritated or angry with you several times a week. When you ask why she denies it or makes you believe it's your fault.
- ✓ When you feel hurt and try to talk to him, issues are never resolved because he refuses to discuss it, dismisses your feelings, or claims you're just trying to start an argument or be right and make them wrong.

✓ You frequently feel frustrated because she can't understand you when you try to discuss things with her.

✓ You feel upset about the poor communication between you – what he thinks he said and what you heard him say are completely different.

✓ You sometimes think, "What's wrong with me? I shouldn't feel so bad!"

✓ She appears to take the opposite view on almost everything and makes you feel you're wrong and she's right.

✓ You can't recall telling him to "stop it!"

Patricia teaches people to become spell-breakers, by resisting the spell and the intrusion. They do this by standing up and saying, "I have a right to be here, and to have my opinions and desires. I will not be erased or ignored." Just as physical pain tells us something is wrong, psychic pain can be so intense that we can no longer ignore it.

One of the most powerful ways to break the Spell, and block another from defining you is to ask, "What did you just say?" This gives the Controller time to see that it is impossible to define you, and gives the yet another chance to wake up from the Spell.

Spell-Breaking Strategies

♥ Recognize the reality of your inner truth.

♥ Be aware of boundary invasions.

♥ Do not respond to nonsense as if it made sense.

♥ Build your life on truth.

♥ Speak up to break the spell.

♥ If someone tries to define you, say, "What?" "What did you say?" or "What are you doing?"

Many people who indulge in controlling behavior do want to stop. They want to find better ways to authentically connect, rather than settle for the mirage of connection with a non-existent Dream Person.

Examples
Verbal Abuse can be a Death Sentence

Fox News visited an annual retreat for victims of verbal abuse, run by Patricia Evans. There, they met mother of four Gina, who returns to the retreat year after year because of the confidence and renewed vigor for life it gives her. As part of the report, she describes Patricia Evans as the woman who saved her life and who gave her children back their mother. Before working with Evans, she was feeling suicidal, but says, "My mind was not sick from mental illness, but fragmented by years of mental abuse."

Evans explains that verbal abuse can be a death sentence for the sufferer. This is because of the self-doubt it creates; the feeling of being out of control, which can lead many sufferers, both men and women, to want to end their own lives.

Sticks and Stones may Break my Bones but Words can Never Hurt me

Patricia Evans teaches that this schoolyard rhyme is in fact a myth and a lie. Bones mend, yet people suffer 20 years or more after they heard hurtful words from their parents. The members of a retreat were once asked to raise their arm if they ever had a broken bone. 75% of the people raised an arm. "Keep it up if it is still broken." All but one hand went done. "Now, raise your arm if someone has ever said a hurtful thing to you. Keep your arm up if you are still hurting." Nearly everyone still had their arm up.

Words can break your spirit and confidence and even leave a person physically ill. It can happen to anyone from all walks of life – doctors, lawyers, and teachers. Evans once even helped the director of a woman's shelter overcome years of abuse.

She explains that this is because verbal abuse can creep up on you, taking hold of your relationship before you even realize it is happening, with the perpetrator often cleverly being just loving enough at times to make up for their verbally abusive side. It's like a Jekyll and Hyde character.

Patricia Evans Quotes

- *People who frequently indulge in verbal abuse may have little, if any, conscious awareness of what they are doing.*

- *A person is probably in a verbally abusive relationship if there isn't a feeling of goodwill and understanding between two people in their relationship, if one is hurting and feeling constantly put down by actual comments, for instance, "You can't do anything right," "You aren't listening," or is frequently yelled at.*

- *When people "make up your reality" – as if they were you – they are trying to control you, even when they don't realize it.*

- *If someone defines you, even in subtle ways, they are pretending to know the unknowable.*

- *People who have suffered over a period of time from verbal abuse sometimes fear that they are being abusive when they demand an end to it. But, it is always okay to say "No!" or "Stop!" to a person indulging in verbal abuse.*

Books and Media

Patricia Evans has written five books on the topic of verbal abuse and appeared on more than 200 radio programs and 20 national TV programs, including *Oprah* and *CNN*. Her book titles include:

- 📖 *The Verbally Abusive Relationship: How to Recognize It and How to Respond*

- 📖 *The Verbally Abusive Man – Can He Change?*
- 📖 *Verbal Abuse Survivors Speak Out: On Relationship and Recovery*
- 📖 *Victory Over Verbal Abuse: A Healing Guide to Renewing Your Spirit and Reclaiming Your Life*
- 📖 *Controlling People* – this book shows why verbal abusers feel attacked when partners tell them what's bothering them and don't usually see themselves as controlling.

How to Find Out More

- 💻 For more information, go to Patricia's websites: *www.patriciaevans.com* and *www.VerbalAbuse.com*

18. Dr. Jeffrey Young

"Breaking down our life traps"

Background and Qualifications

Dr. Jeffrey Young is a cognitive psychologist and founder of Schema Therapy, a cognitive approach to dealing with relationship and personal issues. He is founder and director of the Cognitive Therapy Centers of New York and Connecticut, as well as the Schema Therapy Institute.

Dr. Young received his undergraduate training at Yale University and his graduate degree at the University of Pennsylvania. He then completed a postdoctoral fellowship at the Center for Cognitive Therapy at the University of Pennsylvania with Dr. Aaron Beck, the founder of cognitive therapy, and went on to serve there as Director of Research and Training.

For the past 24 years, Dr. Young has lectured on cognitive and schema therapies, both nationally and internationally, and has trained thousands of mental health professionals in the use of schema therapy to work with their patients. He is also co-author of a psychotherapy outcome study evaluating the effectiveness of cognitive therapy in comparison to antidepressant medication. He has also served as consultant on many cognitive and schema therapy research grants, including the NIMH Collaborative Study of Depression and on the editorial boards of journals including *Cognitive Therapy and Research* and *Cognitive and Behavioral Practice*. In 2003, Dr. Young was awarded the prestigious NEEI Mental Health Educator of the Year award.

Relationship Philosophy

In his early practice, Dr. Young discovered that cognitive therapy had limitations with patients who presented with problems that stemmed from their early life. He began to discover recurring psychological profiles and patterns in many of these patients which were laid down in early childhood, and which were now shaping their adult thinking patterns, behavior, and in turn their relationships, careers, and life choices.

He labeled these habits "Schemas" or "Life traps." Schemas are established during childhood and adolescence, but can affect our present in dramatic ways. As we go through life, schemas become comfortable and familiar. We cling to them because they become part of our sense of self – who we are – and it often appears frightening to let them go.

Classic signs of schema having a negative impact on a person's life are when they are continually drawn to the same type of partners, over and over again, without their needs ever being met. They may overreact continually to the same emotional buttons, or could be stuck in some area of their life, but cannot find a way to change. They could have low self-esteem, addictions, or constant conflict in their relationship.

Within couples, schemas can play a huge role in how the two individuals interact. One person's schema can trigger the other's schema, causing tension to escalate and exacerbate schematic habits and tendencies.

There are 18 schemas, and a person may be affected or defined by one or many of them in combination. They develop when our childhood needs were not met. For example, overcritical parents can create defectiveness, controlling can cause subjugation, and indulgent parents can cause a person to suffer from feelings of entitlement. The 18 Schema are as follows:

The 18 Schemas

5) **Abandonment:** clinging to others out of fear of rejection.

6) **Emotional Deprivation:** usually these people have never had someone to nurture them, or be completely tuned into their feelings and needs.

7) **Entitlement:** those who hate to be constrained or made to follow rules.

8) **Defectiveness:** these people feel unworthy of love, attention, or respect from others, and believe they'll never be able to get a significant partner to respect them.

9) **Unrelenting Standards:** a desire to be the best at everything.

10) **Mistrust/Abuse:** those unable to let their guard down for fear of getting hurt.

11) **Self-Sacrifice:** putting others' needs before their own, or else they feel guilty.

12) **Social Isolation:** feeling unable to relate well to other people, or that they don't fit in with the group.

13) **Dependence:** feeling helpless or unable to make decisions without help.

14) **Vulnerability to Harm or Illness:** those consistently in fear of illness or being in a catastrophe such as an airplane crash or hurricane.

15) **Enmeshment:** those with a weak sense of personal identity who cling to others in order to feel complete.

16) **Failure:** those who believe they'll never succeed.

17) **Insufficient Self-Control:** those who quit a task at the first sign of failure.

18) **Approval Seeking:** placing extreme importance on other people's opinions, often placing high importance on appearance and social status.

19) **Negativity:** those who focus on the worst parts of life.

20) **Inhibition:** those afraid to show emotion or initiate conversation.

21) **Punitiveness:** those who believe even the smallest mistake deserves punishment. Usually have very high expectations for themselves and others and find it hard to empathize or forgive mistakes – their own and others.

22) **Subjugation:** excessive surrendering of control to others because one feels coerced, usually to avoid anger, retaliation, or abandonment. Can be subjugation of needs or emotions.

The Therapy

Dr. Young's first step is to help them recognize that they have schemas and which ones in particular. This recognition stage helps them to realize they've had a distorted view of looking at the world. They can learn to recognize that schemas cause them to gravitate towards partners who trigger their life traps or those who fill gaps in their own self-esteem. Only from here can people resist the pull of their schema.

Within a couple, each partner can learn to recognize their schema and how it makes them behave and react. When they're locked in conflict, a useful tool is to try to remember to halt the battle by shouting out "Schema Clash!" This helps to stop them in the moment, prevent the argument from escalating, and help them realize this is not about what's going on now, but due to learned patterns of behavior from the past. Over time, couples can learn to let go of their schema and recognize that, while they're not to blame for these habits, they are responsible for learning to control them better. Perhaps they can even get to a place where they can have humor about their own Schemas. "Hey, I'm doing that Approval Seeking again..."

The next step is learning to feel differently about our schema. Using imagery, we can get angry with those who created the schema and empower ourselves to validate our own needs. It's then important to break down our life traps into manageable steps and change the patterns one step at a time. Finally, forgiveness of those who helped to create our schema (if possible) is an important step to healing.

It takes willingness from both parties to concede that there is something wrong in the way each of them is behaving. Once they begin letting go of their schema, they begin to feel the thrill of knowing that there is a reasonable explanation for the unhealthy patterns that have governed their lives and relationships. Slowly, this healing allows them to set out on a different life course.

Examples

Abuse and Mistrust

Madeline is twenty-nine years old and has never had a long-term, intimate relationship. In her early twenties, she was a party girl. She would drink a lot and have sex with strangers; she was promiscuous. When she stopped drinking two years ago, she stopped having boyfriends. She was brought to therapy because of an incident that happened at a party. A man she was talking to and dancing with took a sexual interest in her. He pulled her close and gave her a little kiss. This was too much for Madeline. She got angry and left the party in a huff. She is sure men are out to take advantage of her.

Dr. Young asks her when these beliefs about men developed. She knew instantly. When she was nine-years old her mother remarried. Her stepfather molested her for three years. Her mother was zoned out on tranquilizers, and so could not save her. She learned that she was on her own and that men can be either controlled sexually or ignored. Either way, men cannot be trusted.

In his book, *Reinventing Your Life,* Dr. Young has a life trap questionnaire that helps one uncover if they are being run by abuse and mistrust. He also has questionnaires for the other

schemas, so you can uncover what has been running you, in a gentle and guided way. And that is the first step towards freedom.

Abandonment

People with abandonment issues constantly expect to lose the people close to them. They live in constant fear that people will abandon them, get sick and die, or leave them for someone else, so they are constantly on alert for any sign that someone is about to leave them. They experience anxiety, sadness, and depression, and in extreme cases; terror, grief, and rage. They are typically clingy, possessive, and controlling. As a strategy to prevent the other from leaving, they accuse others of abandoning them. Some patients avoid intimate relationships completely so as to avoid the inevitable loss and misery.

As with other distortions, people with abandonment issues often choose unstable partners – people who are unavailable or unwilling to commit. They often have intense chemistry with them and fall obsessively in love. Then they live in constant fear of the other person leaving. They also may suffer from other associated schemas, such as Dependence/Incompetence, Subjugation, and Defectiveness schemas.

Treatment involves helping patients become more realistic about the stability of relationships. Once treated, people have a reduced need to magnify and misinterpret other's behaviors as signs of impending abandonment, and are far less worried about the other leaving. They feel far more secure in their relationships and don't have to cling, control, or manipulate. They are better at selecting appropriate partners. They learn to enjoy their own company and are not afraid or anxious to be alone.

The patient learns how to have a stable relationship with the therapist, and then transfers this new skill to other relationships. Cognitive behavior retraining helps patients alter their unrealistic expectations that other people should be constantly available and completely consistent, and help reduce their obsessive behavior of checking that the partner is still there.

Often, issues of feeling abandoned in childhood must be relived and recoded. The therapist expresses anger at the abandoning parent and comforts the abandoned child, as the therapist becomes a stable figure. The patient then learns to become a healthy adult to their own abandoned child, and thereby learns to serve as their own stable figure.

Dr. Jeffrey Young Quotes

- *A life trap is a pattern that starts in childhood and reverberates throughout life. It began with something that was done to us by our families or by other children. We were abandoned, criticized, overprotected, abused, excluded, or deprived – we were damaged in some way. Eventually the life trap becomes part of us.*
- *Life traps determine how we think, feel, act, and relate to others.*
- *Long after we leave the home we grew up in, we continue to create situations in which we are mistreated, ignored, put down, or controlled, and in which we fail to reach our most desired goals.*
- *The life trap approach involves continually confronting ourselves.*
- *Somehow, we manage to create, in adult life, conditions remarkably similar to those that were so destructive in childhood. A life trap is all the ways in which we recreate those patterns.*

Books and Media

Dr. Young has been published widely in the fields of both cognitive and schema therapies. He has authored two major books:

- 📖 *Reinventing Your Life: The Breakthrough Program to End Negative Behavior... and Feel Great Again* – a popular self-help book based on schema therapy
- 📖 *Schema Therapy: A Practitioner's Guide* – written for mental health professionals
- 📖 *Schema Therapy: Distinctive Features (CBT Distinctive Features)*

How to Find Out More

- 💻 For more information, go to *www.schematherapy.com*

19. Susan Page

"It's a myth that communication is the most important relationship skill..."

Background and Qualifications

Susan Page has over twenty years experience delivering relationship workshops, with spiritually based advice that bypasses the need for better communication.

She has a Master of Divinity degree from San Francisco Theological Seminary and was Director of Women's Programs at the University of California at Berkeley.

Relationship Philosophy

Susan Page believes you are not dependent on what your partner does or doesn't do in order to be happy. She also believes it's a myth that the most important relationship skill is communication and writes that you don't need to talk about every single problem that arises. Although good communication is valuable, Page is convinced that one partner, acting alone, using loving actions, can create a rapid and positive change, even in the most troubled of relationships. Relationship problems will be outgrown without a need to fix them any longer.

She outlines a number of key factors for achieving the perfect relationship that are very different from the usual relationship advice:

♥ Couples should stop trying to resolve their problems.

♥ Fairness and equality are not the most important factors.

♥ You cannot solve a relationship problem by discussing it – especially if one partner is better at communicating their feelings than the other. Furthermore, Page maintains there's often a hidden agenda behind communication, for

example, "we could solve this problem if... you would stop doing this or making me feel like that." It's often about manipulating our partner into change.

The Therapy

Page replaces communication with a focus on feeling happy together – developing a broader consciousness and allowing the problems simply to disappear by using her principles of Spiritual Partnership.

In Spiritual Partnership, Loving Actions replace communication as the main tool for problem solving and relationship enrichment. In addition, you shift your focus from a partner making you happy, to being happy in relationship with your own spiritual self, and your own spiritual journey.

8 Spiritually-Based Loving Actions of Spiritual Partnership:

- ♥ **Adopting a spirit of good will** – no matter who is right or wrong. Focus on what you can do to make positive changes in the relationship rather than having to be right all the time.

- ♥ **Give up problem solving** – it's an illusion to think solving your problems will make you happy. Most problems have no solution anyway and are more a fact of life. Instead, try working on problems by doing something to create a harmonious atmosphere in your relationship right now.

- ♥ **Act as if** – for example, when you are angry, choose to behave in a loving, rather than angry way. If your husband is two hours late for dinner, instead of attacking him with an argument, welcome him home by putting a glass of wine in his hand, giving him a kiss and saying, "you must be exhausted, darling." He might be thrilled.

- ♥ **Practice restraint** – avoid having to communicate about your problems all the time and constantly criticizing your partner. Focus more on working on your spiritual self and ways to improve how you feel about the relationship.

148

♥ **Balance giving and taking** – keep in balance the times you take care of your partner and the times you stick up for yourself.

♥ **Act on your own** – by voluntarily becoming the "Loving Leader" in your relationship, you will be amazed at the changes you can bring about to improve your marriage.

♥ **Practice acceptance** – instead of searching for reasons for your relationship discontent, accept that your discontent is the actual problem. From here, you can work on improving the relationship.

♥ **Practice compassion** – instead of encouraging your partner to change, work on changing yourself to bring harmony to the relationship.

Examples

Self-empowerment Through Spiritual Partnership

Page uses the story of Bill and Karen to demonstrate how Loving Actions can help a couple outgrow a relationship problem, without the need to resolve it.

Karen was extremely frustrated about her husband Bill's controlling attitude to money. They tried everything to work out their issues and reduce her frustration – talking, communicating, and repeating back what they heard each other say. This went on for years, but defeat and hopelessness were setting in.

Karen worked with Spiritual Partnership and made a complete shift in how she thought about the problem. She gave up trying to resolve the problem and instead simply focused on creating a loving, harmonious atmosphere at home. She became a "Spiritual Partner," finding the courage to practice restraint and not talk about money anymore, or Bill's controlling attitude towards it. Instead, she showed a spirit of goodwill by saving money in several ways and sharing this with Bill. She acted alone, finding ways to meet her own needs without upsetting him.

149

Before this shift in attitude, Karen felt weak and powerless; incapable of change. However, through Spiritual Partnership, she was able to empower herself to take control of her own life. Single-handedly, she had made this relationship problem disappear. Bill was still controlling about money but it no longer affected or bothered her – she had outgrown the issue. She felt an enormous sense of personal power and achievement as well as relief. The problem no longer needed to be solved.

An Experiment in Spiritual Partnership

For anyone who wants work with Spiritual Partnership, Page recommends the following exercise. For a period of time (three to seven days), make a personal pact not to make any negative, critical, or demanding comments to your partner. You'll soon discover how often you make such comments without realizing it, and you'll begin to recognize how much they drag the energy in your relationship down.

First, you won't believe you say negative things. Then, you'll go through a process of hearing yourself make negative comments, such as, "You always do X, or you never do Y!" Soon, you'll begin to realize when you're about to make a negative comment and stop yourself from making it, recognizing how futile and useless the comment actually is! You may find yourself taking care of some of the problems, and saying nothing of it.

This small shift in the relationship can start to have a dramatic impact on the way you and your partner interact. It's about creating an inner shift within you and recognizing your true relationship priorities: not to change or reform your partner, but rather to feel good together, enjoy time together, and to support and love one another.

Admittedly, some people may be afraid to use these principles, lest your partner senses this change as tacit approval of this behavior. Realize that your compulsion to change or not tolerate your partner's behavior *is* the underlying issue. Your unhappiness *is* the issue. Finding authentic ways for you to take control of your needs and create the happiness you want *is* the solution. Remember, you chose this relationship.

Susan Page Quotes

- *At last you can stop waiting around for your partner to change! You can actually get your needs met by the relationship through your own actions.*

- *It's a giant myth that you have to solve your relationship problems before you can be happy together. In fact, it's the other way around. If you can first be happy together, you will find your problems diminish or disappear altogether.*

- *In Spiritual Partnership, if you want more, give more!*

- *More important than having the right partner, is being the right partner.*

Books and Media

Susan Page has been a repeat guest on *Oprah*, as well as appearances on *CNN, Donahue*, and *Good Morning America*. Her book titles include:

- *Why Talking Is Not Enough: 8 Loving Actions That Will Transform Your Marriage*

- *How One of You Can Bring the Two of You Together:*

- *The 8 Essential Traits of Couples Who Thrive*

- *If I'm So Wonderful, Why Am I Still Single? Ten Strategies That Will Change Your Love Life Forever*

- *If We're So In Love, Why Aren't We Happy? Using Spiritual Principles to Solve Problems and Restore Your Passion*

- *Leadership Training Manual: for Spiritual Partnership Couples Groups* for therapists and marriage educators.

How to Find Out More

- Go to Susan Page's website: *www.susanpage.com*

20. Dr. Gary Smalley

"Make your spouse feel truly honored."

Background and Qualifications

A family counselor and author of many books on family relationships from a Christian perspective, Dr. Gary Smalley has over 35 years teaching and counseling experience, drawing on hours of research through surveys as to what strengthens and weakens a relationship.

Born in 1940, Dr. Smalley has been married for forty years to wife Norma, and has three children, and 7 grandchildren. He founded the Smalley Relationship Center to provide couples counseling and marriage seminars across the country.

Relationship Philosophy

Dr. Smalley believes a marriage cannot exist without trials and irritations – these actually form the secret to intimacy. Creating a successful relationship is about establishing the key relationships in your life – with God, with others, and with yourself – each of which involves choice, because all love is a decision. You have to decide whether you want to love or not. Dr. Smalley outlines 6 keys to love and a successful marriage:

6 Keys to Love and a Successful Marriage

- ♥ Make your spouse feel truly honored
- ♥ Learn the art of touching tenderly
- ♥ Keep courtship alive
- ♥ Re-open a heart closed by anger
- ♥ Build or rebuild trust in a relationship
- ♥ Become best friends

These are all key components of a good relationship. Although couples always start out wanting to build deep intimacy, in his practice, Dr. Smalley has found that people often develop alone and apart, apparently stranded from one another. He suggests there are four pillars that support a fulfilling marriage. Each of these need to be present for both partners to feel safe, open up to each other, and feel loved.

4 Pillars

- ♥ Security. This is the structural support for a marriage.
- ♥ Meaningful communication. Finding common ground that spans differences.
- ♥ Creating emotions, moods, and romantic experiences that bind. This helps to stabilize a marriage, particularly through difficult times.
- ♥ Meaningful touch. This is the silent language of love.

The Therapy

Delivered to over 2 million people, his seminar, *I Promise*, outlines 5 promises that couples can make to increase their marriage security and satisfaction. These promises are tied to the Christian path.

From his book *I Promise,*

"If your spouse does not feel safe enough to open up his or her heart without fear of being judged, criticized, blamed, or rejected, nothing you do will be effective. It's only when couples feel emotionally *safe* that they can truly become one as God intended." The "five heartfelt promises you can make to your mate are guaranteed to build trust and help your spouse become the true soul mate, lover, and friend you desire."

The 5 Promises

- ♥ To conform our beliefs to God's truths,
- ♥ To be filled by God,
- ♥ To look at each trial as an instrument of growth from God,
- ♥ To communicate with love, and
- ♥ To serve the spouse throughout our lives.

One of the tenants of Dr. Smalley's marriage philosophy is that couples have to honor each other above all others and to live in oneness. A marriage forms a bond that is the blending of two selves together into a loving union. Therefore, each person needs to help nurture the other's needs on a daily basis and repair any damage immediately before resentment sets in.

In order to express honor, we need to wake up on a daily basis and set our priorities to honoring our partner. We have to decide everyday that our mate is the most valuable person on earth to use, and to look after their needs before worrying about our own.

He also examines the keys to having great sex, which are the same ingredients as the keys to having a strong and intimate marriage, including honoring your spouse, tender touch, courtship, trust, and reopening an angry heart.

Dr. Smalley says it's also important to acknowledge the differences between men and women and bridge those gaps in order for a relationship to flourish. These 12 keys help keep your love alive and flourishing.

The 12 Keys

- ♥ **Praise:** it's such a great gift and so easy to give. Examine the things that make your spouse unique, and praise them for those special qualities.

- ♥ **Emotional trials and disputes are valuable:** managed conflict is a way to learn, grow, and transform.

- ♥ **Don't go it alone:** welcome fresh insights into keeping your relationship alive from extended family, friends, good marriage books, or a qualified marriage counselor.

- ♥ **It takes two:** in order for a relationship to be mutually satisfying, both people's needs are expressed and they both have the flexibility to give and take.

- ♥ **Honor goes hand in hand with love:** it's about doing worthwhile things for someone who is valuable to us.

- ♥ **Trials increase our intimacy:** they increase our love for life and love for others.

- ♥ **Balance:** oneness does not mean that one mate dominates the other or that the stronger controls the weaker.

- ♥ **Anger is our choice:** it is up to us to recognize anger's destructive power and take steps to reduce it within us. Otherwise, anger will have the effect of obliterating love.

- ♥ **What are our motivations:** if we understand what moves us, this can help us achieve personal and marital satisfaction.

- ♥ **Sharing:** discussing and opening up about our deep feelings is described as emotional intercourse – a concept vital for sexual satisfaction.

- ♥ **Reach out to one another:** this enables our own needs for fulfillment and love to be met.

- ♥ **Even more praise:** give seven or more praises or compliments for every one fault-finding suggestion.

The most powerful concept he has ever seen for connecting with a loved one is using emotional word pictures. This concept adds life, power, and depth to your words, by using a story to simultaneously engage a persons emotions and intellect, and causes them to experience our words, not just hear them. In his

book, the Language of Love, he gives many tear-jerking examples of emotional word pictures, and offers a 7-step method for their creation.

Creating Emotional Word Pictures

- ♥ Establish a clear purpose for enriching your relationship.
- ♥ Carefully study the other person's interest to touch their heart.
- ♥ Draw from the four inexhaustible wells:
  - o Nature
  - o Everyday objects
  - o Imaginary stories
  - o "Remember when…"
- ♥ Rehearse your story.
- ♥ Pick a convenient time without distractions.
- ♥ Milk your work picture for all its worth.

Examples

Getting a License without any Training!

After 43 years of a great marriage, Dr. Smalley believes that marriages are continually on a journey everyday, either towards decline or towards growth; there is no middle ground. In his own marriage, he and his wife have to refocus several times a year on what the most important priorities for them in their marriage are, in order to keep the relationship growing. However, the marriage skills he and his wife Norma now possess had to be learned very quickly during the early years. He admits he felt completely untrained when he was first married, and it took his wife and friends many years to help him become a more loving husband.

A man, who just 18 months into his marriage feels he's made a mistake, asked Dr. Smalley what to do. Despite his parent's warning him not to marry his current wife, he got married – because he felt madly in love. Now, they're both frustrated, spending less time together and having very limited conversations.

Dr. Smalley feels that this is a situation common to many couples. Before marriage, very few couples have acquired the skills needed to emotionally, mentally, and physically care for their partner. "One of the ironies in our society is that a person has to have four years of training to receive a plumber's license, but absolutely no training is required for a marriage license!"

Prioritize your Marriage!

Dr. Smalley explains that many men get married without any idea of how to communicate with their wife and are completely unaware of her sensitive nature. Women also lack the knowledge that men need admiration in the same way that women need romance. He advises any couple to invest in marriage counseling. "If you had a painful, large kidney stone, you wouldn't walk around saying, 'Oh no! I'm just going to let it go because it costs about $6,000 to have the surgery and I don't want to spend the money.' Yet, all too often, couples are walking around doubled over emotionally from their unhealthy marriage situation. The pain is crippling, yet they're not willing to get help or pay for it!"

Dr. Gary Smalley Quotes

- *If you want to wake up each and every morning excited about your marriage, then deciding to do this is the first step.*
- *A great marriage can be compared to doing the tango. If you don't know the steps, you'll land on your head.*
- *If a man truly wants to communicate with his wife, he must enter her world of emotions.*
- *How do you discover what your mate's needs are? Well, you might consider just asking!*

💬 *The basis for genuine love is doing what is right, no matter what the other person does or says.*

Books and Media

Author and co-author of 28 best selling books and videos, with more than 6 million copies sold worldwide.

- ☐ His infomercial, *Hidden Keys to a Loving Relationship,* was broadcast nationwide.
- ☐ Dr. Smalley has made appearances on many national TV programs, including *Oprah, Larry King Live, Extra, The TODAY Show,* as well as a number of radio programs.

His book titles include:

- 📖 *The Language of Love: How to be Instantly Understood by Those You Love* (with John Trent)
- 📖 *I Promise You Forever: 5 Promises to Create the Marriage of Your Dreams*
- 📖 *I Promise: How 5 Commitments Determine the Destiny of Your Marriage*
- 📖 *Change Your Heart, Change Your Life: How Changing What You Believe Will Give You the Great Life You've Always Wanted*
- 📖 *If Only He Knew: What No Woman Can Resist*
- 📖 *The DNA of Relationships*
- 📖 *The Language of Sex: Experiencing the Beauty of Sexual Intimacy*
- 📖 *Making Love Last Forever*
- 📖 *Winning Your Wife Back Before It's Too Late*

How to Find Out More

- 💻 Find out more about Dr. Gary Smalley at his website: *www.smalleyonline.com*

21. Susan Campbell

"You are most loveable when you are most transparent."

Background and Qualifications

Susan Campbell has been an executive coach and a personal and business coach for 44 years. She has a Ph.D. in psychology from the University of Massachusetts and was formerly a faculty member of their Graduate School of Applied Behavioral Sciences, teaching courses in Humanistic Counseling, Couple and Family Therapy, Gestalt Therapy, Jungian Psychology, Community Development, Group Process, and organizational development. She is currently on the Adjunct Faculty of Saybrook University in San Francisco, teaching in their Peace and Conflict Studies Department.

A recognized leader in the "Honesty Movement," Susan currently trains Getting Real Coaches, publishes a free newsletter, *Truth in Dating, Love, and Marriage*, and hosts Honesty Salons, where people practice her "10 truth skills." These skills focus on present-centered communication and help people bring more awareness and authenticity to their business and personal relationships

Dr. Campbell has authored nine books on relationships and conflict resolution, has delivered hundreds of seminars and workshop internationally, and has counseled thousands of individuals and couples. Susan has appeared on numerous talk shows over the past twenty-five years, including CNN's "News Night," "Good Morning America," "The Dr. Dean Edell Show," and "People Are Talking."

Relationship Philosophy

Dr. Campbell sees intimacy as a spiritual path and shows people how to use their relationships to help each other heal

past wounds and realize the deeper aspects of their humanness. In her 1980 best-seller, *The Couple's Journey*, she outlined five stages that couples pass through on their path to wholeness.

5 stages of the Couple's Journey
1) Romance
2) Power Struggle
3) Stability
4) Commitment
5) Co-Creation

Her book, *Beyond the Power Struggle,* explores how the outer struggle between two people often mirrors the inner struggles within each person. One way this shows up is when something that initially attracted you to your partner, ends up being the thing that annoys you. Another way this shows up is aspects of yourself you have a hard time accepting, you project onto the other person. The book shows how to re-own the power and potential that tends to get projected onto "the other".

As you learn to accept your uniqueness, and your shadow aspects, you feel more confident. You feel at ease in situations you used to avoid or fear.

Relate or Control

People are usually not conscious of the hidden intent or need that motivates their communication: Is it to Relate or to Control? According to Dr. Campbell, almost 90% of all human communication comes from the (usually unconscious) intent to control. Controlling is a way to avoid or reduce anxiety, and comes from the fear of stepping outside your comfort zone. It often shows up as a compulsive need to be right or to avoid appearing uncertain, awkward or foolish. She believes that the more you try to control things, the more out of control you feel.

The telltale signs of "Controlling" are whenever you:

- ✓ play it safe or avoid rocking the boat;
- ✓ assume you know what the other is really feeling;
- ✓ assume you know why the other did what he did;
- ✓ lie to avoid someone being upset with you;
- ✓ try to impress others and look good in others' eyes;
- ✓ attempt to appear more "together" than you really are;
- ✓ manipulate others to get what you want;
- ✓ make assumptions or jump to conclusions rather than live with the uncertainty of your situation;
- ✓ resist listening to viewpoints that differ from yours.

The alternative to control-motivated communication is Relating. Relating is motivated by the desire to know and be known. Relating means revealing what is going on for you, in this moment. No one can argue with your present-time experience. You do not need to convince anyone that you are right. You are motivated by your intent to be open to all possibilities and all information so you can make good decisions and connect with others in satisfying, mutually beneficial ways.

When you're Relating, you are curious about the other's experience; open to discovering the other's motives or feelings, and open to learning and hearing the truth, even if it's uncomfortable. Your sense of self-worth will be based on your ability to know and express what you notice, think, and feel – in each moment – rather than on whether you get a predictable or comfortable result. Thus, you learn to "surf life," rather than needing to "control life." The result is an unshakeable sense of self-trust and trust in life.

The honest expression of thoughts and feelings can clear the fog that clouds perception, and release a tremendous amount of creative energy.

The Therapy

Susan's therapy is based on enhancing one's capacity for love and trust by bringing awareness to this present moment. She believes that being honest is the quickest, most direct path to wholeness.

Her theory is that the excitement, energy, trust, and love of truly being alive come from being with the truth of your experience, as distinct from your judgments, assessments, generalizations, withholds, projections, and explanations – particularly of why things, and others, are wrong.

Her practices help you to be candid with yourself (and eventually others) about what's real. These skills help you to stay with your current experience of what you see, hear, smell, sense, feel, remember, think, imagine, and intuit.

The 10 Truth Skills

1) **Experience what is**: to get where you want to go, be where you are

2) **Being transparent**: freedom is just another word for nothing left to hide

3) **Notice your Intent**: is it to relate or to control

4) **Welcome feedback**: it's how we learn

5) **Asserting what you want and don't want**

6) **Taking back projections**: discover your dark side

7) **Revising an earlier statement**

8) **Holding differences**: seeing other viewpoints without losing your own

9) **Sharing mixed emotions**: you are not crazy, you are complex

10) **Embracing the silence of now knowing**

The result of this practice is self-realization – making real all the parts of you that you thought you had to keep hidden in order to survive and be safe. You learn to appreciate and enjoy all your parts, not just the pretty ones. As you explore and experiment, you discover where your natural flow is blocked, and you become increasingly free of your personal story and limiting beliefs.

The 7 Keys to Present-Centered Communication

1) Hearing you say that, I feel…
2) I want…
3) I have some feelings to clear
4) I'm getting triggered
5) I appreciate you for…
6) I hear you, and I have a different perspective
7) Can we talk about how we are feeling?

One of the most profound things you can do with another is to really listen to them, and then share the impact their words have on you. Again, if you share with the intent to control them, punish them for what they said, or manipulate them to say something else, that is not relating. This will cloud and confuse your reality and make trust and intimacy unlikely.

To help a listener get grounded in his own experience, Dr. Susan recommends the sentence stem, Hearing you say that, I feel… And example would be: "Hearing you say you want to go out with me, I notice a fluttering in my chest, and an opening in my throat. I feel happy and excited."

Words that reveal where you are at include:

Hearing you say that, I feel… and I imagine… I'm noticing… I sense… I'm feeling… and at the same time, I'm feeling… Right now, I'm saying to myself…, I have a judgment or withhold, I hear what you are saying, and I have a different opinion.

Examples

A major focus of *Getting Real* is learning tools for clearing the air, and cleaning up unfinished business from the past. This allows one to be present to *this* moment and see things as they really are.

Experiencing what is

The most fundamental of Susan's 10 truth skills is Experiencing What Is. In her work, she helps clients notice and get free from all the many thinking habits that interfere with one's ability to perceive reality clearly. One such thinking habit is our tendency to think "I shouldn't be feeling this."

When Mona's 17-year-old son went away to visit a friend for the weekend, Mona's heart felt heavy. "Todd is spending too much time away. I never see him any more. I feel sad. And I'm jealous. He likes being there more that being at home." Then she thought, "I shouldn't be feeling this way. I should be happy for him."

This type of ambivalence is common for people. This time, Mona decided to stay with the feeling. She felt the pain and began to cry. As she allowed the sobs to get deeper and louder, then quieter, an old memory began to emerge. When she was about ten, her dog was killed by a truck, and she was the first to find him. As she held her dead dog in her arms, wailing out in pain, her father, not realizing what happened, yelled, "Shut up Mona. Stop being such a crybaby!"

She stopped immediately, wiped her tears, and went into the house to tell everyone what happened. Although she got plenty of sympathy, even from her father, she never cried about that again--until now, when the thought about her son triggered this old, repressed memory.

So she moved passed the thought, "You shouldn't cry," and continued to sob, feeling each wave of sadness, until anger emerged (a backed-up emotion covering her fear of expressing her needs). She imagined yelling at her father, "I resent you for telling me to shut up. I need to cry!"

Completing her blocked self-expression allowed a sense of safety to emerge. She had a sense of relaxation and relief. Her breathing slowed, her body tingled with excitement, and she felt more whole. A part of her that was lost had come back home again. No longer cut off from feeling grief or sadness, she has a new ability to be present with what is.

Holding Differences Builds Mutual Trust

Carol met Rand through an Internet dating site. Since he had been married for 28 years, she assumed he wanted a monogamous relationship. When she found out that he did not want a monogamous relationship, because he never wanted to feel trapped again, like he did in his marriage, it was too late – she had already fallen in love with him.

She was in the strange predicament of wanting things to be different than they were. She wanted him to be happy, which meant for him to have multiple partners, *and* she wanted to feel safe and secure, which meant having a monogamous relationship. From the Getting Real work, she learned to use the phrase, "I hear you, and I have a different perspective."

So often, in situations like this, the feelings are overwhelming, and one simply bolts, "I'm outta here!" Another "control pattern" is to berate the other person, telling them that what they are doing is simply "wrong!" Still another response is to give in. None of these positions will bring intimacy, or bring you closer to yourself.

Instead, Carol learned to Relate: "I hear that you want to be sexual with other women, and I wish you felt differently. I wish you wanted to be exclusively with me."

If Carol says this as a way to control Rand, such as telling him what he must feel and do, she missed the opportunity to be real. If she is being open and honest and vulnerable, she is revealing where she is at. This is truly a gift.

Other ways that Carol used this truth skill included: "I want to be fully open and vulnerable with you, and I can't seem to stay as open as I'd like because of your lifestyle choice." "I want you to make love only with me, and I want you to have what you want. This is difficult for me to hold, and I love you."

Communicating in this way over the next few months helped Carol experience the complexity of loving someone with different needs alongside loving herself. This seemed to cause an expansion in her sense of self and in her capacity for experiencing life as it is. Before she learned this practice, she had assumed that if a difference in needs existed, she would have to give in or give up her own wants and needs. Using this skill to consciously "Hold Differences," helped her feel more inwardly strong and self-supporting.

Holding Differences – stating the "both/and" of a situation – can help partners navigate the differences in loving someone who wants something different than what you want. The practice takes conscious effort and may feel painful, but experiencing both sides of the conflict often lets one experience a deeper level of what the conflict is really about, and a deeper capacity for relating.

For Carol, she had envisioned finding love from a devoted other, but had always felt undeserving. By expressing her own needs in this way she discovered a capacity for self-love that did not depend on someone else. At the same time, she could feel Rand's love for her expanding as she expressed herself in this way. And as he opened his heart more, he discovered that what he really needed was to "not feel controlled." This was the deeper issue underlying his preference for non-monogamy.

Sometimes amazing things happen when you are able to feel and say, "I hear what you want, and I want something different."

Quotes from the book, *Getting Real*

- You can only be honest about yourself.
- A complaint is a want in disguise.
- You can only be as honest as you are self-aware.
- Freedom's just another word for nothing left to hide.
- Basing our self-esteem on the ability to control people and events actually keeps us feeling out of control.
- Withholding feelings is a way of giving them more significance than they actually deserve.
- We often need to get our buttons pushed so we can notice what they are.
- All news is good news.
- Get comfortable with discomfort.
- Fear is simply a sign that you're moving into unknown territory, not a signal to turn back.
- All attempts at controlling others eventually backfire.
- Through learning to notice your mind chatter or self-talk, you always have a way of getting back into present time.
- Being honest is the best way to stay connected to others, to your own flow, and ultimately to that greater energy source from which you both partake.
- When you blame another person for your pain, it clouds the truth and makes corrective action less likely.
- Life becomes a painful battle when you struggle against what is.

Books and Media

Susan has developed three card games:

- ♠ The Truth is Dating Card Game: a game of radical intimacy and Fun
- ♠ The Getting Real Card Game for practicing the 10 truth skills
- ♠ Truth at Work, for trained coaches and facilitators to open discussions on important topics that often get ignored in the workplace.

She offers a number of Audio CD programs:

- o A Guide to Open Communication
- o Why Opposites Attract
- o Ten Truth Skills You Need to Live an Authentic Life
- o Bringing Out the Best in People Who Bring Out the Worst in You.

Her best-selling books include:

- 📖 *The Couple's Journey: Intimacy As a Path to Wholeness* (Impact, 1980)
- 📖 *Beyond the Power Struggle: Dealing with Conflict in Love and Work* (Impact, 1984)
- 📖 *Getting Real: 10 Truth Skills You Need to Live an Authentic Life* (New World Library, 2001)
- 📖 *Saying What's Real: Seven Keys to Authentic Communication and Relationship Success* (New World Library, 2003)
- 📖 *Truth In Dating: Finding Love by Getting Real* (New World Library, 2002)

How to Find Out More

- 💻 Go to Susan Campbell's website, *www.susancampbell.com* where you will find articles, a list of upcoming events, and links to her books, games and other products.

22. David Deida

"The Way of the Superior Man"

Background and Qualifications

David Deida has developed a technique and approach that revolutionizes the way men and women grow spiritually and sexually. He delivers his message through private practice and in seminars and workshops across the country.

Deida was a founding associate of the Integral Institute and has taught and conducted research at the University of California Medical School in San Diego, the University of California, Santa Cruz, Boston, and Ecole Polytechnique in Paris.

Relationship Philosophy

David Deida believes in practicing love as a living art, and creates a link between spirituality and sexuality by describing lovemaking as a whole body prayer between two people, and an authentic spiritual communion.

To David, there is great value in the distinction between feminine and masculine self-identification, which he has called "sexual essence." Sexual essence does not correspond with the two genders, but is more defined by identification with consciousness or light rather than a biological or cultural gender difference. According to Deida, the masculine sexual essence provides direction and is identified with consciousness, and thus searches for the freedom of consciousness in life. The feminine sexual essence is identified with light, and thus, wants to be seen and loved as radiantly beautiful.

In an intimate relationship, the more feminine-identified character can misunderstand the tendency for the more masculine-identified character to want some time out alone. They often wrongly assume their partner doesn't love them, but

169

the truth is the masculine-identified partner simply wants to feel a release from constraint into the openness of consciousness, not necessarily an end to their relationship.

Similarly, more masculine-identified character can misunderstand the tendency for the more feminine-identified character to want to talk about the relationship or to complain. They often wrongly assume their partner is dissatisfied and they need to fix the situation, but the truth is the feminine-identified partner simply wants to feel related.

A man grows when he learns to "live as freedom," and the woman grows when she learns to "live as love."

Deida also teaches three stages of development or intimacy. The first-stage is a dependence relationship where "men are men and women are women." Sometimes this is characterized as the macho jerk and the submissive housewife. The woman "needs" the man for money or emotional security and will do whatever it takes to keep him. The man "wants" the woman for sexual release and needs to feel trusted or appreciated by her and get her validation for his mission. In this stage, you need something from your partner, and when you aren't getting it, you close down.

In the second-stage, couples are characterized as in a 50/50 partnership. This is based on two independent and autonomous people coming together in fairness and cooperation. Each person is expected to carry their own weight and deal with their own issues. She has her stuff; he has his stuff, and neither of them feels responsible for fixing the other or making the other happy. In the second-stage, everyone is responsible for his or her own happiness.

Although this may be a great working relationship between best friends full of real love, the passion eventually dwindles because there is decreased polarity between masculine and feminine. Deida suggests that polarity *is* the source of sexual passion, which he differentiates from love. In the second-stage, you get what you need for yourself. You may be willing to do deals where you make equivalent trades. However, you would rather be careful and close down than remain open and get hurt.

Deida works exclusively with helping people move into the third-stage. The third-stage is intimate communion. From here, love is something you do, not something you fall into or merely feel. When you do love, or open as love, you feel love. This is love for love's sake. Here, the greatest desire of the feminine to "be seen and known as love's radiance" is realized, and the potential of the masculine to" provide effortless direction and alignment with deep consciousness" is fully actuated.

The partners dance with the knowledge that all will end someday, so it is best to give all you are now. Light and consciousness merge in love. You have the opportunity to hold nothing back. Be who you truly are underneath patterns, and let go in the bliss of consciousness and love, giving everything in every moment. In this stage, history is unimportant. All there is, is feeling this moment as an opportunity to give everything; because that's who you are, and that's the only way you can live.

Even in the third-stage, the other two stages are present. You won't want to give her what she wants when she is closed. So she stops giving you what you want and you close. The third stage practice is to just give anyway, even if you are hurting, and especially when you want to close down.

To give anyway does not mean to share your thoughts and feelings, and especially the judgments of what your partner is doing wrong. It means to "give your love and consciousness" – your presence or your radiance. It means staying receptive and open to being swayed. It means giving your heart completely. Every action should be like a poet trying to express the deepest truth of one's being.

David is the first to point out that, "The only thing you get for loving is love." Do not think of this as a strategy to get anything, because, in an absolute sense, there is nothing to get. In the moment of giving love, you are actually creating love. His best advice is to give that which you most want to receive, because, in the giving of it, you create it.

At times, Deida's work has been accused of being controversial, because of his straight talking nature when it comes to sex. Many have also deplored the link he makes between spirituality and sexuality, with opponents believing sexuality to be a completely separate bodily experience. However, Deida insists that a fulfilling sex life – whether gay or straight, celibate or raunchy – can be an integral part of one's spiritual journey. He also advocates talking openly and honestly about sex as an important step toward achieving a fulfilling spiritual and intimate relationship.

A Yogic/Artistic Practice

David's work is clearly not therapeutic in nature. People looking for help to deal with childhood wounds, past relationship issues, or communication strategies should look elsewhere. Deida aims to help couples and individuals move from a place of first-stage scarcity and neediness, through the second-stage safe independence, to a place of third-stage practice of trust in devotional love. In his weekend workshops, he helps couples become exquisitely open and vulnerable with each other, and navigate the differences between men and women's internal sexual circuitry.

Throughout his teachings, couples are taken on a transformative path that addresses spiritual awakening in mind, body, and heart to enable intimacy on a level never experienced before. He teaches the ability to love openly, with strength and compassion. Often, this isn't something that comes naturally. He effectively shows couples how to stop searching for love, and instead learn to radiate it through their entire being. They are taught to live love and be love. Couples can develop a freedom of consciousness and humor amidst anger, lust, and jealousy; or any type of conflict situation between them.

He proposes a unique reason for people to come together as a couple: to grow spiritually and to serve each other and the world to openness. According to Deida, the masculine in each of us is turned on by the radiance of feminine energy, and the feminine in each of us is turned on by the authenticity and integrity of deep consciousness. If men and women don't get the radiance and depth they desire from their partner, they begin to seek elsewhere, or try to provide it to themselves.

In third-stage practice, boundaries are gently released and love is more fully inhabited. You practice a third-stage relationship with someone you trust more than yourself to see you and know you, at least in certain areas. The way a third-stage relationship is established is by each partner saying to the other, "I know sometimes you are going to be wrong, and I'm willing to suffer through that, because, in general, you open me more than I can open myself." You each commit to inspiring each other to their highest good for all beings. Through moment-by-moment practice, everything is revealed as divine: every part of me, every part of you, and every part of everything.

In many ways, Deida uses the power of sexual attraction to teach people how to wake up and embrace life – to live open as love, to give yourself fully to everyone and everything. By transcending the fear of death, you transcend the fear of others and the fear of failure, and are able to live fully. Anything less than living fully open and giving completely is painful – to yourself and others.

Examples
Deconstructing Fantasies

At a seminar for young men, one member of the audience offers up his desire in life to sleep with many beautiful women and

have enough money to enjoy them. Men often have the fantasy of being sexually gratified by multiple partners.

David helped to deconstruct this fantasy and get to the root of desire. He asked the participant to describe, in detail, his greatest fantasy. "What would that get for you? What emotions would you feel if you had exactly what you wanted?" In this case, it was a sense of power and of being important. David suggests that *that* is his real need, and that if the women could provide *that* feeling in even greater depth than a mere sexual union, he would actually be much more satisfied, and at a much deeper level. In this way, Deida helps men to feel past the superficial levels of fantasy, and deeper into desire itself.

A Life Worth Living

In order to attract a woman with depth to her heart, Deida advises his young male audience that a man needs to ask himself, "What do I need to do before I die, so that I can die complete?" If this question cannot be answered within 10 seconds, any woman will be turned off. Women can sense superficiality. One response could be knowing that each day you've given a gift to someone else's life. Deida takes up this example as an opportunity to explain the concept of giving – which is what truly makes us happy in life, rather than receiving. A man must know his purpose and be willing to give 100%.

If a man attracts a woman who is radiant and open to her raw yearning, he has the opportunity to experience with her a sexual occasion that could prove to be the deepest of their lives – an intense communion that would inevitably change them both forever and serve as a true mutual gift for them, and the world.

Sexual Crock-Pots

During his seminars and conferences, Deida delivers his message of love as a living art with great passion, humor, and extreme clarity. In discussing the differences between many men and women, he explains how most men respond to visual clues at the very moment they are expressed, whereas, a woman responds to moods and emotions over hours and days.

Using the analogy of masculine blow-torches and feminine crock-pots, he advises how a man can heat up a woman's crock-pot over a number of days. If a husband or boyfriend has spent the last few days staring deeply into his partner's eyes, into her soul, then walking away just as she starts to feel the passion and intensity, within a few days her crock-pot would be bubbling with fire. As he explains: "Once they're heated up, you can't turn them off!" By the way a man touches or doesn't touch his partner, the use of his voice, and the things he does for her over several days, he is able to heat up her crock-pot and guarantee a sexual communion full of intensity.

David Deida Quotes

- *"If you are waiting for anything in order to live and love without holding back, then you suffer."*

- *It is time to evolve beyond the macho jerk ideal: all spine and no heart. It is also time to evolve beyond the sensitive wimp ideal: all heart and no spine.*

- *You can live in fear... or you can dance with her.*

- *Practice intimacy right now, in the present.*

- *Give all your love. I mean ALL your love. Why not? What do you think you can gain by holding back?*

- *No man can be fulfilled unless he has ceased searching for release and is founded in the present relaxation of true being. No woman can be fulfilled unless she has ceased searching for a way to fill herself and is founded in the present relaxation of radiant love.*

- *"Closing down in the midst of pain is a denial of a man's true nature. A superior man is free in feeling and action, even amidst great pain and hurt. If necessary, a man should live with a hurting heart rather than a closed one.*

175

He should learn to stay in the wound of pain and act with spontaneous skill and love even from that place."

● *"Every man knows that his highest purpose in life cannot be reduced to any particular relationship. If a man prioritizes his relationship over his highest purpose, he weakens himself, disserves the universe, and cheats his woman of an authentic man who can offer his full, undivided presence."*

Books and Media

Deida has written 10 books, printed in over 20 languages.

📖 His MUST READ book, *The Way of the Superior Man,* is a spiritual guide for men to master the challenges of women, work, and sexual desire, enabling them to unify "heart and spine."

📖 *Dear Lover: A Woman's Guide to Enjoying Love's Deepest Bliss,* teaches women to attract and keep a man capable of meeting what they most passionately yearn for – to give and receive love fully.

📖 *The Enlightened Sex Manual: Sexual Skills for the Superior Lover*

📖 *Instant Enlightenment*

📖 *Wild Nights*

📖 *Blue Truth*

📖 *Finding God Through Sex*

📖 *Naked Buddhism*

○ *Enlightened Sex: A 6 CD box set*

How to Find Out More

🖥 For more information and links, go to David Deida's website *www.deida.info*

23. Alison Armstrong

"Making sense of men!"

Background and Qualifications

Alison Armstrong has been leading transformational programs for adults for the past 20 years. In 1995, she created the *Celebrating Men, Satisfying Women* workshop to share her findings from years of research and observation of men. She then founded PAX Programs Inc., with the mission of transforming the way women relate to men. PAX stands for Partnership, Adoration, and Xtasy and is also the Latin word for peace. The idea behind the organization is to create peace between the sexes and provide unique and immediately useful information for women.

Alison began to study men when she realized she had been a "frog farmer:" turning princes into frogs. She had been emasculating men for many years, including ex partners and even her own son. She realized her behavior came from her own sense of weakness and feelings that she didn't have enough power. She knew that she would never experience her true power as a woman until she allowed men to have their power too.

Alison fully admits to having no formal psychology background. Nevertheless, psychotherapists are great fans of the PAX method, because it offers information that you cannot study at any university. While many universities offer women's studies, there isn't a single one that offers the study of men.

Alison lives in Southern California with her husband Greg and her three children.

Relationship Philosophy

The PAX philosophy stems from the belief that over the past 50 years, women have seen tremendous growth in opportunities and choices in their life. These cultural changes have brought about an expectation that men and women are equal and the same in character. The problem is that these new expectations cause conflict and confusion in all types of relationships because men and women are fundamentally different.

Women want men to be sensitive and emotional, while remaining ambitious and protective. Basically, women want a man who is a version of the ideal woman. Many of these same successful, self sufficient, independent women are dismayed when they find they'd actually love to have a good, strong, dependable man. These conflicts in desires and emotions have lead to confusion, disappointment, and frustration for women, and struggle within relationships between men and women.

Armstrong discovered from her research and countless interviews with men, that the two sexes are fundamentally different in the way they think, feel, react, listen, speak, and generally behave. For example, men tend to be single focused whereas women can multitask. All too often, women mistake this for men being stubborn and having a desire to ignore them, but it's just a different way of thinking and behaving. Most women know what happens if they get in the way of a man while he's focusing on something – whether that's the TV, newspaper, or his work. Women have to understand that they are not being ignored. They can save a lot of heartache and unnecessary hurt feelings if they realize that their man is simply focused on something and cannot focus on anything else. They can't even focus on ignoring them because that would be two things!

The Therapy

Alison teaches women a new way of relating to men that takes into account the fundamental differences between the sexes. She teaches women that men can be their partner, rather than their adversary. There doesn't need to be a "battle of the sexes" where men are emasculated and women abandon their femininity. If we accept our differences and work with them in order to create trust and support, we can have truly satisfying relationships.

Alison gives women and men practical tips for creating harmony with their partner. For example, she teaches women how to truly listen to men and create the kind of environment in which men really want to open up and express themselves. In order to do this, she shares a number of tips including:

How to LISTEN

- ♥ If you want to ask a question, make sure it's a good time – when he's not doing anything else, including things you don't think are important.

- ♥ After you ask a question, give him time to think before he responds.

- ♥ Once he starts talking, don't interrupt – even head nodding or verbal agreeing are forms of interruption.

- ♥ When it seems like he's finished, listen one minute longer to listen for anything else he might like to add.

- ♥ Make sure you are safe to talk to. If his answer is likely to get him in to trouble with you, he can tell this, and may not answer at all.

- ♥ Men are most alive when talking about their passions, especially to someone who is interested.

- ♥ Appreciate him for answering your question, even if it isn't the way you would like it answered.

Alison offers a simple test to see if you too are a frog farmer.

Frog Farmers

- ✓ Do men keep their distance instead of seeking emotional intimacy?
- ✓ Do you feel ignored instead of adored?
- ✓ Do you feel taken from instead of given to by men?
- ✓ Are men defensive with you instead of open?
- ✓ Do you experience being objectified instead of cherished?
- ✓ Have you been told you intimidate men?

If you say yes to any of these, consider that you are not making it safe for your man. You may, in fact, be a frog farmer.

Female Archetypes

Women are very familiar with common feminine stereotypes, such as "Femme Fatale," Damsel-in-Distress," "Southern Belle," and the like. She likes to talk about the energy of "Temptress," "Mother," and "Queen," because it is easier to see the feminine qualities.

Special among these qualities is the Temptress. The Temptress is subtle, and playful, inviting the pursuit of men, not aggressively pursuing them. Men will instinctively describe her as sexy. When women "get hit on," it is often because they are expressing the Temptress energy. It is important to consciously choose when and where to express this with laser-like focus on the man of your choice. Bringing out the Temptress with other men will cause great stress in your primary relationship!

Women usually relate easily to this archetype early in a relationship, and sometimes lose this when children come along, or the stress of work is too much. Sometimes, women focus more on nurturing or mothering their husbands. This will pull women out of the more playful energy. When you crave more attention from your mate, you just need to bring out more of your Temptress. Alison offers these tips:

Bring Out Your Temptress

♥ Work less, and sleep or rest more.

♥ Engage in activities that give you physical pleasure, for example, a massage, or bubble bath.

♥ Practice loving your body, regardless of its shape or size

♥ Climb back in your body instead of dragging it around. Express yourself through your body. Get physical with dancing, yoga, exercise, or your favorite sport.

♥ When you have energy, save it for play, instead of spending it at work or on the endless projects in your home. Other things will wait; your mate may not.

Male Archetypes

There are specific stages men go through during their lives. Knowing what stage a man is at can provide tremendous insights into their behavior.

♥ **Page** – Until puberty. They are knight wannabes.

♥ **Knight** – Puberty to late twenties. This stage is characterized by adventure. Knights love damsels, but are not ready to settle down.

♥ **Prince** – This stage is about building. A prince can either find a woman first, and build a castle with her, or he will want to build his castle first, and then find a woman. He is acutely aware he is not yet a king and is concerned about what he will be king of. The compulsion to work is very intense.

♥ **Tunnel** – This is the transition between a prince and king. This is better known as a mid-life crisis. He finally has the resources to live out some of his earlier dreams.

♥ **King** – This stage is characterized as being a provider. Kings have a strong sense of self and are clear about who they are, and what they can bring to the world.

♥ **Elder** – Few men reach this stage, which is characterized by people seeking them to share their wisdom.

Examples

Conversation with Ellen

Alison received the most important phone call of her life from her good friend back in 1991. Ellen said, "Men are attracted to you like bees to honey, but when you are done with them, it's like they have been with a vampire." That got her attention. "What are you talking about?" Alison asked back meekly. For the rest of the call, Ellen told her about all the ways she had seen Alison emasculate men. Although Alison squirmed with recognition, she sloughed it off with, "Well, that's what all women do; its standard practice."

What Ellen said next really hit home for Alison: "You've even done it with Jeffrey, your 3 year old son." It was like Alison was trying to train, squash, badger, and drive the maleness right out of her son. Alison could see that she was secretly afraid of men: "They are bigger and stronger and they will hurt me."

Realizing that her need to make men weak stemmed from her own fear helped her to come to a realization: she knew that she would never know her own power until she allowed men to have their own power. This was the beginning of a new life as she gave up power games of manipulation and began to be a partner with communication.

Alison Armstrong Quotes

- *The next time a man is watching TV – or fishing, or driving – and you plop down next to him and ask him, "What are you thinking about?" When he says "nothing," believe him. A glorious benefit of single focus is getting to think about nothing. I envy men for this!*

- What women crave more than anything else is intimacy, connection, and closeness

- *Men only talk about what really matters to them to someone who is "safe," meaning non-judgmental, interested, and not competing for talk time*

182

- *Interrupting men is like de-railing a train. He won't be able to keep opening up if you're saying, "But what about...?" and "Oh, me too, I did that and it was..."*

- *When men judge us by our looks, please understand that it is much more than the various shapes and sizes that make up our physical presence. Our looks really do manage to reflect who we are on the inside.*

- *When a man looks at a woman's body, he can see much more than the size and shape of her various parts. He can tell by the way she carries and moves her body if she's aggressive or receptive... he can tell if she is self-confident or unsure of herself...*

Books and Media

PAX's flagship program, Celebrating Men, Satisfying Women, is a weekend educational workshop for women to transform the way they relate to men. It facilitates the reconciliation many women are seeking with men, and outlines the skills required to realize powerful, satisfying relationships with all the men in their lives.

- Alison's latest book *is Making Sense of Men: A Woman's Guide to a Lifetime of Love and Attention*

- She is also author of *Keys to the Kingdom,* a novel that brings to life the teachings of the *Celebrating Men, Satisfying Women* workshop

- Alison also narrates and has written various CDs and DVDs to accompany the PAX program, including *Celebrating Love,* and

- *Understanding Women: Unlock the Mystery* and *In Sync with the Opposite Sex*

How to Find Out More

- For more information about Alison Armstrong, go to *www.understandmen.com*

183

24. Dr. Harville Hendrix

"A conscious relationship is a spiritual path which leads us home again"

Background and Qualifications

Dr. Harville Hendrix is a father of six and grandfather of four. He has over 35 years experience as a therapist, author, lecturer, workshop leader, and pastoral counselor. He specializes in studying intimate partnerships.

Dr. Hendrix graduated from The Union Theological Seminary in New York with a theology degree, has a PhD in psychology and theology from the University of Chicago, and an honorary doctorate from Mercer University.

Alongside his wife, Helen LaKelly Hunt PhD, Hendrix created Imago Relationship Therapy, which specializes in group seminars or 6-hour private intensives in conscious marriage and partnering. Harville Hendrix has seen over 2000 couples during his practice as a therapist, and Imago Therapy is now based in over 21 countries with trained therapists carrying out his message.

Relationship Philosophy

Dr. Hendrix believes that when we choose relationship partners, we often choose someone who we unconsciously believe will help us heal our childhood wounds. We seek out a person without even realizing that they possess the positive and negative traits of our original caretakers. How many times have you heard a woman say, "It's like I've married my father!"? Well Hendrix explains the reason why.

People tend to marry someone who activates the deepest fears of their childhood, almost recreating those traumas to resolve and grow from that experience. When we are first in love, we feel a joyful wholeness. This can start to disappear when emotional traumas arise and we realize we are with someone who is similar to our original caretaker. We begin to have an expectation of that person that they will react to us in a certain way. If we can become aware of the unconscious purpose of our marriage to begin to heal each other and grow into a new part of ourselves, this can become the means by which we recover our wholeness.

In a conscious marriage, we are able to find a relationship that heals these issues in a positive way. If we can commit to the healing and recovery process to the point where we heal enough of ourselves, this state of conscious is self-sustaining. We can then live a life of relaxed joyfulness.

The real tragedy of relationships is when people leave at the darkest moments of great pain, when the greatest shift of consciousness and movement towards a deeper understanding is about to happen. Hendrix describes this as a rebirth moment, which cannot happen unless emotional pain and outflow is felt.

The Therapy

In his courses and therapy, he enables couples to replace confrontation and criticism with a healing process of mutual growth and support via practical exercises and advice. Of all the exercises in Imago Relationship Therapy, Hendrix has found that Imago Dialogue has been the most effective tool for satisfying our innate yearning for wholeness and connection. It is an effective communication technique that can restructure the way we talk to each other. This technique involves the following three steps:

Imago Dialog

- ♥ **Mirroring** – reflecting back what we hear from each other
- ♥ **Validating** – acknowledging what your partner is saying rather than deflecting it
- ♥ **Empathizing** – acknowledging your partner's feelings

Examples
A Marriage Beyond Dreams

Filmmaker Chris Brickler interviewed Harville Hendrix and wife Helen La Kelly Hunt about their work and their own relationship as part of the Emmy nominated documentary, *Song of Songs.* The film explores the mystery, chemistry, and challenges of romantic love relationships across the country, with emotional stories that will touch anyone's heart.

As part of the documentary, Harville and Helen discuss their theories on a shift in marriage since the 1950's – towards a new kind of marriage: the conscious partnership. The focus becomes the relationship rather than the individuals, whereby two people come together as partners on a journey through life, going through a continual process of helping to heal each other from the emotional stories created in childhood. It is when two people enter into a relationship such as this, that they can find the marriage of their dreams. During the interview, Harville looks lovingly at Helen and remarks, "Our marriage is beyond a dream; it has qualities and feelings to it that we are still looking for a language for." It is this sentiment that has motivated them to help other couples achieve the same dream.

Witnessing and Sharing without Judgment

Helen and Harville explain their Imago Therapy program as a way to enable couples to realize the purpose of their relationship – to heal one another by committing to healing their childhood wounds together. Using such tools as the Imago Dialog process, it is possible for one person to suspend their own thinking without wanting to contradict and counter the other person, and simply be witness to the other person's thinking without judgment.

After completing the Imago program, several couples gave inspiring testimonials. Bruce and Francine, both psychologists, attended a workshop. Despite working with couples themselves, they couldn't make their own relationship work.

Yet, the Imago Dialog enabled them to interact with one another in a non-blaming way for the first time, with each partner feeling validated and un-judged.

Wife Mikki also describes her experience of the program as a way to help her realize her husband Mike's point of view, and understand what's going on in his world, rather than simply focusing on her own problems. Mike adds that through the dialogue process, he became able to practice listening and curtailing his responses, instead of reacting and causing an argument.

Dr. Harville Hendrix Quotes

- *A conscious relationship is a spiritual path that leads us home again – to joy and aliveness, to the feeling of oneness we started out with.*

- *Without change there is no growth!*

- *Empathy is the most powerful bonding experience you can have. It restores the experience of connectedness and union, overcoming the illusion of separation.*

- *When we understand that we have chosen our partners to heal certain painful experiences, and that the healing of those experiences is the key to the end of longing, we have taken the first step on the journey to real love.*

- *What we need to understand and accept is that conflict is supposed to happen.*

- *Divorce does not solve the problems of relationships. We may get rid of our partner, but we keep our problems, carrying them into the next relationship.*

- *We always marry someone for the purpose of finishing our childhood.*

- *Marriage, ultimately, is the practice of becoming passionate friends.*

Books and Media

Dr. Hendrix has written several books on intimate relationships and parenting, which have been translated into over 50 languages. His titles include:

- 📖 *Getting the Love You Want: A Guide for Couples* (which has sold 2 million copies)
- 📖 *Keeping the Love You Find: A Personal Guide*
- 📖 *The Couple's Companion: Mediations and Exercises for Getting the Love You Want*
- 📖 *Giving the Love That Heals* (with Helen LaKelly Hunt)
- 📖 *Receiving Love: Transforming Your Relationship by Letting Yourself Be Loved*
- 📖 *Receiving Love Workbook: A Unique Twelve-Week Course for Couples and Singles*
- 📖 *Wired for Love: How Understanding Your Partner's Brain and Attachment Style Can Help You Defuse Conflict and Build a Secure Relationship*
- ☐ Harville Hendrix has also appeared on *Oprah* 16 times, and one of his appearances was included in her top 20 shows of all times.

How to Find Out More

- 🖥 For more information go to Dr. Harville Hendrix' webpages:

  www.harvillehendrix.com

  www.gettingtheloveyouwant.com

  www.imagorelationships.org

25. Dr. Marshall Rosenberg

"The language of feelings and needs"

Background and Qualifications

Dr. Marshall Rosenberg is the founder of the Center for Nonviolent Communication, an international peacemaking and training organization. His pioneering work is delivered all across the globe first-hand and through facilitators and trainers to couples, schools, prisons, and large corporations.

A father of three, Marshall grew up in Detroit in a turbulent neighborhood, and it was here that he became interested in developing a new form of communication and a peaceful alternative to the violence that he encountered.

He achieved a doctorate in psychology from the University of Wisconsin in 1961, and it was from there that he developed Nonviolent Communication (NVC). Dr. Rosenberg first used the technique in federally funded school integration projects, and it was in 1984 that he founded the center for NVC, an international non-profit peacemaking organization. The center aims to show people how to connect in ways that inspire compassionate results.

In 2004, Dr. Rosenberg received the International Peace Prayer Day Man of Peace Award, and was the 2006 recipient of the Global Village Foundations Bridge of Peace award. He teaches NVC across the globe in local communities, national conferences, and impoverished war-torn states of the world.

Relationship Philosophy

Dr. Rosenberg discovered through his research and observation that the unmet needs behind all communication – what we do and what we say – are the main cause of conflict and hostility.

He is convinced that humans are not inherently violent and there are four basic attributes of human nature:

4 Attributes of Human Nature

- ♥ All humans share the basic universal needs.
- ♥ Compassion is part of basic human nature.
- ♥ Feelings and emotions are signals telling us whether or not needs are being met.
- ♥ At the core of all conflict, violence, and emotional pain, are needs that are not being met.

He defines violence as not just physically trying to hurt another, but any use of power over people in an attempt to coerce them into doing something. This includes any use of punishment and reward, guilt and shame, duty or obligation. From birth, we are taught to judge, demand, and diagnose; constantly thinking and communicating in terms of people as "right" or "wrong." This hinders communication and causes misunderstanding, anger, and pain. Even someone who has the best intentions can end up causing conflict.

The Therapy

NVC is an effective and easy to grasp technique that gets to the root of violence and pain peacefully. By deepening our own sense of personal empowerment, NVC can help us communicate more effectively, reduce hostility, and strengthen relationships. It scratches beneath the surface to discover what is alive and vital within us – that our actions are based on human needs seeking to be met.

NVC enables people to develop a vocabulary of feelings and needs that help us to more clearly express what is going on at any given moment. For example, it teaches a person not to use language that sounds like criticism, but instead to learn to give from the heart and feel the joy in enriching another person's life without any attachment to guilt or shame from either party. It provides a framework for communicating what we feel and need in a manner that helps ensure understanding.

The 4-Part NVC Process:

1) **Observe** the current situation.

2) Identify **feelings** the situation brings up – hurt, fear, joy, amusement, etc.

3) Find out what **needs** are not being met and what needs are connected to those feelings.

4) Work out what is needed for your life to be enriched and make a simple **request**.

For instance, if one's husband leaves dirty clothes on the floor at night, one could say, "Honey, when I notice your dirty clothes on the floor, I feel constricted and frustrated because I am needing order in the bedroom for me to feel comfortable and relaxed with you. Would you be willing to put your dirty clothes directly in the hamper?"

These four parts can also be received from others without them actually having to go through the process themselves. The person practicing NVC can work with the signals they receive from their partner and hear their needs by what they are saying or doing, with the eventual result of an improvement in the way they both communicate.

The only tricky part of NVC is recognizing the difference between an authentic feeling and a judgment. For instance, the statement, "I feel abandoned" is not a real feeling. It is a judgment that the other person is abandoning you. Of course, each of us understands what it "feels like to feel abandoned," but the real feeling is underneath that. One might feel sad, lonely, or scared. On the other hand, someone may feel elated to be abandoned by a bully!

The best test of whether you are expressing a feeling or a judgment is whether the other person could interpret the statement as an attack. If the other person gets defensive, it is a sure sign that the statement was a judgment rather than an authentic feeling.

When your partner expresses herself using judgmental language, you can either correct her language (and cause increased conflict), or learn to translate her judgments into feelings. For instance, to the statement "I feel abandoned. You are never here!" a great response could be, "Are you feeling angry that I am not here to talk with you?" You may not get the feeling absolutely correct, but the fact that you are reaching out will make a great difference. You may not get the basis of the need (more talking or touching, for example) correct either, but now she has the opportunity to reflect and let you know exactly what she needs.

Examples
"Murderer, Assassin, Child Killer!"

In his seminal book, *Nonviolent Communication,* Dr. Rosenberg recounts a chilling story where NVC saved his life, and established a connection with his attacker. He was presenting at a mosque in a Palestinian refugee camp in Bethlehem. A muffled commotion broke out in the crowd; someone yelled out at the top of his lungs, "Murderer!" Dozens of voices joined in "Assassin, Child killer, Murderer!"

Dr. Rosenberg focused his attention to what the man was feeling and needing. "Are you angry because you would like my government to use its resources differently?" *"Damn Right!"* "So, you are furious and would appreciate some support in improving your living conditions..." "Sounds like you're feeling very desperate, and you're wondering whether I or anybody else can really understand what it's like to be living under these conditions." "I hear how painful it is for you to raise your children here..."

From each response, Dr. Rosenberg dug into the person's underlying feelings and needs and reflected them back. He neither agreed nor disagreed, but rather strove to understand his point of view. He was so successful at defusing the situation, that the "attacker" invited him to dinner that night!

Discovering who my Husband Truly is!

In his book, *Giving From the Heart,* Dr. Rosenberg offers a testimonial from a woman who used NVC to create greater depth and caring in her relationship. She describes learning to receive messages about emotions using NVC, which helped her truly listen to the words her husband was saying and receive his underlying feelings. What she discovered was "a very hurting man to whom I had been married for 28 years."

Just a few days before attending the NVC seminar, he had asked for a divorce, but now their story has a happy ending. She learned to listen to feelings, express her needs, and accept answers that she might not necessarily want to hear. She realized, "He is not here to make me happy, nor am I here to create happiness for him. We have both learned to grow, to accept, and to love, so that we can each be fulfilled."

Giraffe Language

Despite the official name being non-violent communication, Rosenberg also calls his technique "giraffe language," because it is a language of the heart; and the giraffe has the largest heart of any land animal.

He was taught a different language when he grew up, which he describes as "jackal language." A jackal is much closer to the ground and they get so preoccupied with getting their needs met, that they just can't see into the future like the giraffe. So the jackal's form of communication blocks compassion and they are motivated out of fear, shame, and guilt.

In an interview with *Yes Magazine,* Dr. Rosenberg recalls a business training session where he became very emotional and tears came to his eyes. The boss of the organization looked really disgusted and turned away. Dr. Rosenberg says, "It was horrible for a few seconds because I allowed the look on his face to stimulate old jackal programming in me. I thought, "Oh my God, I've behaved inappropriately. He must think I'm a real mess!" But after remembering to direct his attention to the man's feelings instead of his own he asks him, "Are you feeling disgusted and needing whoever is running a meeting like this to have his emotions more in control?" It was at that moment Rosenberg could recognize the man's vulnerability. He was surprised when the man responded by saying, "No, no, I was just thinking of how my wife wishes I could cry. I am getting a divorce right now. She says that living with me is like living with a stone."

Dr. Marshall Rosenberg Quotes

- *One needs connection before correction.*

- *As nonviolent communication replaces our old patterns of defending, withdrawing, or attacking in the face of judgment and criticism, we come to perceive ourselves and others, as well as our interactions and relationships, in a new light.*

- *If we wish to fully express anger, the first step is to divorce the other person from any responsibility for our anger.*

- *The language of life is basically the language of feelings and needs.*

- *All human beings have the same needs, so when people can see the needs of the other person, they don't see an enemy.*

- *We've been taught a language of domination for about 8000 years that's designed to get people to obey authority. It's quite a shift for you to move away from enemy images that define badness in the other person, and to instead just express what's alive in you – what are your needs that aren't being met? It's a radical paradigm shift.*

Books and Media

Titles include:

- 📖 *Nonviolent Communication: A Language of Life*
- 📖 *Nonviolent Communication Companion Workbook: A Practical Guide for Individual, Group, or Classroom Study*
- 📖 *Being Me, Loving You: A Practical Guide to Extraordinary Loving Relationships*
- 📖 *Speak Peace in a World of Conflict*
- 📖 *The Surprising Purpose of Anger: Beyond Anger Management: Finding the Gift*
- 📖 *Living Nonviolent Communication: Practical Tools to Connect and Communicate Skillfully in Every Situation*
- ⊙ *Nonviolent Communication* (Audio CD)

How to Find Out More

- 💻 For more information, go the website:
  www.nonviolentcommunication.com

26. Dr. Margaret Paul

"Heal your relationship through inner bonding."

Background and Qualifications

Dr. Margaret Paul has a PhD in psychology, as well as being an educator and chaplain. She has taught classes and seminars for couples since 1967, and has created the highly successful Inner Bonding technique alongside her colleague Dr. Erika Chopich. Clients who have used the Inner Bonding technique with success include actress Lindsay Wagner and singer songwriter Alanis Morissette.

Relationship Philosophy

Dr. Paul believes that the #1 reason for relationship problems is self-abandonment. When people get married, they each have this secret hope that the other will give them what they never received before: fill up their emptiness, make them feel good about themselves: happy, loved, worthy, safe, and lovable. When both people want this from the other, they both end up very disappointed.

You can't love another until you are able to love yourself. To Margaret, this means taking responsibility for your own feelings. When you make another responsible for how you feel, you give up your power to another.

The wounded self bounces between fears of rejection/ abandonment on one hand, and engulfment/ smothered on the other. In any relationship, these fears often manifest as controlling behavior, such as focusing on who is at fault or who started it. You desperately want the other to see what they are doing that (you believe) is causing you to feel hurt or afraid, with the expectation that if they only knew what they were doing, and how you felt, they would stop. But this only activates their fear.

Through Inner Bonding, Dr. Paul helps couples to heal those underlying fears so that they can give up needing to control, and can joyfully share love together. She believes that relationships offer us our greatest challenge and are the most powerful arena for emotional and spiritual growth.

The Therapy

For many, the pain of childhood was too great: the loneliness, heartbreak, fear of rejection, abandonment, engulfment, or failure. We developed many addictive ways to avoid these feelings, such as substance abuse: food, sex, drugs, or alcohol; process addictions such as anger, compliance, withdrawal, or resistance; and co-dependence: controlling others with anger, guilt, compliance, or violence; and even addicted shame for somehow being wrong and unlovable. In each case, resentment is certain to build as the fundamental conflict goes unresolved.

By learning how to manage the underlying feelings, these outdated schemes are no longer needed, and one can move into loving relationships with yourself and others.

The Inner Bonding Process helps individuals and couples to move out of fear and into love. The process helps you learn to manage core feelings, take care of yourself, and connect with a source of spiritual guidance. In other words, this is learning to connect, bond, and take care of your Inner Child. This lets you take care of yourself in any life situations or conflicts with which you are faced.

The technique provides a 6-step process to rapid healing of fears and false beliefs that control our lives. If practiced regularly, it can give you the power to become more loving towards yourself and others, enabling peace, joy, and empowerment. Other benefits include overcoming limiting beliefs, healing fear, pain, anger, guilt, shame, depression, anxiety and addictive behavior. The 6-step process involves mind, body, and spiritual healing.

197

6 Step Inner Bonding Process

1) **Choose to be aware of your feelings, and choose to feel your pain.** This step involves coming into the present and tuning into and truly experiencing your feelings.

2) **Choose the intent to learn:** the willingness to find out what you may be doing or thinking that could be causing the pain (as opposed to the intent to protect yourself from fear and pain with addictive and controlling behaviors). Making this choice is about opening your heart. Ultimately, it is about taking responsibility for the ways you may be causing your own pain with your thoughts and beliefs.

3) **Choose to welcome, embrace and dialog with your wounded self and reclaiming your core self.** When you realize there is a good and compelling reason for your feelings and actions, this helps you discover what is causing your fear and pain. You come to understand that these fears and associated believes were the only way you could feel safe as a child. They were your survival mechanism. Your core self contains your unique talents, natural gifts and wisdom, and your curiosity and sense of wonder that allows playfulness and spontaneity, and your ability to love.

4) **Dialogue with your Higher Guidance.** What is the truth about your false beliefs? What is the loving action you could take toward yourself and others? Look for the action that will take care of your Inner Child, and any anxiety or fear that might arise.

5) **Take the loving action that came from your Higher Guidance.** This included learning to love both the core self and wounded self. It also includes being kind to yourself in a compassionate, non-judgmental, observing fashion, rather than condemning yourself if you slip. You heal your false beliefs when you learn to be accepting of all parts of your wounded self, including the anger, shame, and hurt.

6) **Evaluate your action.** Are your pain, anger, and shame getting healed?

By going through the 6-step process, a person can learn to recognize their true worth, discover passion and purpose in life, and take loving care of their heart, mind, body, and spirit. It also enables them to take responsibility for their own feelings of pain, joy, safety, and self-worth. In doing so, people create deeply satisfying and enduring relationships.

Many people insist that, if their partners changed, then their relationship would be happier. Instead, Inner Bonding instructs people how to take loving action on their own behalf, which in turn can create powerful changes in their relationship.

Inner Bonding helps one to stop seeing oneself as a victim, and helps one overcome the illusion that there is something inherently wrong and unlovable about you, and that you could develop a self that will make people love you. You can accept that you can't control your partner's desire, or their ability to love you. You can learn to define your self-worth using eternal internal standards, rather than fleeting external standards, over which you have little real control.

So much conflict in relationship is stuck in power struggles, as each person tries to control the other by blaming them, getting angry, or simply withdrawing. By giving up on the power struggle, a person can start to take care of him or herself, and be open to the learning their partner is offering them. This is when true relationship change can occur.

Examples
Celebrity fan of Inner Bonding – Lindsay Wagner

Emmy award winning actress and author, Lindsay Wagner, describes Inner Bonding as "One of the most powerful tools I've come across." On the Inner Bonding website, she describes the six step process as something which has brought "Immeasurable peace and joy into my life," enabling her to

enhance relationships with her children, partner, friends, and work colleagues.

In the forward to Dr. Paul's book, *Do I Have to Give Up Me to Be Loved By God?*, Wagner describes how the book and its teachings will take the reader on a life-changing journey down a path full of awakenings, tears, compassion, reunion, joy, and peace. "I am eternally grateful to this 5 foot 2 sparkly eyed spiritual warrior some of us call "The Samurai," for all the courageous work she's done on herself, and the exceptional gift she has to help others realize that peace, love, and security are an inside job."

Should I give up Me to not Lose You?

In an article on the Inner Bonding website, Dr. Paul discusses how far a person should bend their values to preserve their relationship. How much should one change to avoid losing a partner?

Dr. Paul advises against looking at a relationship in terms of changing oneself in order to accommodate a partner's needs and personality traits, but instead, looking at it as a learning and growth opportunity as a result of the differences. Problems arise when one or both partners are not open to growth and this "accept me the way I am" attitude can lead to an unhealthy situation.

Examples of such differences include: Joe is extremely neat, while Julia has a hard time putting things away. Roberta is always on time while Cecelia is always late. Maggie is a spender while David is a saver. Carl has a high sex drive while Andrea has a low sex drive. Angie is an authoritarian parent while Curt is a permissive parent. Ronald is highly social while Greg is a homebody.

Such differences can lead to conflict: one partner giving in to avoid difficulties, or growth: both partners opening to the opportunity to learn from each other. Without this willingness to grow, the problem becomes not the differences themselves, but the refusal to learn from them. "The key is to be willing to come up against conflict and rejection and even lose the other person rather than continuing to accommodate. On the emotional and spiritual level, you can afford to lose your partner but you cannot afford to lose yourself."

With Inner Bonding, you will have the tools to face the feelings of loneliness, heartbreak, despair, and helplessness that come with being human, rather than believing you are at fault for having these feelings.

Dr. Margaret Paul Quotes

- *Most problems in life come from self-abandonment*

- *Work on the premise that true peace and joy come from the intent to be a loving human being.*

- *We cannot experience deep spiritual connection until we love ourselves, but we cannot love ourselves until we experience the love that comes from a deep spiritual connection.*

- *Deal with conflict in a relationship from the intent to learn rather than the intent to protect against pain.*

- *Positive energy flows between two people when there is an attitude of gratitude. Constant complaints create a heavy negative energy, which is not fun to be around. Practice being grateful for what you have rather than focusing on what you don't have.*

- *You heal your false beliefs when you learn to be loving toward your wounded self.*

- *Your life and relationships will greatly improve when you are conscious enough to stop thoughts of self-judgment and judgment of others, and instead focus on kindness toward yourself and others.*

Books and Media

📖 Dr. Margaret Paul has written many books, including her bestseller with Dr. Jordan Paul, which has sold over 1 million copies: *Do I Have to Give Up Me to be Loved By You?* There is also a *workbook* to accompany this title.

📖 *Inner Bonding: Becoming a Loving Adult to Your Inner Child*

📖 *Healing Your Aloneness – written with Dr. Erika Chopich*

📖 *The Healing Your Aloneness Workbook–written with Dr. Erika Chopich*

📖 *Do I Have to Give Up Me to Be Loved By God?*

📖 *Do I Have to Give Up Me to Be Loved By My Kids?*

📖 *Free to Love*

How to Find Out More

💻 For more information go to Margaret Paul's Inner Bonding website: *www.innerbonding.com*

27. M. Gary Neuman

"The destructive power of emotional infidelity"

Background and Qualifications

M. Gary Neuman is a Florida psychotherapist, rabbi, and creator of the internationally recognized Sandcastles Program for Children of Divorce, which is a mandatory program in over a dozen countries. Through his clinic and the Sandcastles Program, Neuman has helped thousands of couples in crisis, with the overriding belief that many couples in crisis simply need to refocus their energy into their marriage and stop the emotional infidelity.

Neuman has a Master of Science in Mental Health Counseling from Barry University in Miami and has been in private practice for over 20 years. He works with the Miami Family Court as a consultant and is also Director of the Family Court and Custody Investigation Unit.

Relationship Philosophy

Through working with thousands of couples, Neuman has found that the major problem in relationships is not to do with communication problems. Most commonly, relationship problems stem from emotional infidelity through failing to put enough focus on their marriage.

If you're not emotionally committed to your marriage, you're draining it of the energy it needs to be great. It could be that you don't invest enough time in your partner, you could be placing more importance on your job than your spouse, you may have relatively little loving touch or affection between you, and you may be getting a secret thrill out of flirting with co-workers, thinking it is safe because it can't go any further.

Neuman's research with men has revealed that men cheat not because of the sex. The number one dissatisfaction in marriage that contributed to men cheating was emotional disconnection. So to prevent infidelity and get more out of your marriage, Neuman advises finding ways to emotionally reconnect with your spouse on a daily basis. It takes work to be constantly in touch with each other and be there no matter what, without constant criticism or judgment. Having a great marriage is a truly rewarding experience, but in order to achieve this, your marriage has to be the number one focus.

The Therapy

Neuman offers a 10-week program that creates emotional fidelity, by uncovering 10 secrets to a great marriage that couples can work on each week. These practical guidelines enable couples to make the commitment to change their focus and transform their marriage. He challenges couples to dare to limit contact with the opposite sex, dare to need each other, dare to put in writing a marriage plan, dare to put your marriage before your kids or job, dare to make love in a whole new way.

10 Secrets of a Great Marriage

- ♥ Commitment is the glue of marriage. Insulate and protect your marriage against emotional infidelity by avoiding friendships with members of the opposite sex.
- ♥ Co-dependence is a necessary ingredient for a great marriage. Spouses must need each other.
- ♥ Spouses need clear, realistic goals and a specific action plan of how to achieve them.
- ♥ Like any strong working partnership, marriage needs well-defined roles for each spouse.
- ♥ Acceptance is about appreciating, not settling.
- ♥ Your marriage has to come first – before job, kids, anything else.

♥ Your childhood has a great deal to do with your ability to enjoy a great marriage.

♥ Great sex comes not from great sexual skill, but from sharing your deepest, shyest self, while trusting your partner.

♥ Your marriage comes before your child; but your child is one of the best tools for creating a great marriage.

♥ Time is on your side. A great marriage has many stages and takes many years to develop properly.

♥ **Bonus Secret:** Focus energy on creating a healthy relationship with your spouse's parents.

Neuman offers a four-point connection plan to help couples to reconnect. These are:

4 Point Connection Plan

♥ **Have five touch points per day** – where you touch each other lovingly. This could be a kiss, cuddle, or sexual intimacy.

♥ **Have four talk points per week** – at least 45 minutes long. Most couples only spend a few minutes talking every day!

♥ **Have a weekly date night** – where it's forbidden to talk about money, business, or the kids, or to use cell phones.

♥ **Have a monthly honeymoon night** – where you plan a romantic dinner and enjoy blissful lovemaking.

These skills are aimed at the prevention of an affair, but once infidelity has occurred, honesty is the key to re-establishing trust. It's also important to find out what happened and go over all the details before you can move forward. You have to be prepared to be vulnerable with your partner who has cheated and trust yourself to them again.

Examples
Expectations

Carla's beliefs about marriage came from how her father cared for her depressed mother. She had seen great devotion, and learned that was the way a man expressed love for a woman. "He always found a way to get her smiling." However, whenever Carla was in the doldrums, her loving husband, Sam, "gave her space." Carla spent five years being angry with Sam because he "wasn't trying hard enough." However, that meant "doing what dad did," which was putting everything on hold to spend hours taking care of, and coaxing his wife. Carla misunderstood what marriage offered, and she had misplaced expectations from her childhood experiences.

Carla would have done better to have appropriate expectations and to communicate to Sam what she needed and what it meant to her.

The Marriage Should Run by Itself!

Frank and Helen came to see Neuman to strategize about how to divorce with the minimal impact on the children. They were eloquent, insightful, and even complimentary. They could not think of anything dramatic that caused them to seek divorce. They had started fighting years before, and hadn't had sex for over a year. They were just tired of each other. They felt like a burden to each other.

When Neuman explored where this burden came from, he saw a couple who were completely overbooked with complicated lives. Weekends were filled with errands that could not be completed during the week. It was exhausting just listening to their story!

Neuman asked them to think back to when they first met and fell in love. What kind of conversations did they have? Were they about credit card debt? How to spend less? About dirty diapers? Were romantic dinners interrupted six times by cell phones and business talks? They never realized how much they ignored working on their relationship. They assumed that after falling in love, they didn't have to work on it anymore. Couples often reason, "If it takes so much energy, we must not be made for each other." Neuman helps people realize the fallacy in this type of thinking.

However, great marriages take an enormous amount of energy to create and maintain. They take fully engaged connection, require constant attention, and an ability to look deeply within and give everything fully. Putting your marriage first is a state of mind that will dramatically impact the quality of your marriage.

M. Gary Neuman Quotes

- *I don't believe in OK, decent, or solid marriages. I'm against them. I believe only in great marriages and that you should expect and reach for nothing less.*

- *We really have to make our lives a marriage-centered lifestyle, where we're really regularly thinking, "What have I done for my spouse today to put a smile on his or her face?"*

- *I'm dismayed that the world around us seems to have lost the pleasure of commitment, the energy to stick with the responsibility, and the determination to develop the greater goal of marital bliss.*

Books and Media

- ☐ M. Gary Neuman has made ten appearances on *Oprah* as well as countless other TV shows. He has also been featured in *People Magazine*, *Time Magazine*, *Parenting Magazine*, and *Parents Magazine*.

He is author of the following self-help books:

- 📖 *The Truth About Cheating: Why Men Stray and What You Can Do to Prevent It*

- *Emotional Infidelity: How to Affair Proof Your Marriage and 10 Other Secrets to a Great Marriage*
- *Helping Your Kids Cope with Divorce the Sandcastles Way*
- *How To Make A Miracle, Finding Incredible Spirituality in Times of Happiness and Struggle*
- *Sandcastles Workbooks – for 4 different age groups*
- His most recent book, *Connect to Love: The Keys to Transforming Your Relationship*, shows couples how to grow stronger by understanding what women really need from a romantic relationship
-

How to Find Out More

For more information, go to *www.mgaryneuman.com*

28. Drs. Gay and Kathlyn Hendricks

"Absolute honesty is key to any relationship"

Background and Qualifications

Drs. Gay and Kathlyn Hendricks are a husband and wife team with over 25 years experience counseling singles and couples who are interested in conscious relationships, and professional to incorporate their body-centered principles.

Kate is a registered dance-movement therapist, has a PhD, and is a consultant and educator specializing in the field of body-mind relationship transformation. She also is the director of training for the institute. Gay has a PhD from Stanford University and is a leading theorist in the field of body-mind integration. He was a Professor of Counseling for 21 years at the School of Education at the University of Colorado. Gay met Kate when he was 35 years old, and says they both went through a series of disastrous relationships before they created conscious loving with each other.

Together, the Hendricks developed *The Relationship Solution*, an online course designed for couples and singles looking to find a conscious, lasting relationship. They have helped over 20,000 couples through group and private sessions.

Relationship Philosophy

Their work has grown out of the heart-felt commitment to create a thriving and conscious relationship with each other. They only teach principles and practices that have made a profound effect on their own life and relationship. They assist people in opening up to more creativity, love, and vitality. They believe there's no point simply focusing on the differences between you and your partner, but instead prefer to work on enhancing the common and shared interests of partners and their common core issues.

209

Five Required Lessons

1) Feel all of your feelings deeply

2) Seek your true self

3) Let go of the uncontrollable

4) We are all made of the same thing

5) Life is fullest when we're most true to ourselves

Absolute honesty is the key to any relationship, including the relationship you have with yourself. People should make a commitment to scrupulously tell the truth about their feelings and actions to their partner. There is absolutely no point in lying to protect the feelings of the other. They also highlight the way arguments start when someone points the finger of blame, which wastes endless energy in an attempt to get the other person to fulfill the role of the villain. Both parties to the relationship learn to take healthy responsibility by shifting from blame to wonder and focusing on creating what each really wants.

Commitment is also a key area for the Hendricks, and crucial for creating relationship harmony in body, mind, and soul. They also teach the importance of learning to appreciate other people and how to receive appreciation, rather than trying to get other people to appreciate us.

The Therapy

The Hendricks primarily teach professional coaches, counselors, and facilitators to work with couples. Through their sessions, the Hendricks aim to create a path to relationship harmony and a vibrancy of body and mind, with activities designed to shift us out of a state of consciousness in which problems occur, to a state of consciousness in which problems can be resolved with more ease. Their methods teach couples and singles how to avoid relationship-killing mistakes.

Relationship Saving Techniques

♥ Learning to communicate clearly on difficult subjects without hurting each other's feelings by speaking unarguably.

♥ Learning to eliminate blame, which they term a relationship killer.

♥ Taking 100% responsibility for your own life's outcomes.

♥ The importance of making time to be close to each other and time for your own individual creative activities. Creativity is an essential key to relationship harmony, because if you can't express it very often, you tend to feel your partner is opposing it.

The Hendricks believe that relationship problems can very often be solved with five simple questions.

The Five Questions

♥ What am I not facing?

♥ What truths have I not spoken?

♥ What have I been blaming others for that I need to acknowledge responsibility for?

♥ What choices do I need to make?

♥ What actions do I need to take?

These questions rely on a skill the Hendricks call "Presencing" becoming aware of what is happening, in the present. From this point, feeling abandoned by your spouse is transformed to "feeling butterflies in my stomach and a tightness in my throat." Both feelings that are unarguable.

There are three practices of presencing that are sure to make you feel more alive: being present to wonder (turning a fear or worry into wondering how), being present to your spiritual essence, and listening while being present to your spirit.

211

Ego centered listening is to find fault, rebut, be right or to fix the other. It is used to get approval, gain control and focus on only your needs. Spirit-centered listening, on the other hand, gets to the real issues quickly, because you don't have to fight the defensiveness and resistance.

Examples

Stop an Argument in its Tracks

Kathlyn Hendricks answers a question from a website reader: "What is the quickest way to stop an argument?" She explains that anyone taking part in an argument is saying something which is arguable – it's not about who is right or wrong. All too often, people believe their role in an argument is to make the other person realize they are saying or doing something wrong, in other words, to reform them. This is what causes a power struggle.

She advises the quickest way to stop an argument is to say something unarguable. For example, partners learn to describe a bodily sensation, such as, "My shoulders are tight," My palms are sweaty," or, "I don't know what I'm angry about." It's the quickest way to stop an argument in its tracks. Alternatively, she advises taking some time out to appreciate yourself for whatever you're experiencing, take a moment to be sensitively aware of what you're feeling, which gives you a break from the power struggle. The third way to stop an argument is to open your body posture to make yourself undefended. During an argument, often our body language is contracted – such as hugging our knees up to our chest. The best way to change your mind is to change your body. By opening your posture, this can help open your mind up to other possibilities.

Do I have to give up myself to be close to my partner?

The Hendricks were asked this tough question about identity – whether getting together with someone means giving up oneself. They explain that there is a common "relationship dance" in couples – between the spouse who likes to get close and the other who likes to feel separation and needs some space. Often, these two personality types are attracted to each other and succeed in a relationship when they don't try to change their partner's personality style. They do this by consciously allowing time for shared intimacy as well as space individually. When a couple can express and listen to their spouse's desires for space or closeness, they can bypass arguments that occur when partners do make clear requests.

Relationships also flourish when each partner commits to learn from the other's differing personality traits. Those who need time apart can teach those who like to get close how to open up a direct link to the universe through unstructured time alone – just "being." Those who like to get close can teach their personality opposite how to open up to feelings more easily.

Drs. Gay and Kathlyn Hendricks Quotes

- *If you are in a committed relationship, you and your partner feel connected on the spiritual level in times of stress, as well as in times of joy and abundance.*

- *You feel an abundant flow of creative energy if you don't squander it on recycling conflicts or self-sabotage routines.*

- *Love as much as you can from wherever you are.*

- *If you tell the truth at all times, you will have clear relationships with everyone. If you do not, things will get out of control very quickly.*

- *When you withhold, you keep inside yourself things that should be expressed. The very act of hiding these things takes you one step back from the relationship.*

- *Human beings have deep needs, both for closeness and for independence. We need unity with others and we need space for ourselves. Thwart either of these needs and we create misery beyond belief.*

213

Books and Media

The Hendricks have written 11 books on relationships which include:

- 📖 *Conscious Loving: The Journey to Commitment*
- 📖 *The Conscious Heart: Seven Soul-Choices That Create Your Relationship Destiny*
- 📖 *Conscious Living: How to Create a Life of Your Own Design*
- 📖 *Learning to Love Yourself Workbook*
- 📖 *The Ten-Second Miracle: Creating Relationship Breakthroughs*
- 📖 *Centering and the Art of Intimacy: A New Psychology of Close Relationships*
- 📖 *A Year of Living Consciously*
- 📖 *Lasting Love: The 5 Secrets of Growing a Vital Conscious Relationship*
- 📖 *Attracting Genuine Love: A Step-by-Step Program to Bringing a Loving and Desirable Partner into Your Life* Identify your must haves and deal breakers.
- 📖 *Spirit Centered Relationships: Experiencing Greater Love and Harmony Through the Power of Presencing*
- 📖 *Breathing Ecstasy: Finding Sexual Bliss Using the Incredible Power of Breath*
- 📖 *The Big Leap: Conquer Your Hidden Fear and Take Life to the Next Level*
- 📖 *The Relationship Survival Guidebook* eBook
- ☐ They have also appeared on over 500 TV and radio programs, including *CNN, Oprah,* and *48 Hours*

How to Find Out More

- 🖥 For more information, go to the Hendricks website: *www.hendricks.com*

29. Dr. Bill Doherty

"How to be intentional about your marriage"

Background and Qualifications

Dr. Bill Doherty has been married for over 38 years, is a marriage and family therapist, and licensed psychologist.

He received his PhD in family studies from the University of Connecticut in 1978. He is now Professor and past Director of the Marriage and Family Therapy Program at the Department of Family Social Science, University of Minnesota. He has been granted the Significant Contribution Award to the Field of Marriage and Family Therapy by the American Association for Marriage and Family Therapy Association.

Relationship Philosophy

Dr. Doherty's relationship philosophy is based around teaching couples to be intentional about their marriage. He believes that far too many couples let their relationships drift, in the hope that things will sort themselves out or get better without effort, but as time goes on, often choosing to bail out when things get tough.

He focuses on the need for couples to actually acquire the skills needed for making marriage work in today's fast-paced world, learning to foster attitudes and values to counteract the "me-first" consumer approach to marriage. It's far too easy for couples just to end their marriage and move onto the next without truly thinking of what they are failing to put into their marriage, what they will lose if it ends, and what they may put their children through.

He sees the "divorce epidemic" as coming from the social forces that pull any couple apart. Although every partner within a relationship deserves to be treated with love, fairness, and

215

respect, within a "consumer marriage," Dr. Doherty believes each party focuses too much on what they are *not* getting in their marriage and how their mate is not meeting their needs, often comparing their spouse to the "fantasy spouse" of other relationships.

Marriage takes work, with daily "connection rituals" to facilitate an intentional marriage. Yet nowadays, according to Dr. Doherty, acquiring a spouse or leaving a spouse increasingly sounds like a consumer purchase or sales transaction, with not enough respect for loyalty or commitment. "I am not getting my needs met," "I deserve better," "If only I were married to that one," "My marriage is not as good as yours" or, "My spouse is a flawed person" (without considering one's own flaws), are all thoughts common to a consumer marriage.

The Therapy

The aim of Dr. Doherty's work is to help couples make marriage last, "as long as we both shall live" instead of "as long as we both shall love." He teaches couples to avoid the common marriage mistakes, such as confusing desires with needs.

He also encourages people to avoid the consumer mentality of trading in the old model when you're no longer happy. Couples also need to avoid becoming overtime parents instead of full-time partners, as well as be aware of family and friends who may try to undermine the marriage.

Dr. Doherty teaches that the way to deal with the pressures of consumerism within a relationship is to ensure that each partner chooses to become a citizen of marriage. They have to be intentional, committed, and take responsibility to make things better, instead of being a passive party to whatever happens. By taking a long-term view and valuing their history together as a couple, this can help to reduce the struggle and pain and the tendency to jump ship and look for something they mistakenly believe will be better, when they already really know that they will create a shipwreck in the process.

Dr. Doherty also teaches that it's doing simple things in everyday life that creates the closeness couples desire. Things like having time in the evening to debrief about the day, going out on dates at least twice a month, greeting each other at the end of the work day as lovers instead of business partners, and celebrating wedding anniversaries as the birthdays of the marriage. These simple "rituals of connection" can keep the spark alive over the years, and they don't require that anyone change his or her personality.

Examples
Small choices, BIG losses

In his book, *Take Back Your Marriage,* Dr. Doherty reveals how anyone can bring down a good marriage within 12 and 24 months by making a series of small choices. He explains, "The sad part is the one who initiates it does not realize, until it is too late, that this is a marriage failure path."

The process begins when a person starts focusing on what they're not getting out of the relationship and how their partner is not living up to their expectations. There is no real reason why this begins, but it could be an increase in stress, an emotional drifting apart, or realizing a friend's husband does a better job. Or there may be a member of the opposite sex who truly listens in a way one's spouse doesn't, becoming a secret confidant.

Next, the person begins to obsess about how they're missing out because of their partner's deficiencies. From here, they begin to criticize their partner for how they respond to them and over time, the word "divorce" begins to come up in fights, initially to grab attention rather than actually meaning it. Or a partner may withdraw from their marriage by no longer sharing feelings

217

about anything, as well as withdrawing sexually. Within two years, a couple arrives at a tough decision point: is their relationship worth saving or should they divorce and separate?

Becoming an Active Citizen of Marriage

Dr. Doherty comments that focusing on a partner's deficiencies, as in the above example, is the typical consumer mindset. "If my car doesn't perform well, it's not my fault; it's the manufacturer's fault. Never mind that I drive it too hard or don't change the oil!"

He advises that it's important to become an active citizen within marriage, to become responsible for building and repairing the relationship, rather than approaching our own needs and desires within a marriage with a sense of entitlement or victimization. "Everyone has some needs that do not get met in marriage. This is not tragic unless we make it that way; it is just life."

He recounts the story of Susan, who dragged her husband into therapy every two years to get him to open up and discuss his feelings. During one therapy session, he tearfully confessed that he felt he wasn't built emotionally the way she wanted him to be and he was sad he couldn't be a better husband to her. Susan understood for the first time his non-emotional way of living did not reflect on how much he loved her. In fact, this understanding ended up making it easier for him to open up his feelings to her and their relationship went from strained to strength!

Dr. Bill Doherty Quotes

- *What happens when we approach marriage and family life as entrepreneurs? When the initial glow fades and the tough times come, we are prepared to cut our losses to take what we want from our old marriages in order to forge*

218

new, more perfect unions until they must also be dissolved. Where does it end?

- *You can work your way out of a reasonably good marriage by focusing on what you're not getting out of it and turning negative towards your mate – who will in turn give you even less and thereby help justify your leaving.*
- *An unnecessary divorce is one of the great tragedies of adult life and all roads towards it are unnecessary.*

Books and Media

- Dr. Bill Doherty has been featured in many newspapers, including *USA Today, The New York Times,* and *The Wall Street Journal.*
- He has also appeared on many TV programs, including *Oprah, 20/20, The TODAY Show, CBS Morning Show, CBS, ABC* and *NBC* Evening News Programs, *CNN,* and *Fox News.*

He has authored and edited 9 books for professionals and five books for the public on family rituals, confident parenting, marriage, overscheduled kids, and the family dynamics of wedding planning.

- His most famous relationship book is *Take Back Your Marriage: Sticking Together in a World That Pulls Us Apart*

How to Find Out More

- For more information, go to the Dr. Bill Doherty's website: *www.drbilldoherty.org*

30. Dr. Jeff Bernstein

"Break the toxic thinking cycle!"

Background and Qualifications

With over twenty years experience of counseling children, teens, adults, couples, and families, Dr. Bernstein is a renowned TV relationship expert and couple's counselor. A licensed psychologist, he specializes in breaking toxic thinking in intimate relationships and building up self-esteem, by offering private counseling and group workshops.

Relationship Philosophy

Dr. Bernstein draws from cognitive therapy techniques, which he blends with mindfulness and empathy to create an integrated approach to relationships. Although many therapists believe poor communication is the reason why so many relationships end, Dr. Bernstein focuses on the way we think about our partners that can end up killing trust, erode intimacy, and cripple communication.

The 9 Toxic Thought Patterns

- ✓ The All or Nothing Trap
- ✓ Catastrophic Conclusions
- ✓ The Should Bomb
- ✓ Label Slinging
- ✓ The Blame Game
- ✓ Emotional Short-Circuit
- ✓ Overactive Imagination
- ✓ Head Game Gamble
- ✓ Disillusionment Doom

With emotional pain from toxic thoughts, often we feel we're not getting our needs met and tend to shut down. It is the resentment of unmet expectations about a relationship and how our partner was "supposed to make us happy" that can lead to a toxic relationship.

According to Dr. Bernstein, there are several key reasons why relationships fail: escalating conflict, poor problem solving, withdrawal, and low blows (such as insults) during arguments.

The Therapy

During couple's therapy, Dr. Bernstein focuses on the toxic thought patterns that exist in virtually every relationship, and shows the couple how destructive, negative, and exaggerated thought patterns can end a relationship. Even facial expressions such as a raised eyebrow or raised tone of voice can cause toxicity. The aim of the therapy is to break the toxic thinking cycle and replace it with new and more positive thinking habits for solving relationship stresses.

He goes on to explain that how we argue and resolve arguments says a lot about the strengths and health of a relationship, as well as its level of toxicity. He identifies 5 key negative communication patterns that can erode a relationship, leading each spouse to feel distracted and full of despair:

5 Key Negative Communication Patterns

- ✓ **Using extreme statements:** such as, you <u>always</u> do this, or you <u>never</u> do that. It is more effective and far less destructive to communicate in a realistic way, enabling more effective communication and less hostility.
- ✓ **Making threats:** such as, "If you don't listen to me, then I'll leave!"
- ✓ **Shaming your partner:** offensive comments can cause irreparable damage to your partner's self-image. Statements such as, "You're a lazy slob!" said in the moment of desperation during an argument.

- ✓ **Trying to make your partner feel guilty:** this is a manipulative and coercive tactic to try to force change, which often backfires leaving both parties feeling resentful, unfulfilled, and unappreciated. Changes that occur after a guilt trip typically are not long-lasting, due to a lack of inward desire to make the change.
- ✓ **Throwing the past in your partner's face:** what is the point of dragging up the past? Things that happened 10 days, 10 weeks, or even 10 years ago only distract you from dealing with the present, leading to more arguing and frustration.

It is important that couples learn to handle a conflict without hurting, insulting, and engaging in ugly fights. Alongside "tuning in" to your toxic thought patterns and challenging those patterns so that they don't run you, you can achieve a more balanced perspective. Another relationship key is to learn to handle conflict in an emotionally healthy way. If you have to fight, Dr. Bernstein advocates fighting in a civil way, without letting the argument become ugly or insults being thrown that can never resolve a dispute. He also advises couples not to discuss or resolve differences until you can be calm and relaxed in each other's presence.

Examples
He Will Make you Happy!

Dr. Bernstein uses the example of what happens at a wedding to explain how toxic relationships can begin. What happens is that all the guests go up to the bride or groom and say how wonderful it is that, "He will make you happy," or, "She will make you happy." This is at the beginning of the relationship where huge expectations are set up, yet over time, one or both partners realize that their spouse cannot suddenly make them happy. During stressful times or relationship pressure, some people become disappointed in their partner because they cannot make them happy, and it is this disappointment that often causes toxicity.

Don't Sweep Secrets Under the Carpet!

Secrets can cause a huge rift in a relationship, but according to Dr. Bernstein, there are ways to come clean without getting into destructive conflict. "If handled the right way, revealing secrets can enhance your relationship." He identifies some common secrets that shouldn't be swept under the carpet. Firstly, if your partner has gained weight and you're no longer physically attracted to them, use statements such as, "I'm concerned about your health and I'd love for us to commit to staying active together." This encourages teamwork and prevents a partner from feeling resentment or having their feelings hurt.

Another such secret is when couples conceal a same-sex encounter from their sexual past. Bernstein explains that same sex experimentation is fairly common and that there is no need to hide it, as long as you explain your desire to disclose the experience and for a partner to accept it as a way to be closer to them.

A third common secret is how you feel about your partner's children. Having a relationship with someone who already has children is like walking into a ready-made family, which can cause stress on the relationship. A parent is often so closely aligned with their biological child that this can create resentment towards the stepchild from the stepparent. Rifts can occur, but Bernstein advises discussing the issue with your partner, using words such as, "I understand your desire to protect your children, but I feel making parenting decisions together can accomplish that." Staying calm and working as a team can help diffuse any potential conflict, rather than bringing resentment until it erupts into an argument.

Dr. Jeff Bernstein Quotes

- *Many couples mistakenly think that if they don't argue, that means they have a great relationship. That's often not true, especially if issues are being ignored because one or both partners don't feel comfortable bringing them up.*

- *It's how you and your partner communicate during the argument that's key to success or failure.*

- *The fear of loss – loss of respect, loss of love, or loss of the relationship often fuels poor communication between couples.*

- *Handling conflict in an emotionally healthy way is the single most important skill partners can learn to solve their marriages.*

Books and Media

Dr. Bernstein has appeared regularly on various TV programs as a relationship expert, including *NBC Today Show, CN8's Your Morning,* and *It's Your Call,* as well as being quoted regularly in *Cosmopolitan* and *Men's Health* Magazines.

- He may be most well known for his groundbreaking work about dealing with "defiant children" *10 Days to a Less Defiant Child: The Breakthrough Program for Overcoming Your Child's Difficult Behavior*

- His most popular relationship book is *Why Can't You Read My Mind? Overcoming the 9 Toxic Thought Patterns That Get in the Way of a Loving Relationship*

How to Find Out More

- For more information, visit: *www.drjeffonline.com*

31. Drs. Les and Leslie Parrott

"Save a marriage before it starts!"

Background and Qualifications

Husband and wife team Drs. Les and Leslie Parrott work together to help other couples build a healthy relationship. Drawing on their medical and therapy backgrounds, the Parrott's popularity has led them to teach workshops around the globe that infuse couples with the passion to make their relationships work.

Leslie is a marriage and family therapist, and Les is trained in clinical psychology. Together in 1991, they founded The Center for Relationship Development on the campus of Seattle Pacific University. Here, they teach the basics of good relationships and have pioneered the Marriage Mentoring Program, enabling couples to share their wisdom to newlyweds and those experiencing problems in their marriage.

The Governor of Oklahoma has recently appointed the Parrotts as statewide Marriage Ambassadors.

Relationship Philosophy

The Parrott's vision is to help people to become soul mates for life by "saving a marriage before it starts." They provide practical and useful wisdom to establish the essentials for lasting love and ways to reduce conflict. They believe these habits should be engaged even before the honeymoon begins, so that the techniques of marriage success can be established right from the start.

They offer practical tips for disputes and arguments, acknowledging that disagreements are part of every healthy marriage, but there are ways to prevent conflict from escalating and causing hurt and resentment.

The Therapy

Learning to "fight fairly" is one of the cornerstones for the Parrott's work, offering techniques and strategies to prevent conflict escalating to negative levels.

Tips for Arguments

♥ **The 1 to 10 method:** if you're locked in a disagreement, stop your partner and ask them how important what they're saying is to them, from one to ten. This prevents unnecessary conflict about unimportant issues from escalating. Once locked in a disagreement, often couples lose clarity and end up fighting about semantics. This method enables each person to really work out if the disagreement is worth continuing, or if it's simply a product of a stressful day and not enough food to keep the mind focused.

♥ **What are your hot topics:** early on in the relationship, work out what you disagree on, so if you end up in a dispute about these issues, you can learn to discuss them rationally, when you're not feeling tired or hungry.

♥ **Learning to fight fairly:** conflict can destroy a relationship or make you stronger. When having an argument, steer clear of critical comments that can cause the debate to go in a damaging direction, because it automatically puts the other person on the defensive. Turn generalized critical comments into a specific complaint. Rather than saying, "YOU always do this," learn to say, "I feel frustrated when X happened." Start with I, instead of YOU, to avoid arguments turning into a slinging match of criticism and insults.

♥ **The XYZ formula:** this is one of the most famous techniques for fair conflict. "In situation X, when you did Y, I felt like Z." It's a way of phrasing your complaints and prevents your partner from feeling like they're being criticized, enabling you to communicate your needs and feelings. Limiting to one specific incident reduces the critical nature. Follow with a specific request that would make love flow better.

The Parrott's also advocate the extreme importance of finding time for shared activities, where you dedicate time to each other when you're truly present to the other person, rather than just the leftovers of a busy day. This "hang out" time for couples is essential for maintaining intimacy.

Examples
Love is Not Enough

The Parrotts consistently draw on their own marriage to give guidance and wisdom to other couples. In their book, *I Love You More: How Everyday Problems Can Strengthen Your Marriage,* they tackle how relationship problems can help make a partnership thrive, through learning to cope with relationship stress and how to resolve problems. They believe that couples cannot rely on love alone and need a lot more to make a relationship truly successful.

While on their honeymoon, just a couple of days after their wedding, Leslie was overwhelmed by the deepest sense of love for her spouse – how it was enveloping her being and filling her soul. However, they both remained conscious of the fact that love alone cannot protect their marriage from harm, not even between the most loving of couples. Although love ensures that every marriage starts out well, negative stresses and strains come up that can threaten marriage harmony. If you're not equipped with the skills to deal with these moments, the marriage can encounter problems: "Like two weary soldiers taking cover in a bunker, every couple is bewildered by constant assaults to their love life... we are torn apart by busy schedules, by words we wish we could take back, and in short, by not giving all that love demands." In order to future proof any marriage, it's important to take stock of your relationship and save your marriage before it even starts.

Safety Needs

In an interview with CBN.com, Les and Leslie Parrott admit that at the start of their relationship, like many couples, they struggled to understand each other. "Even though we knew all of the techniques and all the bells and whistles, we still couldn't make it work in our own marriage," Leslie explains. Through research of other couples, they discovered the importance of understanding your spouse's emotional safety needs. There are four main categories of safety needs, and each person tends to fall into one of these categories:

The 4 Safety Needs
- ♥ Gaining control of your time,
- ♥ Winning approval from others,
- ♥ Maintaining loyalty, and
- ♥ Achieving quality standards.

Les reveals that his main safety need is time – wanting to be productive, he presses on in conversations with Leslie and moves forward to make a decision, aggressively solving problems. Yet, Leslie's main need is approval, and wants to check with everyone else before making a final decision, passively solving problems.

Without understanding these changes, friction can occur. Les reveals, "I come off in our conversations like a jerk sometimes... abrupt and abrasive. With her need for approval, how is she reading that? She is taking it personally. I think that happens in a lot of marriages." By truly understanding a partner's safety needs, this can help to reduce marital strain.

Dr. Les and Leslie Parrott Quotes
- ● *Once you know how to fight fair, conflict is often the price we pay for a deeper level of intimacy.*

- *Good communication is the lifeblood of your relationship. How close you feel hinges on how well you and your partner are able to understand each other.*

- *Shared activity is one of the supreme gifts of married life, and it is an insurance policy against the fading of passion and intimacy.*

Books and Media

With over one million books sold, the Parrotts have written a range of relationship guides with easy, effective, and practical tips that will help any couple. Titles include:

- *Saving Your Marriage Before it Starts: Seven Questions to ask Before and After you Marry*

- *Saving Your Marriage Before It Starts (Men's Workbook)*

- *Saving Your Marriage Before It Starts (Women's Workbook)*

- *Love Talk: Speaking Each Other's Language Like Never Before*

- *Relationships: How to Make Bad Relationships Better and Good Relationships Great*

- *Save Your Second Marriage Before It Starts*

- *Trading Places: The Best Move You'll Ever Make in Your Marriage*

- *Becoming Soul Mates*

- *The Love List: 8 Little Things That Make a Big Difference in Your Marriage*

- The Parrotts have also appeared on *CNN, Good Morning America, CBS This Morning, The View, NBC Nightly News, Oprah*, and weekly on *Fox Morning Show* in Seattle.

How to Find Out More

- Go to the Parrott's website: *www.realrelationships.com* Their website contains an extremely useful video problem page with the Parrott's answering questions and emails from readers to camera.

32. Dr. Harriet Lerner

"Anger is a signal, and one worth listening to!"

Background and Qualifications

Dr. Harriet Lerner is one of the US' most respected clinical psychologists, best known for her series of "Dance" books, which began with *The Dance of Anger*. Much of her work has focused on women and family relationships.

She majored in psychology, achieved an MA in educational psychology from the Teachers College Columbia University, and a PhD in clinical psychology from the City University of New York. Her husband, Dr. Steve Lerner, is also a clinical psychologist, and they have a private practice together. They have two sons.

Lerner admits that she never wanted to be a "self-help" writer, not believing in "quick fix" solutions and "10 step guides" to a better relationship. That is because we need to gain a deeper understanding of how relationships work. Even so, her series of books translate complex theory into accessible and useful methods that have been extremely popular, with over 3 million books sold in 35 different languages.

Relationship Philosophy

Dr. Lerner is best known for her theories on the psychology of women and family relationships. The lessons she teaches may seem simple, but nothing is easy. It takes dedication and a commitment to use her lessons. It is well worth it to regain a sense of who you really are and what you really want in your relationship.

Dr. Lerner notes, that as stress increases in a relationship, people tend to blame the other person; they get focused on what the other person is doing or not doing. People tend to focus on changing or fixing the other person, rather than looking at their own options. This puts pressure on the other, who typically responds by either escalating the fight, or withdrawing. Anger is often the result.

According to Dr. Lerner, anger is an important signal to pay attention to. Anger means that we may be hurt, our rights may be violated, our needs or wants may not be met, or something else is not right. Anger often indicates we are not addressing important emotional issues. Anger may be a signal that we are giving too much of ourselves, or others are doing too much for us.

If we fear our own anger, we may block or invalidate our experience. Questions like, "Do I have a right to be angry?" serve to silence us. We may be too worried about the disapproval of others. Better questions include, "What am I really angry about? Who is responsible for what? How can I communicate without becoming defensive or attacking?" In her book, *The Dance of Anger*, Dr. Lerner describes the entire process of how we typically deal with anger as being too nice or bitchy, and presents an alternative where we can use anger to clarify our position, our relationships, and ourselves.

The Therapy

Dr. Lerner's therapy focuses on the positive aspects of anger as a warning sign that "something is not right." The key is to acknowledge the anger and use it for positive growth. She offers a 4-step program to use anger as a tool for change.

Four-Step Program

- ♥ **Learn to Tune in to the True Source of Our Anger and Clarify Where We Stand** – The first step is to become aware that anger is arising. Judging that you should not be angry really gets in the way of noticing what is true for you. "What makes me angry?" "What is the real issue here?"

231

"Who is responsible for what?" "What do I want to accomplish?"

♥ **Learn Communication Skills** – You have the choice of whether you want to blow up at your partner in full-blown anger and accusations, or use skillful language to communicate your truth, what you want, and what you will do.

♥ **Observe and Interrupt Nonproductive Patterns of Interactions** – When Emotions are high, intelligence is low. It can be difficult to stand back and observe yourself in the midst of a tornado. Learning to calm down, stand back, and change your part in the relationship is essential.

♥ **Learn to Anticipate and Deal with Counter-moves or "Change Back!" Reactions from Others** – Whenever one makes significant changes, we will likely meet strong resistance or countermoves. It is never easy to move away from being submissive and towards a calm assertion of who you are. Yet, there is much to be gained by managing old anger, gaining clearer and stronger sense of "I," and opening to a more intimate and gratifying "we."

Most people want the impossible: we want to control not only our decisions, but also how the other person reacts to them. We want to make the change, AND we want our partner to like the change.

Tasks for the Daring and Courageous

There is a lot of advice on how to handle anger: hold your tongue, get it out quickly, count to 10, etc. Its not how you handle your anger that matter most, but whether you can use your anger to realize areas of life that aren't working for you, and to achieve greater self-clarity and discover new ways to navigate relationships. To use Dr. Lerner's work, you will want to read her book *The Dance of Anger* several times because it is worth it. Here are a few practice tasks:

Practice Tasks

- ♥ **Practice Observations** – How do you handle anger? Do you get hurt and cry? Do you blame others? Do you silently submit? Do you pursue or distance yourself? Do you under-function or over-function? These are neither right nor wrong, but just strategies you have developed to manage others and the world. Begin to observe your characteristic style.

- ♥ **Choose a Courageous Act** – Find a way to break out of the circular dance. Think of one or two ways you can more clearly define who you are without criticizing or changing others.

- ♥ **Prepare for Resistance** – As you shift your patterns of behavior, you need to be prepared for intense resistance from others and from yourself. Be clear with who you want to be, and be willing to pay the price while staying connected.

- ♥ **No More Gossiping** – Gossiping about the problem you have with your partner only interferes with healthy person-to-person relationships.

Examples

Sandra and Larry

When Dr. Lerner first asked Larry and Sandra to describe their marriage, she heard an avalanche of complaints from Sandra. "He's a workaholic. He neglects the kids and me. He's a stranger to his own family." As Sandra fell silent, Larry turned away and said nothing. When it was Larry's turn, he had complementary complaints. "Sandra isn't supportive enough. She's always on my back. She cuts me down a lot. If I sit down for five minutes, she's on my back." This is a very common dance among married couples: **He just doesn't respond-She's over emotiona**l. The more she nags, the more he withdraws. The more he withdraws, the more she nags, and on and on.

Sandra and Larry had spent tremendous energy blaming each other for their problems and fights. They keep looking for "who started it?"

Instead of going through the "emotional pursuer – emotional distancer" dance, Lerner recommends taking responsibility for the part you can control: "How can I change *my* steps in the circular dance?"

One night Sandra sat beside Larry on the couch. Larry expected the usual attack. Instead Sandra said, "I feel like I owe you an apology. I've been on your back for a long time. I realize I have been wanting you to provide me with something. It's my problem, and I recognize that I need to do something about it." Sandra asked Larry to put the children to bed two nights a week so she could take a yoga class and socialize with her friends.

After three weeks, Larry began to get nervous and tried to provoke a fight. Next, he started to pursue her, suggesting they go out one of those evenings. However, now Sandra relished her time alone.

Breaking the circular dance was only the beginning. Before, Larry could pretend all the neediness was Sandra's, and she could imagine all the avoidance was due to Larry. Now, they both realized their need for closeness. They still had significant barriers to intimacy, but they could begin to work more productively on their relationship.

Jane and Stephanie

Jane and Stephanie lived together. They had a German shepherd who became very ill in the middle of the night. Stephanie thought it was serious enough to call the vet immediately and wake him. Jane accused Stephanie of over worrying, and to wait to until morning.

The next day, the vet admonished them for not bringing their dog to the clinic right away, "Your dog could have died." Stephanie was furious. "If anything had happened, you would have been to blame!" she yelled at Jane.

What really happened here? This is really about more than just the dog. It is about the patterns in their relationship. One of the patterns that is coming to light is an "over-functioning – under-functioning" dance. The more Jane makes decisions for both of them (over-functioning), the more Stephanie relies on Jane to take over (under-functioning). The more Stephanie under-functions, the more Jane must compensate by over-functioning.

The first step is to be aware of the real source of the anger: autonomy in decision-making. The next step is to communicate with your partner. Stephanie could either lash out at how Jane constantly takes over, or alternatively, Stephanie could focus instead on how difficult it has been for her to make decisions. "When you have such confidence, I begin to doubt my own opinions. I'm planning to work harder to make my own decisions. Our relationship may be tense for a while, but I am not satisfied with things as they are." Then, they would have a real opportunity to relate to each other, and grow together.

Dr. Harriet Lerner Quotes

- *Intimate relationships cannot substitute for a life plan. But to have any meaning or viability at all, a life plan must include intimate relationships.*

- *Even rats in a maze learn to vary their behavior if they keep hitting a dead end. Why in the world, then, do we behave less intelligently than laboratory animals? The answer, by now, may be obvious. Repeating the same old fights protects us from the anxieties we are bound to experience when we make a change.*

- *We cannot make another person be different, but when we do something different ourselves, the old dance can no longer continue as usual.*

- *We never know for sure what motivates other people. Still, the human desire to construct explanations for other people's behavior is very strong.*

- *An intimate relationship is one in which neither party silences, sacrifices, or betrays the self, and each party expresses strength and vulnerability, weakness and competence in a balanced way.*

Books and Media

- The *Dance of Anger* was Lerner's first book aimed at the general public. This is a MUST HAVE book. It has been translated into over 35 languages and was a New York Times bestseller with over 1 million copies sold.

A series of books followed including:

- *The Dance of Fear: Rising Above Anxiety, Fear, and Shame to Be Your Best and Bravest Self*

- *The Dance of Connection: How to Talk to Someone When You're Mad, Hurt, Scared, Frustrated, Insulted, Betrayed, or Desperate*

- *The Mother Dance: How Children Change Your Life*

- *The Dance of Deception: A Guide to Authenticity and Truth-Telling in Women's Relationships*

- *The Dance of Intimacy*

- Her most recent book, *Marriage Rules: A Manual for the Married and the Coupled Up,* explores 100 rules that covers all the hot spots in relationships

How to Find Out More

- For more information about Harriet Lerner, go to *www.harrietlerner.com*

33. Kara Oh

"Draw your soul mate to you like a honey bee to a flower."

Background and Qualifications

Known as *The Heart Whisperer™*, Kara Oh specializes in helping men and women find love and turn it into a joyous relationship that fulfils their deepest hearts desires.

In her books, articles, and on her weekly radio show, Kara Oh shares her unique perspective on what keeps men and women from finding love and why so many people are unable to sustain fulfilling relationships. Kara has spent the last 15 years researching what's required for men and women to attract a high quality partner; then go on to develop a relationship that deepens in love over time. She presents live workshops and private one-on-one counseling sessions for both individuals and couples.

Relationship Philosophy

Kara Oh teaches men and women how to dismantle the barriers that keep them from finding and creating the relationship of their dreams. Her heart-centered approach to dating, relating, and communicating outlines what is preventing many people from finding love. She explains that at the core of what keeps us from being happy and having the life we desire is some kind of Heart Condition.

Kara used to liken this Heart Condition to the "Clogged Heart Syndrome." This syndrome means that a person no longer exudes "falling in love" energy. The heart has almost stopped feeling; it is clogged up with energy, closed, and shut down. Oh describes this energy clog as "emotional plaque" which prevents a person from having a magnetic attraction for the opposite sex that would tantalize a prospective date.

Basically, a newborn baby is completely open to love, with its heart fully trusting. But as we go through childhood, we are wounded in different ways. Each time we are hurt or disappointed, we guard our hearts a little bit more, until eventually, it becomes more and more difficult to open our hearts to love. Kara calls this wounding, "Emotional Plaque."

Most of this build-up of Emotional Plaque occurs as small children, when we don't understand fully what is happening. A child has limited skills and does whatever it can to protect itself. To help people open their hearts and clear away this Emotional Plaque, Kara helps her audience better understand themselves and each other. Only with greater understanding and awareness, can we clear away the Emotional Plaque so we can open our hearts to life and to love.

The Therapy

The goal of Kara Oh's work is to show people how to find a relationship with passion, fun, and a heart connection they have always dreamed of, but never felt before. She offers a step-by-step plan for more effective dating, which involves creating a personalized plan for finding the right person, boosting one's self-confidence, and projecting positive energy so their date can see and even feel how amazing they are.

Kara Oh teaches women to develop their Feminine Grace, because when a man is seeking a long-term partnership, he is attracted to a woman's spirit even more than how she looks. She explains that a super-model with negative energy will lose out to a less attractive woman who exudes a positive, joyful attitude. Any woman can enhance her beauty and attraction quotient by smiling more, standing tall, developing an attitude of acceptance, looking for the good in people, and expanding her self-confidence. Many women, through life-experience – and the Post-Feminist culture – have lost touch with their femininity and need to be taught how to truly enjoy being a woman, which will cause her to be magnetically attractive to men.

As a woman expands her Feminine Grace, she will discover her true inner self: the perfect being waiting within, who is able to love and be loved so deeply it will take her breath away. In becoming her ideal woman and reaching her true potential, a woman can finally attract her ideal man, ideal relationship, and ideal life. When women are happy and positive, they have an inner glow which men find irresistible!

Once they've found the right partner, in her book, *Marriage Made Easy*, Kara Oh shows couples how to use her *RPL Technology of Love* to keep their relationship energized with what she calls "In Love Sparkles." RPL stands for Recommit, Prioritize, and then show Love for each other at least once a day in creative, fun, and romantic ways, of which she offers pages of suggestions. RPL becomes a fun way for a couple to keep their relationship filled with love.

One of women's greatest frustrations with men is their unwillingness to open up. When a woman wants more intimacy, she often means she wants more heart-to-heart communication. But most men have been taught throughout their lives not to show their emotions – to not even feel their emotions. To get a man to open up, Kara Oh advises talking to him when he is not doing something else and asking him a "not too scary question." If you go straight in and ask, "Why do you love me?" this will scare him because he knows you have an agenda and the odds are, he'll get it wrong. Instead, ask more benign feeling questions such as, "What do you like best about your work?" or "What's your favorite thing about playing golf?" These questions are less threatening but still require him to access feelings. Since men are thinking creatures, ask him what he "thinks," rather than what he "feels" about something.

When a woman wants to get her man to open up and share what he's thinking and feeling, she has to learn to be quiet and let him speak. When women talk, they "meander," like a stroll through the park, more interested in having a heart-to-heart

239

connection. They also interrupt each other, excited to add details to the conversation. This just makes men a bit crazy.

There's one more piece Kara discovered that is essential to respect if the goal is to get him to open up. When she was interviewing men for her book, *Men Made Easy*, men opened up to her, often telling her they had never told anyone what they shared with her... and that it felt good. She started paying attention to what she was doing and discovered what she calls men's "Moment of Silence." That's when a man is gathering his thoughts. Women tend to jump in when there's a lull in the conversation. This works with other women but for most men, they've been cut off by women most of their lives and have stopped trying.

To get a man to open up, it is essential that a woman honor every Moment of Silence. Each time he is allowed to gather his thoughts and say a bit more, he will begin to relax and trust that he is really being listened to, maybe for the first time. With trust, he will go deeper and deeper into his feelings. The final key to getting a man to open up is, when he's done – which you'll know because he'll change the subject – is don't judge or comment, just thank him for sharing. And never, ever tell anyone else, or he will never open up again.

Examples
You Helped me Change my Life

Kara Oh has many success stories on her website, which provide a valuable insight into her work and strategies to help dating and relationship success. In one letter, Betty writes about how Oh's book, *Men Made Easy*, changed her life, allowing her to learn much about herself as a woman and the minds and hearts of men. She hadn't realized how selfish and inconsiderate she had been to past mates. "I have always been a tomboy and didn't realize how I compromised my 'Feminine Grace' by trying to be an equal to gain the respect of men. I've learned that I am an individual, beautiful woman with a lot of power I never knew I had."

The Power of Appreciation

Kara Oh believes one of the best ways to win a man's heart is to offer sincere appreciation, especially for those things he values in himself – what are considered masculine qualities. Men get very little appreciation. It will make a woman stand out as someone exceptional when she offers sincere appreciation and even simple compliments.

In her book, *Men Made Easy*, Ms. Oh offers 12 Simple Secrets. The first is to exude attractive energy through the development of Feminine Grace, and the last is to remember that a man wants to be with a woman who makes him feel like a man. The other ten secrets teach women how to do just that.

12 Simple Secrets to a Man's Heart

♥ Using your Feminine Grace opens a man's heart

♥ Men need to feel understood and accepted for who they are

♥ You are his only source of intimacy

♥ Sex is the only way most men know how to be intimate

♥ Men have high hopes for monogamy

♥ If you're not happy, he's a failure

♥ To a man, failure is "death"

♥ Men show their love through action

♥ Men take risks to survive

♥ Men lose when they commit

♥ To be heard, you must speak his language

♥ A man wants to be with a woman who makes him feel like a man

What's something you can go out and do right now? Give men opportunities to be your hero... then appreciate the heck out of him. He'll respond by lighting up because you just made him feel ten feet tall.

Kara Oh Quotes

- *If you are no longer in your twenties, you need to develop a new way of relating to men if you are going to achieve your goals.*

- *If you have a partner that you love and who loves you, let go of anything and everything that keeps you from opening your heart completely.*

- *I believe, deep inside every cell of my being, that we are on this planet to learn how to love and be loved more fully.*

- *When you allow your heart to guide you, your self-love will keep you connected to your intuition – your deep wisdom – so that you make wise choices in what you do and with whom you spend your precious time.*

Books and Media

- Kara Oh most famous book is *Men Made Easy,* where she teaches women how to get him to fall in love. She provides the 12 simple secrets into a man's heart and soul.

She has written several eBooks on finding the right date and building a fulfilling relationship. Titles include:

- *Marriage Made Easy*
- *Flirting Made Easy*
- *How to Date Smart and WIN His HEART*
- *Let the Real You Shine Through*

How to Find Out More

- For more information, go to Kara Oh's websites: *www.KaraOh.com* and *www.AliveWithLove.com*

34. Drs. Peter Pearson & Ellyn Bader

"Tell me no lies!"

Background and Qualifications

For the past twenty years, Drs. Ellyn Bader and Peter Pearson have helped thousands of couples, and trained therapists worldwide. Both have PhD's and work in private therapy, and lead the *Coming from Your Heart* workshop. Married since 1982, they have three daughters and live in Menlo Park, CA

Relationship Philosophy

Drs. Bader and Pearson believe that strong, loving, and healthy relationships provide more than companionship and support. They also encourage both partners to be their best as individuals. They teach that relationships evolve through four stages; getting stuck in any one stage leads to stagnation.

The 4 Marital Stages

1) **The Honeymoon** – This is the stage of symbiosis, or exclusive bonding. This is characterized by the glow of new love. This stage is crucial for establishing a loving bond. One cannot stay at this stage without squelching each other's uniqueness.

2) **Emerging Differences** – This is the stage of differentiation. Partners begin to assert their individual desires. People can be torn between revealing themselves, and thus growing, or wanting to retreat and hide out in happy honeymoon. When one risks confronting one's own truth, one can begin to reap the rewards of honesty.

3) **Freedom** – Interests like career, hobbies, travel, and free time outside the marriage take center stage. The couple has to negotiate time together and apart. The couple must grapple with conflicting interests. When one addresses

their desires truthfully, and with regard to the other, they can reap the benefits of independence within security.

4) **Together as Two** – Partners have become more accepting of themselves and each other. Intimacy deepens, and the marriage becomes deeper as a result. They can respond to their differences with humor and compassion. This is the stage of synergy

As couples progress through these four stages, there are blind alleys that couples can get trapped in.

Detours or Dead Ends

- **The Dark Side of the Honeymoon** – happens when couples refuse to acknowledge any problems during the Honeymoon stage. They are so afraid of tension developing that they avoid significant truths. Couples here lie to hide their discontent and use deception to avoid conflict.

- **Seething Stalemate** – happens during the Emerging Differences stage, when couples fight and brutalize each other in an effort to coerce agreement. People in this Dead End are refusing to take responsibility for their own feelings or actions. People use lies as a manipulative tool, often while holding "the higher ground," to badger the other into accepting your version of the truth.

- **Freedom Unhinged** – happens when independence outweighs togetherness in the Freedom stage, and marital anarchy ensues. One partner "checks out" rather than be truthful. This is the Detour in which "felony" lies, such as infidelity and financial misrepresentations occur. Partners have wandered far off the morality map, and are taking liberties without concern for the other.

Bader and Pearson are experts on how people lie to either protect their partners or to manipulate a situation. They show couples how to analyze the amount of lying that is occurring in their relationship and how it could be damaging their love. Everybody lies at some point, whether it's to their parents, friends, or partner, but those who lie to keep a marriage together, don't realize that in reality they are destroying it. As lying escalates it can cause serious trouble within a relationship.

Bader and Pearson introduce a new concept: the Lie Invitee. The Lie Invitee is unwilling or unable to handle the truth. The may want to run things, and don't want to know the truth. They may be afraid the truth will be another jab at their already weak self-esteem. They may want to avoid ruining the fantasy of the mythical ideal mate.

The Lie Invitee will react in particular ways to block the truth from coming out, through a look, tone of voice, expression, or posture. Sometimes they will withdraw, refusing to acknowledge the other person until they recant the truth, and come up with a more palatable story.

The truth is not the problem, but rather the emotional response to it. If one partner throws a tantrum at hearing the truth, the other can save a lot of grief by inventing a little fib. After all, you wouldn't want to put them through unnecessary hurt, would you? Of course, the lie will eventually eat into your sense of integrity, and will become a problem in its own right.

Imagine you are annoyed at something your partner did at a party last night. When you bring it up in the morning, he gets defensive, and blames you for the situation. He puts up a brick wall. If you continue to be candid about your feelings, you get blasted, so you get quiet. There is no room for honesty here.

The Therapy

Although struggle is an important part of relationships and can bring you together, Bader and Pearson recognize that many couples develop a chronic negative cycle that they can't stop by themselves. Through their therapy, couples learn the difference between constructive lies and those that can destroy the relationship. They learn to reach a state of mutual appreciation and co-operation, and become conscious of lies within a marriage through the understanding of when, how, and why they lie.

The program teaches how to repair, renew, and restore relationships, collaborate as a team, disagree without nasty arguments, negotiate with each other, and most importantly, how to bring out the best in each other. Communication is directed away from defensiveness and towards honesty and openness. Individuals within the relationship are encouraged to recognize and address their own bad habits, even the little ones they may disregard.

All too often, we expect our partners to change first, to relieve us from relationship distress. However, Bader and Pearson believe that if this becomes the foundation for relationship change and improvement, a couple will only hit obstacles and problems: short-term and long-term. This is because the only aim each partner has within the relationship is relief from this distress, rather than a willingness to communicate or learn to create a joyful relationship. It's important to stop telling your partner what to do in an attempt to feel better when distressed, and instead, to spend time working on yourself.

Real success depends on how you think about your differences; manage your feelings; where you focus your attention; how you act and communicate under stress; and how you react to your partner's pain.

Confronting the truth can be a scary process, but by overcoming these barriers, healing and growth between the couple is promoted, along with the ability to create a loving and happy relationship.

Initiator-Inquirer Process

This is a communication tool to help couples talk in a more structured way, so they can listen and share, and understand each other's feelings. This also helps partners from becoming too reactive and starting an argument. Over time, people learn increased tolerance to anxiety, capacity to self-soothe and can experience genuine empathy and compassion. Ultimate, one can learn to not take things so personally.

Rules for the Initiator

- ♥ **Focus on only one issue** – Get clear on your main concern. Stay on track and describe what you want.

- ♥ **Express your thoughts and feelings** – Look for the vulnerability underneath the initial feeling, such as afraid, sad, hurt, jealous, guilt, or shame.

- ♥ **Avoid blaming, accusing, or name-calling** – Blaming stops you from understanding yourself and your role in this situation. This is about revealing yourself and being willing to express yourself to another.

- ♥ **Be open to self Discovery** – Explore your inner experience. This is about your willingness to discover your truth and find out who you really are in this situation.

Rules for the Inquirer

- ♥ **Listen calmly** – Don't defend, argue, fix or cross complain. You don't have to own this problem. You get to manage your own emotions and reactions.

- ♥ **Recap** – Repeat back what your heard as accurately and completely as possible. Check to see if you got it.

- ♥ **Ask questions** – Be interested and curious. Seek to understand your partner thoughts, feelings, and desires.

- ♥ **Empathize** – Put yourself in your partner's position. See how this makes sense for them. Stay with it until a soothing moment occurs

Examples
Marital Honesty

In their *Love that Lasts* newsletter, Dr. Pearson discusses the importance and liberating feeling of being completely honest with your partner. "Being honest involves the willingness to take emotional risks." It is not always easy to be completely honest with your partner, through fear of hurting oneself or them, but it can bring a closeness and intimacy to your relationship as well as freeing feelings of guilt, bitterness, or resentment.

Dr. Pearson uses the story of Terry and Jim. Terry complains that she cannot rely on Jim to follow through with arrangements, particularly with everyday tasks such as putting out the garbage, getting the kids to bed on time, or doing grocery shopping. But Jim feels no matter what he does, Terry is never satisfied – either the job isn't good enough or, he's too slow. Very often, she ends up taking over and doing the job herself in order to avoid being disappointed.

Both are afraid of being completely honest with each other about their needs and wants. Terry is scared of telling him how much she wants to depend on him and also how she's not used to relying on anyone and more used to being in control. She's most scared of relying on someone and being disappointed, so she tries to get Jim to make agreements over what he needs to do and imposes a deadline. She hopes this will solve her emotional fears without having to express how she is feeling. Jim is afraid to say how he feels and talk about his fears of disappointing her.

As Dr. Pearson advises, if each were more honest about their fears, this would be the first step to breaking the pattern, but often communicating in this way makes one feel too vulnerable and insecure. Yet, the so called "safe" option ends up corroding the relationship, and frustration and resentment can set in. "Taking these risks is what makes relationships sing. When each person responds respectfully to the vulnerability, you

249

create a connection of magnificence. When it doesn't happen, you create a relationship peppered with misery."

Hard-Won Honesty

In their book, *Tell Me No Lies,* they relay a story about how honesty can bring light to the dark side of a relationship. Pete was disappointed that Ellyn wasn't living up to his version of "the ideal mate." Their conversation included Pete describing various ways he had thought about getting rid of, or leaving Ellyn. To each comment, Ellyn calmly replied, "So, why wouldn't you do that?" or "What's wrong with that plan?" The fact that she was open and unperturbed, gave Pete the safety and freedom to explore his dark side. The conversation ended when Ellyn asked, "Is there anything I should be seriously worried about?" and Pete responded, "Actually, now that you ask, the answer is no."

The black humor definitely helped them explore the shadowy underbelly of their marriage. "It was like lancing a boil," exclaimed Pete. "It allowed me to stop obsessing. I could express the most reprehensible things, share my darkest feelings, and Ellyn wouldn't drop me." His respect for Ellyn skyrocketed.

One-Liners to Avoid at all Costs!

According to Bader and Pearson there are four one-liners we should always avoid using in an argument. "They slice and dice, causing misunderstandings not easily healed by pacifying words. They inflame like a blowtorch on tinder. They suck the life out of all that they touch."

The first of these one-liners is, "That's not what happened here!" This comment implies "I'm right and you're wrong!" Instead, say, "Well, here's another point of view…"

The second is, "You always…" or "You never…" These over generalizations can be hurtful and automatically put your partner on the defensive. Instead, it's important to be specific and talk to your partner about a particular incident – "When you did that, I felt this."

The third is, "You really know how to hurt me." This implies that your partner would deliberately want to hurt you. Also, it suggests that someone other than yourself has the power over how you feel, making you an emotional victim. Instead, it's important to explain your feelings: "What you just said really hurt me. It was painful because…"

The final one-liner is, "How can you be that way?" This non-question is in fact an assault on your partner's character and suggests they should be ashamed of their behavior. Instead say, "Can you help me understand why you did that?"

It is easy to see that these one-liners are real zingers. You are sure to "win a point" by using any one of these. You will put your partner in his or her place, and walk away feeling like a boxing champ. However, you damage the intimacy beyond anything you could possibly imagine.

Drs. Bader and Pearson Quotes

- *Lies between lovers can be highly electric; they have tremendous potential to both nurture and destroy a relationship. Unfortunately, lies usually undermine a relationship, because, when unchecked by compassion and honest introspection, they tend to feed on each other. Most couples underestimate the power that lies – even seemingly harmless lies – wield in their marriage.*

- *The human capacity to forgive even the deepest wrongs is awe-inspiring.*

- *Forgiving others is liberation from anger and grievance, and it leads to a richer and happier life. Psychologists say there is an even deeper peace to be found through what might be the hardest act of all – forgiving ourselves.*

- *When you're in a tense, difficult, or nasty discussion with your partner, the problem isn't communication. The problem is your distressed emotional reaction about what they are saying.*

- *When you are at your worst, you're likely to bring out the worst in your partner.*

Books and Media

- Drs. Bader and Pearson have appeared on many TV programs, including *The TODAY Show* and *CBS Early Morning News.*

- Their book, *Tell Me No Lies: How to Face the Truth and Build a Loving Marriage,* teaches how to stop lying to your partner and yourself, and how to stop creating the environment in which your partner feels compelled to lie.

- *In Quest of the Mythical Mate: A Developmental Approach to Diagnosis and Treatment in Couples Therapy* presents a powerful therapeutic approach for professional who treat couples

How to Find Out More

- Go to Drs. Bader and Pearson's website: *www.couplesinstitute.com*

35. Dr. David Schnarch

"Marital problems are not situational difficulties to be solved or avoided."

Background and Qualifications

David Schnarch, PhD is the author of numerous books and articles on intimacy, sexuality, and relationships, and is a licensed clinical psychologist with almost 3 decades of experience. He leads workshops and couples therapy alongside his wife Dr. Ruth Morehouse, also a clinical therapist. Together, they have developed the *Passionate Marriage* couples retreats and enrichment weekends and founded the Marriage and Family Health Center and the Crucible® Institute in Colorado.

Dr. Schnarch chaired the Professional Education Committee and served for eight years on the Board of Directors of the American Association of Sex Educators, Counselors, and Therapists (AASECT). He is a certified sex therapist and for 17 years was Associate Professor in the Departments of Psychiatry and Urology at Louisiana State University Medical School s.

Relationship Philosophy

Dr. Schnarch believes that committed relationships can be more fulfilling that we ever dared believe. The Schnarch relationship philosophy is that marital problems are an essential part of individual and relationship growth. They help us to activate deep intimacy, profound desire, and meaningful sex. According to Schnarch, sexuality is a powerful window into who we are.

Romantic love within a marriage is a relatively new concept. We now demand a high level of gratification and fulfillment from our relationships, and the high divorce rate reflects these high expectations, and our inability to achieve them. We are living

longer than anytime in history, but what's the point if our relationships are not alive and vibrant

The 4 Stages of Sexual Drive

1) **Lust**, craving for sexual gratification, driven by testosterone and estrogen

2) **Romantic** love, infatuation driven by dopamine and serotonin

3) **Attachment**, secure bonding, driven by oxytocin and vasopressin

4) **Selfhood**, developing and maintaining a sense of identity and self, driven by need for integrity

People move at different rates through the four stages of sexual drives. The early phases feel so good because the other sees only the best in you. Your "Reflected Sense of Self" is greatly enhanced, and this feels incredibly good. As people get to know one another, they get a better idea of the other, and the Reflected Sense of Self is sometimes in jeopardy. As we demand our partner see is in the way we want to be seen, we put pressure on them to conform. At some point, they are unable or unwilling to continue to play this charade, and the house of cards comes tumbling down.

This is the phase after the attachment phase wears off, and people who are unable or unwilling to develop an autonomous sense of self, while also being in a stable relationship, feel stuck. Sometimes, we will try to control our partner when we face a "two-choice dilemma." A typical example is where you want to buy something, and at the same time, what your partner to not be upset with you. Emotional gridlock develops as each partner thwarts the desires and needs of the other, while at the same time blaming the other.

No longer able to regulate each other anxieties, no longer willing to accommodate or bolster the other's reflected sense of self, gridlock often resembles a Cold War.

Resolving gridlock is how people learn and grow. The secret is "differentiation," which is the ability to maintain yourself while maintaining relationships with others. Differentiation is your ability to soothe your own anxieties and having emotional immunity to your partner's anxiety. While being impacted by your partner's distress, you can still be non-reactive to your partner's reactivity.

Also vitally important is the concept that you don't have to settle for less than a passionate marriage. Sexual development should be viewed as a life-long journey with the reality that people get better in bed as they get older, reaching their peak sexual potential in their 40s, 50s, 60s, and beyond. It's important that people don't confuse genital prime with sexual prime.

The Therapy

One of the most important things in relationship is bringing your authentic self. We have powerful drives to be in relationship with another (attachment) and an urge to drive our own life (autonomy). Being able to manage these two disparate needs is one of the biggest challenges in adult life.

The backbone of Dr. Schnarch's therapy is differentiation – the ability to be okay with being separate *and* together in an intimate relationship. The less differentiated you are, the more you will be dependant on your partner for validation. The desire to be fused with your partner actually means that you will experience *less* intimacy.

People with low differentiation either feel abandoned and need safety and security, or they feel suffocated and controlled, and need space. Dr. Schnarch offers Four Points of Balance™ as the fundamental abilities for an emotionally healthy life.

The 4 Points of Balance™

1) **Solid Flexible Self**™– Having your own identity. Being able to hold on to your values and beliefs, even when challenged

2) **Quiet Mind, Calm Heart**™– The ability to sooth your own mind and heart. Being able to control your own anxiety. Being responsible for your own thoughts and feelings. Being able to pay attention to body sensations

3) **Grounded Responding**™–The ability to stay calm. Neither explosively overreacting or avoiding and creating distance when your partner is upset

4) **Meaningful Endurance**™–Tolerating discomfort for growth

When sex dies in a relationship, partners often withdraw emotionally from each other or look elsewhere. Couples need to realize that sexual relationships develop by the willingness to do new, creative, and spontaneous things. The sexual relationship matures as each person shifts the focus of from the desire to reduce tension, to the desire *for the other person*. This is the shift from impersonal sex to connected intimacy.

Since the brain is the largest sexual organ, Dr. Schnarch helps people pay attention to the mental dimensions of sex. What you think about during sex has a profound effect on your function and the level of connection you and your partner feel during intimacy. He talks about three dimensions: sexual trance, where one is focused on body sensations; partner engagement, where the emphasis is on the emotional bond with your partner; and role playing, in which shared fantasies take center stage.

Schnarch offers practical tools to promote a rapid change that improves connection, enhances intimacy and sexuality, promotes self-regulation, and improves relationship stability and individual function by enhancing differentiation. Some of the practical techniques Schnarch teaches couples are:

Five Practical Techniques to Enhance Intimacy

- ♥ **Hugging until relaxed** – learn to self-soothe while touching.

- ♥ **Eyes open sex and orgasms** – according to Schnarch only 15% of couples have their eyes open during orgasm, which means that most people tune out from their partner at the moment that is supposed to be the most intimate.

- ♥ Actively **feeling while touching**

- ♥ **Foreplay as a language** – your words and actions always communicate an emotional tone and meaning.

- ♥ **Heads on pillows** – this technique is a great way to jump-start your sex life. All you have to do is lie on the bed, naked or clothed, and maintain sustained eye contact for five minutes. Really look into each other's eyes. Focus on the best in your partner. For some couples, this can feel even more intimate than intercourse.

Examples
Differentiation

Bill and Joan are the perfect example couple: married twelve years with two children, ages 6 and 8. He manages several sporting good stores; she gave up her career to become a full-time mother and homemaker. He is easygoing, but overly passive; she is intelligent, but high strung. When Joan loses her temper, Bill patronizes her or walks out. Both are in pain; both are desperate for the others agreement and approval.

Bill complains that he wants more sex; Joan complains she feels used and wants more intimacy. Bill thinks Joan is clingy and dependent; Joan thinks Bill is afraid of getting close. Both are upset at how the other handles almost everything, wishing the other was more like them.

Dr. Schnarch pulls them out of their fighting with the perfect question: "What makes you think you shouldn't have the

problems you are having?" They are shocked at the possibility that this might be normal. Joan retorts, "We shouldn't have this level of difficulty if we really loved each other." Dr. Schnarch explains that people often think that, or that no one else has the sort of problems they do. "Most people believe that it is their disagreements that are killing their relationship, when it is really what you agree on that makes you miserable. For instance, you agree that you shouldn't be having the problems you do."

There is always a low desire partner and a high desire partner. This is true not only for sex, but for many other decisions, such as should a parent move in when they are unable to take care of themselves. This is a profound paradigm shift, and one that will make looking at desire differences much easier.

Dr. Schnarch explains that it is their "fusion" that is making them miserable. As long as they feel the need to be fused, their needs for the relationship and for time alone will be in conflict. Differentiation means that one is able to maintain an independent sense of self while remaining emotionally close to another. Differentiation allows one to maintain their own course, even with pressure from friends, family, or one's lover to change or conform. Well-differentiated people can either agree or disagree without feeling pressured or alienated. They can stay connected to people "no matter what."

Hugs from Dad

David started studying his father's reaction to receiving hugs 20 years ago. "Hugging my father was like hugging a tree trunk; he was stiff and awkward." As his father warmed up to the value of hugs, he didn't want to miss out on one, but was still afraid to initiate a hug. Now, his father holds him for a several seconds and says, "Have I told you recently that I love you?" Later, his father apologized for being so long without hugs. "My own father wasn't physically affectionate. We never touched. When you were growing up, I wasn't comfortable showing the kind of affection we now share." He was overwhelmed with love.

Dr. David Schnarch Quotes

- *You can badger your spouse into having sex, but you can never badger him or her into wanting you.*
- *Marriage is a natural "people-growing process", and sexual boredom, lack of passion, and communication difficulties are what drive it.*
- *Relationships are driven by more than your feelings – and your feelings are not always accurate.*
- *Facing relationship realities produces the personal integrity necessary for intimacy, enduring eroticism, and a lifetime of loving marriage.*
- *Marriage takes your lowest, weakest, and darkest parts and stuffs them up your nose until you can't stand yourself as you are.*
- *Relying on your partner to give you a positive reflected sense of self (as most people do) limits intimacy and desire.*
- *Better sex doesn't automatically create a better relationship. However, the personal growth required to enhance sex and intimacy also improves marriage in other ways!*
- *Some find the discomfort of wanting so intolerable that they don't let themselves want sex or their partner.*
- *The process of becoming can lead you to act in ways that exceed your self-image. In doing what you aspire to be, you become that person.*
- *You don't think your way to a new way of living. You live your way to a new way of thinking.*

Books and Media

- Dr. Schnarch serves on the editorial board of AAMFT's *Journal of Marriage and Family Therapy.*

- 📖 In 1991 Schnarch released his book aimed at therapists and industry experts, *Constructing the Sexual Crucible: An Integration of Sexual and Marital Therapy.* This book is now used in clinical training programs worldwide.

His books aimed at the mass market include:

- 📖 *Passionate Marriage: Sex, Love, and Intimacy in Emotionally Committed Relationships.* This is a key book for the tools of connection. Chapter 10 will blow you away!

- 📖 *Resurrecting Sex: Resolving Sexual Problems and Rejuvenating Your Relationship*

- 📖 *Intimacy & Desire; Awaken the Passion in Your Relationship*

How to Find Out More

- 💻 For more information on Dr. David Schnarch and his work, go to *www.passionatemarriage.com*

36. Dr. David Richo

"Choosing a life of love, realism, and acceptance..."

Background and Qualifications

Dr. David Richo is a PhD psychotherapist, teacher, and workshop leader. He offers practical and spiritual exercises for couples who want to have mature and loving relationships, by helping to release the past, and thereby prevent the previous experiences from being transferred to new relationships.

Relationship Philosophy

Dr. Richo believes that people are programmed to replay the past, especially when it includes emotional pain or disappointment – whether that's an abusive childhood, an ex partner who cheated on you, or a marriage that broke down acrimoniously. Many go through life, transferring that pain to new experiences and relationships, casting new people in the roles of their parents or previous partners with whom they have unfinished business.

He describes this unconscious transference of feelings, needs, expectations, defenses, beliefs, fantasies, and attitudes as prime inhibitors of our current relationships. He teaches couples and individuals to become adults psychologically, rather than staying in the mindset of a hurt and wounded child.

He notes that our early experiences in childhood form, or distort our adult relationships. We all had basic emotional needs for attention, acceptance, appreciation, affection, and allowing, and if these were met well in childhood, we had a good foundation for adult relationships. These five A's allow us to become healthy, individuated people. We have childhood wounds in whatever way our parents were unable to fulfill those needs. As we enter relationships we looked for someone who is a replica of our parent, only better.

261

The Therapy

By learning to live life at the "heart level," Dr. Richo shows couples how to take small steps that lead to the expression of wholesomeness and loving-kindness, with increased joy and compassion. As we learn to live more permanently on this level and in the present, we experience an interior shift that increases love and virtue in our lives on a day to day basis, with less and less effort.

Dr. Richo teaches that this is achievable by learning to notice the clues about our past that are still alive in our present relationships. Since our childhood designs our adult intimacy, we reenact childhood scenarios so they come out differently. We either pick the perfect partner, or we train them so that they will play exactly as needed, or we project onto them the characteristics we need. We are looking to complete the past. What we didn't receive, we look to receive; what wasn't resolved, we are looking for resolution on the stage of adult relating.

By clearing up old business and forming a healthy, "adult" relationship, we no longer need to replicate the past and can be truly authentic. This is what it means to be a psychologically healthy adult, both on a personal level and within a relationship. This requires trust that right here, right now, in this relationship, is a place you can rely on to receive what you need. This takes doing the personal work to confront the three challenges of adulthood: fear, anger, and guilt. Tremendous self-esteem is available from meeting those challenges, as well as a deeper level of trusting yourself, that when the other is reliable and trustworthy, you can receive with appreciation.

By understanding the five "givens" within a relationship that always exist, we can learn to stop fighting against what is, and learn from our experiences. These five givens are:

The Five Givens
- ♥ Everything changes and ends
- ♥ Things don't always go according to plan
- ♥ Life is not always fair
- ♥ Pain is part of life
- ♥ People are not loving and loyal all the time

By accepting these relationship givens, and the fact they may cause a struggle within and without us, we can start to feel safer within the world, learning to embrace what is, rather than trying to resist and control it. In time, we start to see these givens that exist in all relationships as gifts that help us to grow in character, depth, and compassion. The universe has a power to bring about synchronicity; to bring the right people to us at the right time who can teach us who we are, what we can be, and how to let go of previous baggage.

Yet, one of the biggest barriers to pure joy is the ego, which Richo describes as the **F.A.C.E** we are afraid to lose – **F**ear, **A**ttachment, **C**ontrol, and **E**ntitlement to special treatment. The ego becomes neurotic when overtaken by fear and desire, creating self-defeating habits that keep one at the mercy of one's habitual beliefs or the past. Fear constructs walls so that people won't get too close or love you too much. Dr. Richo believes that if you can enter the "jungle of fear" surrounding love, loss, aloneness, and abandonment, you can find the inner resources so that fear can no longer stop you.

He also teaches an effective approach to resolving conflict without our egos getting in the way combined with the ability to grieve from the past and move onto a place filled with joy and free of resentment and expectation.

Seeing the Real Person

Being truly present and mindful to our partner and the relationship between us takes practice. Richo discusses one of

the best ways to achieve presence and avoid transference or projection of our own feelings onto our partner is to be present to the five A's:

The Five A's

Attention: Am I paying **attention** or am I planning what I'll say next? Am I noticing feelings and body language as well as words?

Acceptance: Am I **accepting** my partner as he is or passing judgment on his or her behavior or lifestyle?

Appreciation: Am I **appreciating** him or her, cherishing her, valuing his place in my life? Or am I taking him or her for granted?

Affection: Do I feel **affection** or do I fear closeness and distance myself from her? Do I show **affection** and intimacy by holding and touching her, or only through sex?

Allowing: Am I **allowing** him to be himself? Or am I trying to control his behavior?

In these moments, we can let go of our past long enough to "be here now," be attuned to the other, and truly let the love unfold between us.

These are the same 5 A's we need to feel self-respect, self-worth, and lovable, and to have the freedom to seek our own deepest needs, values, and desires. Although we needed 100% of these 5 A's from our parents when we were very young, in adult partnership, we expect only 25% of these needs to be met by our partner. The other 75% we achieve on our own, through friendships, work, hobbies, and other activities.

Dr. Richo points out that there are two fears built into relationship: the fear of abandonment or the fear of engulfment. When we have an uncomfortable feeling, we typically follow:
- ✓ Shame for having the feeling
- ✓ Blame others for causing us to have that feeling
- ✓ Desire for the feeling to go away
- ✓ Attachment to the outcome of getting over it
- ✓ Judgment of self and others
- ✓ Control the feeling

Instead, Dr. Richo recommends the triple A approach.

The Triple A Approach
1) **Admit** you have the feeling. This has the dual meaning of to say it is true, and to let it in.
2) **Allow** the feeling fully. Learn to savor the feeling.
3) **Act** as if (so that) the feeling cannot stop or drive you.

In other words, how would you act if you didn't have that fear? This allows you to act with the feeling, rather than thinking the feeling must go away before you can act. This means the feeling is no longer a compulsion.

When a couple has a difficult issue together, Dr. Richo recommends a rather straightforward process: address the issue and process (look for the projection, seek out ego wounds, and see how this is like wounds from earlier life) leads to resolution (new agreements and commitments).

3 Phases of Relationship
1) **Romance**: Two egos meet 2 ego ideals.
2) **Struggle**: 2 egos butt-up against 2 egos. One starts to see the shadow side. You begin to work out unfinished business. It is necessary to drop all ideals.

3) **Commitment**: Together, you have learned to handle obstacles and keep agreements. A real connection with growth is an authentic possibility here.

Examples
A Difficult Situation

A husband and wife are having intimacy issues. He doesn't share his inner life with her, and she wants more intimacy. He has a new female friend at work with whom he opens up and can share himself. He admits there is no sex involved. The wife is very annoyed, jealous, and upset.

She may first have to go through the Triple A approach where she admits to herself that she is feeling jealous, feel that feeling fully, then approach him in such a way that the jealousy doesn't interfere.

Then, she will need to address the situation with her husband. Rather than ignoring it and resenting him, or playing the blame and shame game, which is guaranteed to lead to closure and wounding, she might say, "I'm glad for you that you found someone with whom you can share and open up, and I would like to share with you the impact on me." The key to this step is to be heard. If he is defensive, or argues back, she will need to bring this up another time, until she feels understood.

As she processes the emotion, she would look for the projection: I wanted someone with whom I can share myself, and I want the intimacy that comes from someone sharing with me. The ego wounding may be: "I wanted to be the centerpiece of your life. I am wounded that I am not the most important person in your life right now." It may remind her of when her brother was born, and she didn't get the attention she was used to and wanted, and so this brings up the old, unresolved pain. As they move to the resolution phase, they want to move hidden expectations into the open, and make agreements. They may decide that he will spend more time with her, the three of them may become friends, or he may need to demote that other friendship. The result is a new way of being together that brings more trustworthiness and closeness.

A Basic Exercise in Becoming Truly Aware of your Partner

You may live with your partner but how aware of them are you really? How present to them are you? Learning to be mindful to your partner helps you to begin the journey of being truly <u>with</u> your partner, without dwelling on previous problems.

A simple way to practice relationship mindfulness is to begin by monitoring the physical details of your partner at this very moment – how are they standing, talking, holding their arms, looking to the side? This focus on the raw details of here and now allows you to break through the downward spiral of an argument. It also prevents you transferring your current or previous emotions onto the situation and what they are saying.

Attention to the here and now is a reminder that everything is continually changing – in life and in your relationship – that nothing is what it was a few moments, hours, days, weeks, or years ago.

Asking your partner what he or she is really saying or feeling, and repeating back what you hear – to make sure you've understood – can help you in becoming mindful of them. This prevents you from transferring your own reality onto what they are saying.

Dr. David Richo Quotes

- *Mindfulness can help us to compensate and no longer be held back by the past.*
- *How can we give up trying to get from other adults now, what we missed out on in childhood?*
- *We learn to grieve – and even bless – the past so that we can really live in the present.*

- *Humility means accepting reality, with no attempt to outsmart it.*
- *A hero is one who has lived through pain and been transformed by it.*
- *Our wounds are often the openings into the best and most beautiful part of us.*
- *The foundation of adult trust is not, "You will never hurt me." It is "I trust myself with whatever you do."*

Books and Media

- Dr. David Richo's latest book is *Daring to Trust: Opening Ourselves to Real Love & Intimacy*, where he explores the fear of commitment, insecurity, jealousy, and the tendency to want to control. He offers insights and exercises to learn to trust oneself, and one's partner. Other titles include:
- *When the Past Is Present: Healing the Emotional Wounds that Sabotage Our Relationships*
- *Coming Home to Who You Are: Discovering Your Natural Capacity for Love, Integrity, and Compassion*
- *How to Be an Adult*
- *How to Be an Adult in Relationships: The 5 Keys to Mindful Loving*
- *When Love Meets Fear: How to Become Defense-less and Resource-full*
- *Everyday Commitments: Choosing a Life of Love, Realism, and Acceptance*
- *The Five Things We Cannot Change: And the Happiness We Find by Embracing Them*
- Dr. Richo has also produced a CD series, based on his workshops entitled: *Making Love Last: How to Sustain Intimacy and Nurture Genuine Connection*

How to Find Out More

- For more information, go to Dr. David Richo's website: *www.davericho.com*

37. Dr. Willard Harley PhD

"Restore love rather than resolve conflict."

Background and Qualifications

Dr. Willard Harley has been married for 44 years, has two grown children who also work as marriage coaches, and four grandchildren. He has saved thousands of marriages from the pain of unresolved conflict, and the disaster of divorce.

Dr. Harley achieved his PhD in psychology from the University of California at Santa Barbara in 1967. He has been a licensed psychologist since 1975, and has lectured at undergraduate and graduate level. When he began work as a counselor, he became frustrated at his lack of success in marriage in counseling. He then made a startling discovery that marriage therapy had a less than 25% success rate, which all marriage therapists were discovering. He set out to discover why marriages were failing and a new therapeutic approach that would be more successful.

He discovered that couples fall out of love and tend to fight instead of resolving their conflict through mutual care and respect. But he realized it went beyond communication; it was about restoring love, and that was the key factor to marriages that failed – they had fallen out of love.

Once he changed the focus of his marriage counseling to restoring love rather than resolving conflict, his success increased to 90% repaired marriages. In the late 80's, Dr. Harley decided to give up private counseling and dedicate himself to improving his marriage building therapy. He went on to write 15 more books, and alongside his wife Joyce, works across the US delivering their Marriage Building seminars.

Relationship Philosophy

In his work helping couples restore their love, and in turn rebuild their marriages, Dr. Harley also discovered that love is a conditioned response. It is important to realize that just about everything one person does, affects the feeling of love you each have for each other. It takes willingness and the ability to care and protect each other. When love resonates in a relationship, the instincts to be affectionate, sensual, conversational, honest, and admiring come naturally. However, when you do not feel love, everything feels unnatural and your instincts cause you to shut down and turn against your spouse and your marriage.

Harley describes a Love Bank that we use to keep track of the way people treat us. When our partner "meets our needs", or does something for us that makes us feel good, "love units" are deposited in the account. When he or she does something that feels bad, love units are withdrawn. We check this balance automatically to know who is taking care of us, and who isn't. When the Love Bank is above a certain threshold, we feel romantic love, and have an added incentive to spend more time with that person. Of course, men and women have different needs in a relationship.

His Needs	Her Needs
Sexual Fulfillment	Affection
Companionship	Conversation
Attractive Looking Spouse	Honesty
Domestic Support	Financial Support
Admiration	Family Commitment

People usually start relationships irresistible to the other, because they meet all of each other's needs. However, couples sometimes become incompatible, as they don't think their needs are being met, and therefore leave the other's needs unmet.

When that happens, partners have lost interest in making one another happy, and end up making one another miserable, through fighting, sarcasm, and disrespect. They develop habits that drain the Love Bank. He calls these "Love Busters." These repeated behaviors continually cause large withdrawals of the Love Bank.

The 6 Love Busters
- ✓ Selfish Demands
- ✓ Disrespectful Judgments
- ✓ Angry Outbursts
- ✓ Dishonesty
- ✓ Annoying Habits
- ✓ Independent Behavior

The first three Love Busters are a form of marital abuse, because these are ways to get your way in marriage, and are deliberate efforts of one spouse to cause the other to be unhappy. However, the abuser rarely acknowledges that it was done deliberately, and tends to hide behind the excuse that it was unintentional.

When these Love Busters are present, an affair can begin when someone outside the marriage offers to meet those needs. The lover then looks irresistible. Usually, the lover is only meeting one or two basic needs, while the spouse fulfills the rest. Thus, the unfaithful spouse may feel a strong need for both people.
For the marriage to survive and thrive, the couple must move back to being irresistible to one another. Dr. Harley teaches that the fastest road to becoming irresistible to one's mate is to meet the other's most important emotional needs.

The Therapy
Dr. Harley has developed a number of methods to overcome marital conflicts and easy ways to restore love. He has written hundreds of questionnaires and articles to help clients in

therapy and in his workshops. He has a number of basic concepts to restore love and build a happy marriage:

9 Basic Concepts to Restore Love

♥ **The Love Bank:** an analogy that helps couples visualize and keep track of the way each person in the relationship treats the other. When you associate good feelings for a person, deposits are made into that person's account at the Love Bank. Once a certain level of deposits is achieved, then love is triggered. In order to experience a long-term feeling of love, the Love Bank must be held above the threshold. Likewise, associating bad feelings about a person causes withdrawals from the Love Bank. If it goes into debit, the Love Bank can even turn into a Hate Bank.

♥ **Instincts and Habits:** a good or bad habit or relationship instinct adds a credit into or makes a withdrawal from the Love Bank.

♥ **The Most Important Emotional Needs:** meeting each other's emotional needs can make huge Love Deposits.

♥ **Policy of Undivided Attention:** set aside time with complete undivided attention to each other. Dr. Harley recommends at least 15 hours per week in order to avoid feelings of neglect.

♥ **Love Busters:** we should pay attention to our everyday behavior to prevent becoming each other's source of greatest unhappiness. Love Busters include anger, disrespect, being demanding, insensitivity, or dishonesty.

♥ **The Policy of Radical Honesty:** reveal as much information about yourself as you know: your thoughts, feelings, habits, likes, dislikes, activities and plans for the future. This honesty guarantees the safety and success of the relationship and brings you closer emotionally.

♥ **The Giver and Taker:** during Giver mode, you will do anything to make your spouse happy. The Taker mode is when you're willing to let your spouse be unhappy in order to make yourself happy. It's important to achieve a balance between Giver and Taker.

♥ The Three States of Mind in Marriage:
- o **The State of Intimacy**: when you are in love and happy.
- o **The State of Conflict**: the taker is in control of the relationship.
- o **The State of Withdrawal**: when either party or both give up entirely.

♥ **The Policy of Joint Agreement:** never do anything without enthusiastic **agreement** between both partners, through safe and pleasant negotiation.

Guidelines for Successful Marital Negotiation

♥ Be pleasant and cheerful throughout the negotiation

♥ Put safety first. Do not make demands, show disrespect, or become angry

♥ If you reach an impasse, or rule 1 or 2 are not being followed, take a break and come back to the issue later

♥ Identify the problem from both sides

♥ Brainstorm with Abandon and Creativity

♥ Choose the solution that creates mutual and enthusiastic agreement and deposits into the Love Bank

Examples

Honesty and Openness... it's the Only Way

In his website advice page, Dr. Harley received a letter from a woman who is struggling to overcome her partner's dishonesty. When they first met, her husband was dating a woman she knew and he denied having a sexual relationship with her. Recently, the woman discovered that he had lied; he did in fact have a sexual relationship with this woman. She is not angry about the fact they had sex, but angry that he lied when she'd asked for complete honesty in the relationship. She feels bitter

and can't help questioning what else he may have lied about. She's always been honest with him and wants to know how to resolve the situation because she feels like she's been stabbed in the back.

Harley offers his stance on honesty – "Honesty at all times, especially on instances of sex with others before or after marriage." He admits it is often an unpopular belief – many other therapists believe discussing previous sexual partners or confessing to an affair is cruel to a spouse and usually only done in a bid to make one's self feel better and relinquish their guilt. Harley says, "I am horrified whenever I hear such nonsense... honesty is the door to understanding, and it's what each of us deserves from our spouses... honesty does not make up for the harmful act that has been hidden, but it does prevent another harmful act: dishonesty, being repeated throughout the marriage."

He advises that this woman let her husband know what she wants is the truth at all costs. He may have been dishonest about other things and should tell her about those too. She herself might not have been completely open with him about her emotions either. He recommends that they can use this as an opportunity to create a relationship that places honesty above all other values, which could help improve the intimacy levels between them even more. He suggests they follow the policy of joint agreement – never doing anything without an enthusiastic agreement between spouses. He also advises against any behavior that would make him lie again in the future – crying, screaming, hitting, or making threats. Instead, she needs to be safe to tell the truth to, and together, they need to plan and work to achieve a more honest marriage.

Lessons in Affection

A wife asks Dr. Harley for advice on giving her 14-year marriage another go. She tells of how she needs more affection from her husband, as he doesn't understand that she needs him to show her his love with physical attention. Harley explains that affection is something that is learned and many men have never been taught. When he counsels a man who doesn't know how to show affection, Harley gives him a list of things to do every day; things he must tick off as he does them. For example, to hug and kiss his wife every morning before he gets out of bed, to tell her he loves her over breakfast, to call her during the day to ask how she's doing, and to buy her flowers at least once a week. Some wives complain that this can't be real affection because their husbands have to be told what to do. Yet Harley insists this is not fake affection; it's real, because the husbands really do love their wives, but they've just not learned to express how they really feel. What this exercise does is teaches them how to show their wives they care by the little things they do every day – until it becomes second nature!

Dr. Willard Harley Quotes

- *If you want a marriage that satisfies both you and your spouse, you must have a passionate marriage.*

- *Without an effective plan of action, it's unlikely that you'll achieve your objectives in life, and that's particularly true of marital objectives.*

- *The difference between my approach to saving marriages and the approach of most other therapists is that I focus on building love between spouses, rather than simply focusing on the conflict.*

- *Couples should not waste their time trying to understand each other's failures, but rather, they should try to overcome them as quickly as possible so the issue doesn't have time to drain their Love Banks.*

- *If you want a happy marriage, you must be able to discuss your conflicts safely and enjoyably.*

- *In successful marriages, spouses expect to change to accomplish each other's needs, so when a spouse requires a compliment it's a signal for action. In failed marriages, on*

the other hand, spouses expect to be accepted as they are, without change.

Books and Media

- Dr. Harley wrote his first book in 1986, *His Needs, Her Needs: Building an Affair-Proof Marriage.* The hardcover American edition alone has sold over one million copies and has now been translated into 16 languages worldwide.

- *I Promise You: Preparing For a Marriage That Will Last a Lifetime.*

- *Surviving an Affair*

- *Love Busters: Overcoming Habits That Destroy Romantic Love (2002)*

- *Love Busters: Protecting Your Marriage from Habits That Destroy Romantic Love (2008)*

- *Five Steps to Romantic Love: A Workbook for Readers of Love Busters and His Needs, Her Needs*

- *Fall in Love, Stay in Love*

- *Draw Close: A Devotional for Couples*

- *Effective Marriage Counseling: The His Needs, Her Needs Guide to Helping Couples*

- Dr. Harley also has his own live radio show that airs from 10 to 1 PM, called *Marriage Builders Radio,* with live call in advice.

How to Find Out More

- For more information, go to Dr. Harley's website: *www.marriagebuilders.com*

38. Michele Weiner-Davis

"Divorce is NOT the answer!"

Background and Qualifications

Married for over thirty years with two children, Michele Weiner-Davis has been a marriage therapist since the 1970s, and has developed a successful strategy that helps prevent couples going through what she terms, "unnecessary divorce."

Having been a child of divorced parents herself, as she began to work as a marriage therapist, she became deeply influenced by her parents' divorce and how it had affected her growing up. She was looking for something that would be more effective than regular marriage advice she had learned throughout her education, and decided to come up with realistic and effective strategies and solutions to help couples prevent divorce, rather than spending sessions simply analyzing what the problems were that were pushing them to divorce.

Michele has a Masters degree in social work and is Director of the Divorce Busting Centers in Woodstock, IL, and Boulder, CO. She has also received an award from the American Association of Marriage and Family Therapy for Outstanding Contribution to the Field of Marriage and Therapy.

Relationship Philosophy

The underpinning message to Weiner-Davis' relationship therapy, is that divorce is NOT the answer. She has developed a program of working with couples experiencing a variety of different marital problems. She warns against the pitfalls of unnecessary divorce and aims to help make marriages work and keep families together. She believes the vast majority of divorces are unnecessary and most relationship problems are solvable. Marriage can be brought back on track, even when your friends and family are telling you to move on.

Weiner-Davis aims to rescue marriages that seem beyond help. She believes affairs are not a marital death sentence and through working on ways to move forward and forgive the affair, the resulting intimacy can make the marriage even stronger.

The Therapy

From one or two day private intensives with just one couple, to workshops and seminars for hundreds of people, Weiner-Davis believes change can start with one person in the relationship. As that person changes, their marriage can take on a new meaning and new life, with significant growth towards a happy and successful future. She coaches couples towards working out what to do about their problems, with helpful solutions, rather than analyzing why they have the problems.

7 Steps to Saving Your Marriage

- ♥ Start with a Beginner's Mind
- ♥ Know What You Want
- ♥ Ask for What You Want
- ♥ Stop Going Down Cheeseless Tunnels (conversations where there is no positive payoff)
- ♥ Experiment and Monitor Results
- ♥ Take Stock
- ♥ Keeping the Positive Changes Going

She believes hopelessness is the number one marriage killer, preventing the capacity to re-open our hearts to one another. Other common dilemmas she deals with are: infidelity, depressed spouse, midlife crisis, and passion meltdown.

Examples

Sex-Starved Marriage

Some couples engage in a "cat and mouse" game around sex. Perhaps you pursue your spouse to be sexual, and your spouse turns you down repeatedly. What do you do? If you are like most people, you become obsessed with being sexually connected, and you do more of the same to get their interest. Every interaction is another opportunity to express your sexual interest. The problem is, what you were doing in the first place wasn't working, and doing more is likely to make your spouse feel annoyed, rather than turned on.

Instead of evaluating your approach, you decide to discuss your unhappiness with your spouse, i.e. pursue even more. They are likely to feel cornered and shut the door on any intimacy. Although your differences may have been small at one point, they can easily become a huge focus point in your marriage.

People are typically blind to how their behavior affects their partner, and so conclude that it is their spouse who is changing, becoming less caring and more stubborn. You end up blaming your spouse, rather than look at what you're doing. The first step to solving this is to identify what you're doing that isn't working, and quit doing that. She offers step-by-step solutions to move forward.

The willingness to change is the key to success. It is the Law of Relationships that change causes a chain reaction: as one person changes the other one does too; it doesn't matter who starts first.

A Case of Faulty Genes

Kim was preparing to leave her second marriage to her husband Glen, because he was unable to form a close bond with Todd, her child from her first marriage. As they discussed this problem with Dr. Weiner-Davis, it was clear that they both thought there was something wrong with Glen. It was just "a fact" that Glen could not bond with a male child, as if he lacked the gene for a father-son relationship. When Kim finally realized that it was going to be this way forever, she decided to end her marriage. "He can't change now," Kim exclaimed.

Meeting with Glen on his own, Weiner-Davis discover that Glen *did* reach out to Todd, but Kim never noticed. She kept expecting to see no interaction, and so she filtered for that – she saw only what she expected to see. Receiving no positive feedback from Kim, Glen assumed he was a failure. Glen also assumed that his interactions with Todd should have felt more natural. As Glen learned that feeling comfortable takes time, he was willing to work on his relationship with Todd. He started watching TV together, doing chores together, and initiating conversation. Perhaps because of the therapeutic intervention, Kim was now able to see this and was amazed. She decided to keep her marriage, and they began to enjoy each other again.

Michele Weiner- Davis Quotes

- *Forgiveness opens the door to real intimacy and connection.*

- *Forgiveness doesn't just happen. It is a conscious decision to stop blaming, make peace, and start tomorrow with a clean slate.*

- *Anger imprisons you. It casts a gray cloud over your days. It prevents you from feeling real joy in any part of your life. Each day you drown yourself in resentment is another day lost out of your precious life.*

- *Spend more time trying to figure out what might work as opposed to being hell bent on driving your point home.*

- *Stop waiting for your partner to change in order for things to be better. When you decide to change first, it will be the beginning of a solution avalanche.*

Books and Media

- Michele Weiner-Davis has written 7 books. Her career as a relationship author began in 1992 with the bestseller: *Divorce Busting: A Step-by-Step Approach to Making Your Marriage Loving Again.*

Other titles include:

- *A Sex-Starved Marriage: Boosting Your Marriage Libido*
- *The Divorce Remedy: The Proven 7 Step Plan for Saving Your Marriage*
- *Getting Through to the Man You Love: The No-Nonsense, No-Nagging Guide for Women*
- *Change Your Life and Everyone In It: Do-It-Yourself Strategies*
- *A Woman's Guide to Changing Her Man: Without His Even Noticing It*
- Her latest book is *The Sex Starved Wife: What to Do When He's Lost Desire*
- Weiner-Davis' work as featured in the *New York Times, LA Times, Cosmo, Glamour,* and *Time*
- TV programs such as *Oprah, 48 Hours, 20/20, CBS This Morning* and *Evening News, The TODAY Show, CNN,* and *Bill O'Reilly.*
- She has also recently completed a reality show for the BBC to help couples save their marriage.

How to Find Out More

- Go to Michele Weiner-Davis' website: *www.divorcebusting.com*

39. Terrance Real

"In the last generation women have radically changed, and men, by and large, have not"

Background and Qualifications

Known for his no nonsense approach to therapy, Terry Real has been a family therapist and teacher for over twenty years. He's helped thousands of couples take their journey to greater intimacy and greater personal fulfillment through private therapy, workshops, audio programs, and books.

He describes his own life as a journey of self-awareness, grief, and acceptance, as he came to terms with a painful childhood with a depressed father who abused him. This lead to a troubled adult life tainted by feelings of disconnection, until he eventually healed himself and found his calling to help others, through therapy. He decided to dedicate himself to teaching as many people as possible how to become "relationally skilled" as well as training other therapists in the techniques.

Terry served as a senior faculty member of the Family Institute of Cambridge in Massachusetts, is a retired Clinical Fellow of the Meadows Institute in Arizona, and founded The Relational Life Institute – which is dedicated to teaching mental health professionals the practice of Relational Life Therapy (RLT™), and teaching the general public how to live relational lives. He lives with his wife, Belinda Berman, who is also a family therapist, and they have two sons together.

Relationship Philosophy

According to Terrance Real, the rules of marriage have changed. Women in particular have changed over the past few decades, becoming more powerful, independent, and self-confident. The problem is that most men have not kept up with those changes and often remain emotionally detached and at times irresponsible. As women demand more from their marriages with a wish that their husbands become lifelong friends and lovers, they often don't have the correct strategy to communicate to their partners what they truly desire from their relationship.

Often, women become over critical: blame, complain, and vent their frustration, with the opposite effect they desire from their men. Out of frustration, men can become more arrogant: bully, stonewall, and withdraw. Real shows women how to replace accusation with understanding, and shows men how it is possible to become emotionally mature and step-up to the plate in a twenty-first century marriage.

He also believes that conventional therapy can cause people to become over empowered, meaning, they often put themselves first without thinking of the relationship or ever focusing on their partner's good points. This can pave the way for poor relationship behaviors that can be thought of as "losing strategies."

Losing Strategies
- ✓ **Being right**
- ✓ **Controlling your partner** – trying to get him or her to bend to your will
- ✓ **Unbridled self-expression** – an "adult temper tantrum"
- ✓ **Retaliation**
- ✓ **Withdrawal** – either becoming walled off and superior, or walled off and defeated

The Therapy
Relational Live Therapy (RTL™) focuses on action rather than insight. In order to have a successful relationship, you need to be proactive. Far too many people focus on the negatives, yet, it's impossible to get what you want unless you actually decide

283

what you DO want, rather than simply what you don't want. It's important to actually sit down and decide on the relationship goals, rather than waiting for things to go wrong and reacting to the dissatisfaction. If you work as a team, you can empower each other to achieve your relationship goals – *"What can I give you to help you give me what I want?"* Real focuses on five core relationship skills:

5 Core Relationship Skills
- ♥ **Relational esteem** – Hold the relationship in high regard
- ♥ **How to speak** – tell the truth with skill and love, responding constructively
- ♥ **How to listen** – generously, without defensiveness or comeback, with curiosity, without taking things personally
- ♥ **Negotiating with wisdom**
- ♥ **Relational integrity** – How to stay on course

Therefore, how you communicate is essential. For example, many women criticize their partner in a manner that is entirely unconstructive. Being critical is often aggressive and extends back in time, such as, "You are so insensitive. You never listen to me." Instead, it's better to complain constructively about a specific incident (and make clear requests) while coming from a position of love, always holding in mind the reason why you're complaining – to make things better, not to belittle or shame your partner. They are not the enemy; they ARE the person you are in love with. He sets out the constructive complaining strategy in four steps (with credit to Janet Hurley's Feedback Wheel as the source):

Constructive Complaining Strategy
- ♥ **Explain what you've observed** – this should be specific actions not an attitude or feeling you think your partner was demonstrating.
- ♥ **Explain the meaning it had for you**.

- ♥ **Explain what you felt at the time** – and not that they MADE you feel this way; you have to take responsibility for your feelings.
- ♥ **Make a request** – tell them what they can say or do to make you feel better.

When couples have the core relationship skills, know how to constructively complain, and have the intention to replace the "control, revenge, and resignation syndrome" with "harmony, disharmony, and then repair," their future is much brighter. They can start asking the question: "Am I getting enough here that makes it worthwhile to let go of what I'm not getting?" If the answer is yes, then it's time to step up to the relationship. Stop whining, stop complaining, stop acting like a victim, and embrace the other person and the relationship.

Examples
Jenna and Joe

Instead of waiting until their relationship was at the bitter end, Jenna and Joe come to one of Real's "Fight Less, Kiss More Relational Boot Camps" to tune up their relationship. Jenna relates a typical fight for her and Joe. "While I'm talking, Joe gives me his 'hurry up and get to the point' hand gestures that I find absolutely infuriating." "How do you react when he does this?" asks Real. "I growl, call him a jerk, and storm off," declares Jenna.

Terrance offers Jenna an alternative script: "Just now, when you made that hand gesture, what I made myself feel was frustrated and angry. What I'd like you to do in the future is to listen patiently when I speak. Try not to use your hands. Can you do that?" Joe will be free to say yes or no. However, since he is invested in this marriage and wants to make her happy, he is likely to honor her request. As Joe always says, "Happy wife, happy life." Most men feel this way.

Rage-a-holic

"I'm a rage-a-holic," declares Renee. She is on her third marriage and it is at the verge of divorce. She has two young sons and she fights all the time with her husband. Real asks, "Do you have a photo of your children? Take it out, look in their eyes, and repeat after me: 'As much as I love you, and as much as I know how horrible it is to live in a hostile household, I am more committed to violent displays of anger than I am to your emotional well-being. I apologize, but I choose my dysfunction over your happiness.'"

"I can't say that!" sobs Renee. "You are saying that everyday. They hear it, and they know it," says Real.

Real teaches people to pay attention to their losing strategies when they fight, and turn them around. If it isn't working, find the option that has the best odds for successful outcome. If you can't interact with respect, take a time out. If you are fighting about "who's right," he asks the killer question, "Do you want to be right, or be happy?"

Terrance Real Quotes

- *Real intimacy is the collision of your imperfections with those of your partner, while still holding one another with love and respect.*
- *People in good relationships know how to manage the heat, not avoid it.*
- *The person you bring into your second marriage is still you!*
- *For most of us, whatever we learned growing up about relationships is simply not sophisticated enough to deliver all that we hope for... you have been trying to negotiate a 21st-century relationship using 20th-century skills.*
- *Men are not unhappy in their marriages. They are unhappy that their women are so unhappy with them.*

Books and Media

- *I Don't Want to Talk About It: Overcoming the Secret Legacy of Male Depression,* was Terry Real's breakthrough best selling book.

- *How Can I Get Through to You? Reconnecting Men and Women*

- *The New Rules of Marriage: What You Need to Make Love Work*

- Real has also created several CD and DVD programs, including *Relationship Turnaround, Making Love Work* and *Starter Kit for Relationship Repair*

- He has numerous media credits, including appearances on *The TODAY Show, CBS Early Show, 20/20, Oprah,* and has been featured in *The New York Times*

How to Find Out More

- Go to the website *www.terryreal.com*

40. Dr. Gail Saltz

"Get real with yourself!"

Background and Qualifications

Dr. Gail Saltz is a psychologist, columnist, and best-selling author who teaches the power of becoming real with yourself and dealing with patterns of behavior learned in childhood, in order to improve our relationships.

Married with three daughters, Dr. Saltz is Associate Professor of Psychiatry at the New York Presbyterian Hospital Weill-Cornell School of Medicine. She also has a private practice out of Manhattan.

Relationship Philosophy

Dr. Saltz believes the key to having fulfilling relationships as well as a satisfying work life is being authentic, confident, and comfortable with yourself. This is a process she defines as becoming REAL with yourself.

The stories we tell ourselves as children to make sense of the world cause many of the problems we face as adults. For example, stories such as, "I can't depend on anyone but myself," or "There must be something wrong with me that no one sticks around." These stories keep us from authenticity, personal freedom, true strength, self-acceptance, and intimate relationships. It's as if time hasn't passed; we still remember the insults and comments from our childhood, and previous relationships that keep playing over and over like a tape recorder in our brains.

Often, as adults, we end up punishing others, and ourselves in order to play out these stories, attaching ourselves as a matter of security to adults who can't truly satisfy our emotional needs, but fulfill these childhood myths. We become lodged in unconscious, destructive, and non-productive behavior in order to shield off emotional stress. This narrative plays out every time we meet a new person, have sex, or get intimate.

The Therapy

Dr. Saltz' relationship therapy involves understanding and rewriting the stories from your childhood to free yourself from your past, to prevent history from repeating itself, and to allow you to pursue healthy and fulfilling relationships with other people, as well as with yourself.

The steps involved include taking the time to work on changing and rewriting these stories, making the decision to no longer be a victim, and taking control of your own thoughts and feelings. Instead of saying in your mind, "They say I'm too ugly to be loved," for example, it's important to change this to your own feelings. So turn it around to, "I feel too ugly to be loved," and then work on evaluating that statement and finding out if it really makes sense. Could it really be true that someone would love you any less because of the way you look? If so, take action.

Finally, take new actions so that you can replace that old statement with a new story, such as: "I am loveable and worthy. I am smart, sexy, and attractive!" You are then able to take control, be strong, and have truly magical relationships and marriage longevity.

Although some of Dr. Saltz' techniques are deeply rooted in psychoanalytical theory that require careful studying and concentrated effort, her exercises and methods for achieving personal freedom are well worth the time and dedication.

Dr. Saltz believes it's important to fully feel negative emotions, such as sadness and anxiety, in order to be authentic with yourself. If you have serious issues, it's important to deal with them. On the other hand, having a persistent pessimistic

attitude is also unhealthy, and finding something fun to do can help you snap out of it.

She also combines her therapy with simple step-by-step guides to improving your relationship and ensuring marriage longevity:

Step-by-Step Guide

- ♥ **Be flexible:** accept that your partner may not always share your views. Otherwise, pick someone who shares your ideas. But you'll never find someone who agrees with everything you do, and it is here that flexibility is required.

- ♥ **Give 80% of your time:** ensuring you leave around 20% of the time to put yourself first.

- ♥ **Love on balance:** there are things about your partner you won't like… take the bad with the good!

- ♥ **Determine the source of your unhappiness:** too many couples blame personal unhappiness on their marriage. Work out exactly what it is that is making you unhappy and if it's personal to you, it won't matter whom you are with – you'll still have the same unhappiness issues in the next relationship.

- ♥ **Treasure your life history:** you and your partner have shared many experiences intimately and intensely, which you should learn to cherish.

Examples

I'm not Attracted to my Wife… Help!

Dr. Saltz received a letter from a man who is no longer physically attracted to his wife – her appearance has always been an issue and she's put on a lot of weight. He's tried to tell her in a sensitive way, but she gets offended. They're now having communication problems, intimacy problems, and much less sex.

Dr. Saltz suspects that his turned-off feelings probably have to do with more than just weight. She's not suggesting having an overweight spouse has no impact on a sex life, and a negative message could be received; she doesn't care enough about herself, the marriage, or whether or not they have sex. However, she recommends also figuring out what the real problem in the marriage is, and confronting the underlying emotional issues. Why is his wife using food as a comfort? Why doesn't she recognize how her husband is feeling?

Her advice is to discuss the problem by beginning talking about the marriage, his feelings, and their sex life. Then, he can ask her how she feels her weight affects those things, without being critical and distant. If she wants to lose weight, they can work on it together, through exercise and cooking healthy meals. Yet, Dr. Saltz makes a final observation – that this man's wife could be keeping the weight on to avoid having sex, which is common in many women, and in that case, the sexual problem needs addressing.

Our Deeply Embedded Story

Everyone has within them a deeply embedded story that can shape everything they do, according to Dr. Saltz. In adulthood, this story can hold us back, trapping us in repetitive and destructive behavior. To illustrate the power of these stories, in her book *Becoming Real,* Dr. Saltz uses the story of Sydney, a woman in her early thirties who came to her, desperate for help. She had always been an animated and upbeat person, with a fiancé who adored her. But as their wedding day approached, she became cold and angry towards her fiancé, Brian, for no apparent reason. He kept asking her if something was wrong and she insisted all was fine. While Brian was worried he could be marrying the wrong woman, Sydney was scared that an angry woman with an engulfing rage that erupted for no reason was replacing her usually accommodating nature.

Dr. Saltz explored with Sydney the turmoil she was going through, and helped her realize it could be a useful tool to enrich her life and let go of her childhood stories. Sydney's story began to unravel – that inside she feels insufficient as a woman, never good enough for any man. Throughout her life to protect herself from pain, she had become a people pleaser, always trying to make people around her happy, including Brian, who had fallen in love with her compensatory personality. He had no idea who the real Sydney was, and she was scared of showing him. Instead, she ended up freezing him out.

Together, Dr. Saltz and Sydney uncovered the vulnerable child who created this story – at aged 11 Sydney's father left her mother for another woman, and for years, Sydney listened to her mother argue with him. She was left believing, "No wonder he left," and she blamed her mother for him going, creating the belief that all women who yelled at their man risked abandonment. She herself also didn't feel lovable enough for her father to stay. So in order to avoid becoming her mother and experiencing the same fate, she had become a submissive, pleasing woman. Her story had stopped her feeling true intimacy and real connection in an attempt to protect herself from pain. She now had a tough choice to make – keep the story and risk losing Brian, or take the journey to becoming real by embracing and understanding these painful and negative emotions.

Dr. Gail Saltz Quotes

- *Nothing solidifies love and trust like being thoughtful and giving towards your mate. Nothing breeds love like giving love.*

- *Marital dissatisfaction often has its roots in personal unhappiness – which can be related to work, level of success, health, or weight. Often these personal shortcomings are blamed on the marriage.*

● *If you feel it's your relationship that is making you miserable, try to step back and see if it's really you!*

Books and Media

□ Dr. Saltz is the regular health, sex, and relationship counselor to *The TODAY Show,* as well as regular appearances on *Oprah, Dateline, CBS News, CNN,* and *Larry King Live.* She is a regular contributor to *O, The Oprah Magazine* and the emotional wellness coach for iVillage.com.

□ In 2004, Dr. Saltz became the host of a series of 92nd *Street;* interviewing celebrities and extraordinary individuals on psychology related issues. Interviewees have included Woody Allen and Rosie O'Donnell.

Her books include:

📖 *Becoming Real: Defeating the Stories We Tell Ourselves That Hold Us Back*

📖 *The Anatomy of a Secret Life: Are the People In Your Life Hiding Something You Should Know?*

📖 *Anatomy of a Secret Life: The Psychology of Living a Lie*

📖 *The Ripple Effect: How Better Sex Can Lead to a Better Life*

How to Find Out More

🖥 For more information, go to Dr. Gail Saltz' website: *www.drgailsaltz.com*

41. Dr. Barry McCarthy

"Desire is the core of sexuality"

Background and Qualifications

Dr. McCarthy specializes in sex therapy for individuals and couples. He is a tenured professor of psychology at American University and has been a licensed psychologist since 1972. He has an MA and PhD from Southern Illinois University, and is also a certified couple therapist (American Association of Marital and Family Therapy) and a diplomat in sex therapy (American Association of Sex Educators, Counselors, and Therapists). In addition to teaching and his clinical practice, he has presented over 350 professional workshops nationally and internationally.

Relationship Philosophy

Dr. McCarthy helps couples in low-sex or no-sex marriages improve their sex lives. The statistics show that 20% of married couples have a no-sex marriage, and in non-married couples who've been together more than 2 years, a third no longer have sex. McCarthy believes that the major sexual dysfunction is lack of sexual desire. However it's more difficult to admit, "I'm not interested in sex," than to look for a specific dysfunction, such as premature ejaculation, erectile problems, or inability to orgasm.

There are 4 phases of sexual response – desire, arousal, orgasm, and satisfaction. Desire is the easiest to disrupt. There are some common "poisons" which can get in the way of desire. These include shame, guilt, anger, and passivity, but also side effects from many common medications as well as some people being genuinely afflicted with a biologically-caused sexual dysfunction.

However, perhaps one of the biggest poisons is comparison of marital sexual patterns to pre-marital sex, which is a self-defeating and unrealistic standard of comparison. Pre-marital sex is based on newness, illicitness, risk-taking, winning the partner over, and exploring sexual boundaries. On the other hand, marital sexual desire is based on dealing with the whole person and sharing complexities of life, including emotional and sexual intimacy. Ideally, romantic love, based on unrealistic expectations, would be replaced by mature intimacy; hot sex would be replaced by intimacy, non-demanding pleasuring, and erotic scenarios and techniques specifically learned with your partner to please him or her.

Many sex problems occur because people are too embarrassed to speak about their problem, including not being able to communicate about it with their partner. For example, a man may have erection problems and feel ashamed because he thinks he's the only one going through this. The truth is, 90% of men have occasional erection problems by the age of 40. According to Dr. McCarthy, couples need to view erection problems as a "common enemy" and recognize that it happens to the majority of men at some point in their life. In fact, this could be transformed from a problem to a new way to be sexual.

Another focus for Dr. McCarthy's work is middle-aged and older clients. He encourages them to learn new ways to experience sexuality and eroticism. He challenges the view that sex should play a smaller role in our life as we age. Sexuality does change with the aging of the person and the relationship, as well as side effects of medications, but this does not end sex. The healthy sexual focus is on desire; pleasure and satisfaction will be the natural result.

Now more than ever, people need help with their sexuality. Contrary to media myths, sexual problems have become more frequent with the release of pharmaceutical sexual aids such as Viagra. What is needed alongside such prescriptions is help for the couple to integrate the medication into their style of intimacy, sexual pleasure, and eroticism. A crucial concept is to adopt a

"Good Enough Sex" approach, rather than clinging to the pass-fail criterion of perfect intercourse performance.

The Therapy

Dr. McCarthy encourages couples to resolve sex problems by committing to sharing and working on the problem as an intimate team. It's important not to blame or apologize, but to find ways to be intimate without every encounter having to end in sexual intercourse with climax. It's important to talk about sexual desire and function, but without falling into unhealthy extremes:

Unhealthy Extremes

- Avoiding sexual intercourse
- Becoming obsessed with intercourse and orgasm as a pass-fail sex test

The keys to sexual desire are positive anticipation and knowing that you deserve sexual satisfaction in your relationship. Each person needs to be responsible for his/her desire. Revitalizing desire is the couple's job, with each partner acting to nurture and enhance desire.

He teaches that the worse time to talk about sex is in bed after a negative experience. Much better is to chat while out for a walk or over a cup of coffee. Female non-arousal or non-orgasmic response or male ejaculation inhibition is the "joint enemy," and you commit to sharing pleasure and working together as an intimate, erotic team.

The essence of sexuality is giving and receiving pleasurable touch. Touching needs to occur both outside the bedroom as well as in the bedroom. Touching has value in and of itself.

Dr. McCarthy also believes that couples should look at sex as a concept of "five gears of touching" rather than merely an end goal of intercourse. Like in a stick shift car, you gradually build up to the fifth gear. Just because you don't get to fifth doesn't mean you've failed or can't enjoy the journey. The 5 gears of touching are:

The 5 Gears of Touching

1) **Affectionate touch** – holding hands, hugging, kissing. Affection is very important in terms of intimacy but it's not sexual.

2) **Sensual touching** – this is where you can begin to think of touching as something sexual. It's still non-genital touching that can include cuddling together, kissing, massage, or holding each other when you wake up or go to bed at night.

3) **Playful touch** is the third gear. It can be with or without clothes and mixes genital and non-genital touch. It can be whole body massage, showers or baths together, or sexy dancing.

4) The fourth gear is **erotic** but non-intercourse touch, including manual, oral, rubbing stimulation to high arousal, and/or orgasm.

5) The final gear is **sexual intercourse.** A key concept is to transition to intercourse at high levels of arousal.

Sexuality has a number of positive functions for the relationship: shared pleasure, a means to reinforce and deepen intimacy, and a way to reduce the stress of life. Healthy sexuality can energize your bond and generate special feelings of desirability. On the other hand, non-existent sexuality can play a powerful negative role in a relationship.

In his book, *Rekindling Desire,* Dr. McCarthy outlines 10 steps to help a low-sex or no-sex marriage. The first step is understanding why this happens, that it is a joint problem, uncovering the turnoffs of anger, guilt and anxiety, inhibitions, obsessions, and shame, and overcoming sexual dysfunction. The full 10 steps are listed below.

297

10 Steps to an Erotic Marriage
- ♥ **Understanding** – The First Step
- ♥ **Nurturing Anticipation** – Bridges to Sexual Desire
- ♥ **Feeling Close** – Enhancing Intimacy
- ♥ **Let's Play Feely-Touchy** – Non-Demand Pleasuring
- ♥ **Just Do It** – Challenging Inhibitions
- ♥ **Making It Special** – Creating Erotic Scenarios
- ♥ **Keeping It Vital** – Preventing Relapse
- ♥ **Enhancing the Bond** – Intimacy Dates
- ♥ **Lusting for Life** – The Erotic Marriage
- ♥ **Your Parents Were Wrong** – Valuing Marital Sexuality

Examples
Unrealistic Expectations

For Danielle and Jacob, the first 6 months of their relationship was a very exciting time. They hid the fact that they were dating from their colleagues, which added to the excitement. Jacob, who was 13 years older than Danielle, felt sexually revitalized. Danielle was totally in love, and amazed that she was in a relationship with such a mature and professional man. Their weekends away were amazing; they cut loose and forgot about everything. Danielle especially likes Jacob's excellent sexual skills. It seemed like a match made in heaven.

Their romantic bubble burst because of a series of non-sexual factors, Jacob's adolescent children weren't thrilled about Danielle. The relationship was a source of gossip, and Danielle had to find another job – one that was less than satisfactory. They married in the hope that this would restore the romance.

Romantic love and passionate sex are often fantastic at the beginning of a relationship. However, this sets a couple up for disappointment and resentment later, if the sex does not compare. In their case, sex became a strain. Both wanted the other to initiate sex. Jacob responded by having performance anxiety, about which he apologized. Danielle found his tentativeness and apologetic nature repellent, and they descended into a vicious cycle.

In therapy, both could identify the "poisons" of guilt, anger, shame, and withdrawal that drained their sexual desire and exhausted their marital vitality. They introduced "non-demand" pleasure to reconnect. Pleasuring served as a way to connect and build intimacy. Danielle enjoyed pleasuring Jacob, and her arousal was arousing for him. Once they dealt with Jacobs's obsession about whether intercourse would succeed or fail, they were able to enjoy each other more fully. In the 10th week they discussed creating erotic scenarios. Although hesitant initially, once Danielle assured Jacob that she was open to erotic adventures, they were able to open up to each other.

They were able to complete therapy knowing their marital bond was solid and secure. Although sex was less frequent than during the first 6 months, it was based on genuine sexual attraction and openness to each other's needs. They were committed to maintaining a vital sexual relationship and followed Dr. McCarthy's relapse/prevention strategies.

Getting it Right

Michelle and Carter met for the first time at a college football game, years after each one had graduated. Michelle was now living in Boston and had a career as a financial analyst. Carter was near Washington, DC, and ran a home restoration company. Two months later, when Carter was in Boston, he called Michelle and they spent the Saturday together walking. They found they had a lot of common interests.

Their romance evolved over 8 months, with Michelle finding a lower paying job near Carter. Michelle asked for what she needed: a room of her own for an office. She wanted an

intimate, stable marriage and children, and wanted to make sure they had the same values and expectations. They created the time and space to talk about the serious issues. Both enjoyed individual time and interests; they loved to disclose and solve problems; they were not overly emotionally expressive. They were clearly a complementary couple style.

They divided couple's tasks based on strengths and interests rather than gender roles. They appreciated each other's skills and successes. At least once a month, they would create time to discuss their issues and concerns. They realized that marriage is a complicated balance of his-her-our needs. When they added a baby, they made a promise to continue to share feelings with each other, to problem solve, and to value their marriage.

Problems with Money

Leanne and Alex were married only 14 months when the battles about money began. For Alex, this was his second marriage and he had a 5-year old son from his first. Since Leanne and his son hit is off, they assumed it would be clear sailing for their marriage.

Much of their problems can be traced to the fact that they did not discuss issues around income, spending, parenting, etc., before getting married. Alex had just started a small business, and could not afford insurance. He insisted that Leanne keep her full-time job that had full health insurance benefits, and attacked her as selfish when she wanted something different. She counterattacked with, "If you were a real man you should be able to support both of us and not leech off my health insurance, especially for *your* son." The arguments spiraled into personal put-downs, character assassinations, and attacks. It had become a blaming, disrespectful disaster.

Although they could enjoy other aspects of life, they became almost hopeless when it came to discussing money. Each talked to their own friends, who supported their anti-other stance. It was going downhill fast.

When they took a course on money management, their eyes were opened. As they tracked their income, Leanne was able to feel compassionate about the insecurity Alex felt because of his highly variable income. As they tracked their expenses, they were shocked at how much money they spent on "Miscellaneous." They finally realized the huge drain that financial illiteracy had been on their marriage. They started to share information and feelings about money. They also started to see how their upbringing caused them to view the other as the enemy when it came to money. As they understood each other's hopes and fears, shared information, and planned together, they started to work together as a functional financial team.

Dr. Barry McCarthy Quotes

- *A common mistake is thinking about sex as intercourse or nothing. You either hit a home run, or you failed and don't want to play.*

- *As men and women age, two things happen that are a real plus: they need each other more, which makes the sex more personal and human. The second is that sex becomes more of a team sport. Sex is more a genuine experience where you enjoy each other and really value sensual, playful erotic, and intercourse experiences.*

- *Desire and satisfaction are the core of sexuality.*

- *Non-demand pleasuring can be a way to connect physically, a means to share pleasure and/or a bridge to sexual desire.*

- *The functions of marital sexuality are to create shared pleasure, to reinforce and deepen intimacy, and to use as a tension-reducer to deal with the stresses of life and marriage.*

- *No-sex and low-sex marriages become devitalized, especially when this occurs in the early years of marriage. Unless something is done to reverse this process, divorce is a likely outcome.*

- *The longer the couple avoids sexual contact, the harder it is to break the cycle. Avoidance becomes a self-fulfilling trap.*

- *Personal turn-ons (fantasies, erotic scenarios, being playful or spontaneous) and external turn-ons (X-rated videos, candles, sex toys, being sexual outside the bedroom) facilitate sexual anticipation and can increase desire.*

Books and Media

Barry McCarthy has authored over 85 professional articles, 20 book chapters, and 12 books for the general public including:

- *Discovering Your Couple Sexual Style*
- *Rekindling Desire: A Step by Step Program to Help No-Sex and Low-Sex Marriages* (with Emily McCarthy)
- *Coping with Erectile Dysfunction: How to Regain Confidence and Enjoy Great Sex*
- *Getting It Right the First Time: Creating a Healthy Marriage*
- *Getting it Right This Time: How to Create a Loving and Lasting Marriage*
- *Men's Sexual Health: Fitness for Satisfying Sex*
- *Male Sexual Awareness*

How to Find Out More

- To find out more about Dr. McCarthy's writings, go to *www.routledgementalhealth.com/Barry-McCarthy*

42. Dr. John Welwood

"Integrating Western psychology and Eastern spiritual wisdom."

Background and Qualifications

Dr. John Welwood is a psychotherapist, teacher, and author with more than 30 years experience of couple's therapy.

Dr. Welwood studied philosophy at Bowdoin College, spent two years at Sorbonne in Paris studying existentialist thought, and was awarded his PhD in clinical psychology at the University of Chicago in 1974. He is a former director of the East-West Psychology program at The California Institute of Integral Studies in San Francisco, and is now Associate Editor of the Journal of Transpersonal Psychology.

Dr. Welwood has been married twice and has one stepson. It was after the breakdown of his first marriage, that he was inspired to write his first book, *Journey of the Heart.* He couldn't understand, "How we could love each other so much and still have the whole thing blow up?" His book was an attempt to discover what relationships are all about, and what serves as the basis for an enduring and enriching relationship. It took 10 years to finish the book, and by the time it was in print, he was already married to his second wife, Jennifer.

Welwood now dedicates his time to teaching psychotherapists how to employ psychology within a spiritual framework as well as running workshops for couples alongside his wife Jennifer.

Relationship Philosophy

Dr. Welwood's relationship philosophy centers around a psycho-spiritual approach, with particular focus on love as a living process. Relationships need to be conscious and changing. Relationships inevitably take the couple on a transformative

path that brings up emotional conflict from the past and challenges about the future. Being present to our relationship is the key, as well as learning from its teachings of who we are and how to be a human being.

According to Dr. Welwood, deep relationships often bring up in us issues that we prefer to avoid. That is really a blessing. The test is whether we can work *with* the issues, as they arise. In this way, personal love is a call to awaken to our deepest nature.

Typically, people react in defensive ways, and are therefore incapable of real intimacy. Genuine intimacy is only possible when people connect being-to-being.

Many people say they want unconditional love. This openness of the heart is tender, responsive, and eager to reach out. It is a basic openness to reality. Our heart's desire to circulate love – warmth and compassion – without putting limits or conditions, alters our perception of the world.

Yet, we live in the earthly realm, with conditioned likes and dislikes, needs, wants, and desires. When we meet someone who fits our ideal, we feel attraction. This is conditional love, and can fade when the other person no longer continues to meet our needs and fulfill our desires.

The real mystery of love is when we overcome the moments of disillusion, and face the rawness of our broken-open hearts. You may glimpse the truth that you cannot avoid pain, so you develop an invincible tenderness and compassion. The obstacles to love can help you realize your capacity to love by helping your heart stretch to encompass and embrace all that you are.

John points out that love between partners can provide a powerful glimpse of the sacred vision. Perhaps the trap has been that we turn to intimate relationships to fill our hunger for the sacred, to fill the vacuum we feel inside. If we inflate romance and regard it as salvation, we are set up for despair and emptiness as we inevitably wake up from the delusion.

The Therapy

Dr. Welwood presents a new vision of relationships, enabling us to understand and use challenges as opportunities for personal transformation. As part of having a conscious relationship, he focuses on the importance of feeling and being aware of emotions. If your partner hurts you, it's important to let yourself feel that hurt in order to be able to cleanse – to connect with the heart and the moment.

The best intimate moments between a couple are those when each person is simply present; being themselves, without having to do anything or prove anything to the other. Learning to be vulnerable with each other, a process that Welwood describes as "rawness," is about letting go of control, showing who you really are, not only to your partner, but also to yourself.

This takes the skill of staying present in one's body and staying connected with oneself first. Being able to consciously inhabit the "wisdom body" – your bodily felt experience, your sensitivity, and your depth gives you the capacity to relate freshly to experience – just as it is.

Meeting your experience fully, and holding it in compassionate awareness is incredibly healing. By tracking your sensations and felt experience, you can unhook from stories, beliefs and judgments. This process helps you relate to the energy of an emotion, without the added fuel of limiting beliefs that make strong emotions seem overwhelming and consuming.

This practice is best done when you have several uninterrupted minutes when you can focus on yourself, allowing whatever arises to be okay and allowing yourself to feel whatever is there, without judgment, blame, of remorse.

Unconditional Presence Practice

1) Choose some experience that is causing you difficulty.

2) **Turn towards** the experience and explore how it affects you,

3) **Acknowledge the feeling**, pay attention to the sensations. Name the emotion, and say hello to it.

4) **Allow the sensations**. Let them be there without reactivity or judgment that it shouldn't be there. If this is not yet possible, allow the resistance to the emotion to be there.

5) **Admit the emotion**. Open your heart to the sensations. Find the part of you that authentically feels that emotion. Realize that "it makes sense" to feel that way.

6) **Enter the emotion**. Actually walk into it and feel all the energy of the emotion. Become one with the sensations as you dissolve into it. Explore and awaken to the direct and immediate experience, from within the emotion.

7) Notice if anything new becomes available to you, such as relief, peace, openness, tenderness, or strength. If so, acknowledge that new feeling, and open to it. Feel it fully and pay attention to how this feels in your body. Drink it up and see if you can be nourished by it.

Working with the Fourfold Truth

When a couple is caught is deadlock, one way to work with is to reveal how each side contains particular truths as well as particular distortions. When working with a couple over difficulty with sexuality, Dr. Welwood begins by asking Karen to say what's true for her. She responds that she would like to be able to respond to her husband in a passionate, erotic way when he is interested in sex, but she cant. She often feels like a failure. Looking deeper, her truth is that she actually wants compassion, love, romance, and tenderness.

David wants there to be more freedom in the way he is sexual. It seems to him that she puts demands on him, and that this is all her problem. As he looks deeper, he realizes that he doesn't want to have to summon up all those feelings. He wants to be free from having to please her. Owning this truth allows him to realize he never really knew his truth because he was so wrapped up in trying to please his mother.

As each partner hears the other's truth, they each relax. Karen's distortion is that she doesn't know how to ask for what she wants. She believes that she is too needy, and so she judges her desire, and that disconnects her from her body, and she feels even more needy. David's distortion is that it is hard to respond to desire for intimacy when he feels that he has to please her, and he doesn't know how.

Prior to this exploration, each person's truth was hidden, and each person's distortion would trigger the other's distortion. When truth and distortion come up together, and are seen and acknowledged, we get a chance to really know our partner. Defensiveness softens, and connection arises. Each person becomes more present and real, both with themselves, and with each other.

Examples
The Clouds Metaphor

In order to help relay his relationship philosophy, Dr. Welwood uses the metaphor of clouds to describe a personality that has been conditioned through the accumulation of fears, hurt, defense mechanisms, and complaints. These clouds end up hiding or partially covering the sun, which represents the presence of love in our lives.

In the beginning of relationships, the sun is fully out for both partners as they either fail to notice their new partner's flaws and imperfections or they don't give the flaws any importance. However, as the relationship progresses, the clouds of each individual's personal issues get in the way. In addition, old wounds from the past are projected onto the new relationship, causing clouds to block out the sun. Therefore, it is important to

identify one's clouds, that is, the emotional issues that shut our heart and block our soul from fully shining. It is probably a good thing to understand the other person's clouds as well.

Eros and Psyche

A story that brings Dr. Welwood's therapy to life is the story of Eros, the god of love and Psyche, who represents consciousness. He uses this as a metaphor to explain the power of conscious relationships.

In the story, Eros tells Psyche he will come to her in the middle of the night, when they can be lovers; then he'll leave before dawn. As long as she never sees his face, everything will be fine. For a while that arrangement works, but Psyche inevitably becomes curious about who her lover is. One night she secretly lights a candle to see his face, and he immediately disappears. She eventually manages to win him back, but only after going through many difficult and emotionally painful challenges, after which they can enjoy their love in the light of day.

Dr. Welwood compares this story to relationships and explains that so many people experience "love in the dark." However, with consciousness, we can discover what the relationship is truly about, which requires hard work and can be extremely challenging. A conscious relationship puts any human to the test and ensures they become clear about what they are doing in that relationship and what is required of them. It's about learning how to be oneself; how to simply "be."

The Power of Truth-Telling

Every couple knows the feeling of being in an unproductive, repetitive argument, going around and around without resolution. It is possible for this to turn into a sacred combat, which penetrates the pretense, and each person becomes more authentically present. The way to do this is to address the real issue – not the present argument. The real issue is how this argument touches an old sensitivity, and leaves one feeling vulnerable, uncertain, isolated and afraid.

To cut through an argument, the couples need to talk about their raw edges – what is really happening inside, behind the façade. Typically, there is some sort of underlying fear. Revealing this takes trust, and the ability to listen to the other without blame or fault, so both partners can be present with one another in the pain of the conflict. Moments of genuine connection are possible, with immediacy and self-revelation, being totally exposed, totally present with oneself and with the other, and feeling held in love and compassion.

Partners soften hearing what is really going on for the other. Often, partners realize they are both in a similar situation, having similar feelings, fears, wants, and needs. Remaining, and staying present in this feeling space is open and infinite, and a profound feeling of love may envelop the two of you.

Dr. John Welwood Quotes

- *Love is the recognition of beauty.*

- *If there is one thing I've learned in 30 years as a psychotherapist it is this – if you can let your experience happen, it will release its knots and unfold, leading to a deeper, more grounded experience of yourself. No matter how painful or scary your feelings are, your willingness to engage draws forth your emotional strength, leading in a more life positive direction.*

- *If we are to cultivate a new spirit of engagement in our intimate relationships, we need to recognize and welcome the powerful opportunity that intimate relationships provide – to awaken to our true nature.*

- *The more two people open to each other, the more this wide-openness also brings to the surface all the obstacles to it: their deepest, darkest wounds, their desperation and mistrust, and their rawest emotional trigger points. Just as the sun's warmth causes clouds to arise by prompting the*

earth to release its moisture, so love's pure openness activates the thick clouds of our emotional wounding, the tight places where we are shut down, where we live in fear and resist love.

- *When we connect deeply with another person, our heart naturally opens towards a whole new world of possibilities.*

- *This is how love ripens us... by warming us from within, inspiring us to break out of our shell, and lighting our way through the dark passage to new birth.*

- *A soul connection is a resonance between two people who respond to the essential beauty of each other's individual natures, behind their facades. It is a sacred alliance whose purpose is to help both partners discover and realize their deepest potentials. A soul connection opens up a further dimension - seeing and loving them for who they could be, and for who we could become.*

- *A soul connection not only inspires us to expand, but also forces us to confront whatever stands in the way of that expansion.*

- *The words "I love you," spoken in moments of genuine appreciation, wonder, or caring arise from something perfectly pure within us - the capacity to open ourselves and say yes without reserve. Such moments of pure openheartedness bring us as close to natural perfection as we can come in this life.*

- *Not knowing that we can be loved for who we truly are prevents us from trusting in love itself, and this in turn causes us to turn away from life and doubt its benevolence.*

Books and Media

- Dr. Welwood has written several books about relationships, *Journey of the Heart: the Path of Conscious Love* was a bestseller after its release in 1990.

📖 *Towards a Psychology of Awakening: Buddhism, Psychotherapy and the Path of Personal and Spiritual Transformation*

📖 *Love and Awakening: Discovering the Sacred Path of Intimate Relationship*

📖 *Perfect Love, Imperfect Relationships: Healing the Wound of the Heart*

📖 *Awakening the Heart: East/West Approaches to Psychotherapy and the Healing Heart*

📖 *Challenge of the Heart: Love, Sex, and Intimacy in Changing Times*

📖 *Ordinary Magic: Everyday Life as Spiritual Path*

📖 *The Meeting of the Ways: Explorations in East/West Psychology*

○ He has a series of audio works, including a 4-CD box set of a workshop based on his book, *Perfect Love,*

📼 *Sacred Fire,* a 2-audio cassette seminar on conscious relationships.

How to Find Out More

💻 For more information on Dr. John Welwood, go to his website *www.johnwelwood.com*

311

43. Dr. Steven Stosny

"Compassion is Power"

Background and Qualifications

Dr. Steven Stosny, PhD, the founder of CompassionPower, specializes in anger, resentment, and abusive relationships. He grew up in a violent and emotionally abusive home – his mother left his father 13 times before he turned 11. Stosny says he learned a great deal from his mother and her use of compassion as a tool for healing emotional injury and the resentment that surrounds it. His interest in emotional transformation and the healing power of compassion began in his childhood.

Dr. Stosny has treated over 4500 clients in various forms of anger, abuse, and violence since founding CompassionPower in 1988. He is a consultant in family violence for the Prince George's County Circuit and District Courts. He has also been an expert witness in criminal and civil trials.

Relationship Philosophy

Through research into human and animal behavior, Dr. Stosny has discovered that male and female responses to stress are distinct, even from birth. When a baby girl hears a sudden, loud noise, she looks for someone to make eye contact with. A baby boy will jolt into a fight or flight response. He is usually emotionally neutral but pumped with adrenaline. As girls get older, they frequently want to talk about emotional topics, while boys and men tend to pull away to avoid the shame of failure.

Dr. Stosny also looks at the science behind the stress response and the behavior in men and women. When a man feels shame, his body is flooded with cortisol, a stress hormone. This causes an instant rush and then a crash of energy. Women get a similar cortisol release when a husband shouts, ignores her, or does something that scares her. The after-effects can last for hours in men, but in women in can last for days.

It was these research findings that lead Dr. Stosny to co-write the book *How to Improve Your Marriage Without Talking About It: Finding Love beyond Words,* with Dr. Pat Love. In the book, he explains that a man is likely to become critical, defensive, aggressive, or shut down, if he feels like a failure as a provider, protector, or lover. A woman is apt to become critical, defensive, or aggressive, if she fears harm, isolation, or deprivation. Fear and isolation are the greatest dread of most women, while the shame of failure and loss of status is the greatest dread of most men.

Dr. Stosny believes that one of biggest destroyers of health and happiness is to live with a resentful, angry, or abusive partner. One of the biggest destroyers of the soul is to become resentful, angry, or abusive. Becoming identified as a victim destroys personal power and a solid sense of self. His book, *You Don't Have to Take It Anymore,* helps people overcome abusiveness and the victim identity.

The Therapy

Dr. Stosny has separate approaches to treatment for abusive and non-abusive relationships. For non-abusive relationships, he emphasizes removing barriers to emotional connection. For abusive relationships, he stresses creating a safe environment, so that both parties can decide whether they want to undertake the hard work of repairing the damage of abuse.

In both approaches, compassion is the key to change. Compassion sensitizes angry and abusive men to the vulnerability of their partners, and helps them understand that

their partner is a separate person, with a different temperament, vulnerabilities, and values. They learn to see their partner as they truly are and learn to feel protective without trying to control. Compassion facilitates emotional transformation from a focus on injury – with its inherent revenge motives – to a focus on healing and improving.

Compassion can set victims of abuse free, whereas resentment, anger, guilt, and shame, keep them enchained to their abusers. Through a wiser compassion that rises from her deepest values, an abused woman can see that the abuser violates his own deepest values with the abuse. It is self-destructive to him as well as harmful to her and to their children. If he will not heal himself by replacing his dominance and entitlement with compassion and support, the most compassionate thing for her to do is leave.

In fact, Dr. Stosny believes that compassion is far more important than love; a relationship can survive with low love and high compassion, but not the other way around. A key way to bring more compassion into a relationship is through binocular vision, which is making a conscious effort to see the other person's point of view and to see yourself through your partner's eyes. If you can't see your partner's perspective – and you cannot when angry or resentful – you lose the connection between the two of you.

Dr. Stosny has many emotional regulation and core value techniques to transform abusers. One of his many techniques to enhance connection in relationships that are no longer abusive is the Power Love Formula, which incorporates small moments of connection into daily routine. It takes less than 5 minutes every day and involves four basic steps:

Power Love Formula

- ♥ Acknowledge your partner's importance to you at four key stages in the day – waking up, leaving the house, coming home, and before you sleep.
- ♥ Hug at least six times per day for at least six seconds each.
- ♥ Entertain at least three positive thoughts about your partner when you're not together.
- ♥ Implement your love contract daily by enacting some brief gesture, such as lighting a candle for her, leaving a love note, sending a love text, or leaving a flower petal on her breakfast plate.

Examples

The Mirror of Love

Dr. Stosny points out that we are affected much more by the behavior of a loved one. If your boss reads the paper while you talk to him, you might be a bit annoyed, but if your husband reads the paper while to try to talk to him; watch out! You are likely to conclude that you are unlovable or inadequate, and that your husband is rejecting you. Stosny says that intimate relationships have enormous power to affect because they serve as a mirror of the inner self. We tend to decide how valuable and lovable we are by how the people we love interact with us.

The instinct to believe what others think about us starts in early childhood. Children inevitably blame themselves for their parent's bad moods and anger, concluding that they are inadequate. Although this instinct lessens as we grow older, we still draw conclusion about who we are from the people closest to us. That is why criticisms and put-downs, even if you don't consciously believe them, will have a huge unconscious impact. The mirror of love depletes energy when it doesn't reflect our value, but it can generate energy when it does.

Blame vs. Responsibility

Dr. Stosny helps people realize that the road to power begins with responsibility. He points out that one can't find a good solution to a problem while one is blaming. He gives an example of having someone hit his car while it is legally parked on the street. A natural reaction might be to get angry and blame the hit-and-run driver. As long as he is coming from blame, he will feel anxiety and helplessness, and nothing gets done. However, as soon as he assumes responsibility, he empowers himself to find solutions: find other transportation and get the car fixed. A jolt of self-esteem comes from acting responsibly, rather than a blast of shame and anger. He can take pleasure in his resourcefulness.

Dr. Steven Stosny Quotes

- *Love without compassion is possessive, controlling, and dangerous.*
- *Talking about feelings soothes most women but makes most men physically uncomfortable.*
- *A man's greatest suffering comes from the shame he feels when he doesn't measure up – which is why discussing relationship problems offers about as much comfort as sleeping on a bed of nails!*
- *When couples feel connected, men want to talk more and women need to talk less, so they meet somewhere in the middle.*
- *We need to stop trying to facilitate bonding verbally and instead let words come out of the bonding.*
- *If you want to love big, you have to think small.*

Books and Media

- Dr. Stosny has co-authored two books with Dr. Patricia Love: *How to Improve Your Marriage Without Talking*

316

About It: Finding Love beyond Words and Why Women Talk and Men Walk

📖 *Manual of the Core Value Workshop*

📖 His most recent book is *Love Without Hurt: Turn Your Resentful, Angry, or Emotionally Abusive Relationship into a Compassionate, Loving One*

❑ Dr. Stosny has made several guest appearances on *Oprah*, as well as other TV appearances and interviews in *The New York Times, Wall Street Journal, USA Today,* and *Washington Post*

How to Find Out More

🖥 For more information and links, go to the website: *www.compassionpower.com*

44. Ellen Kreidman

"If you don't have a loving affair with your mate, someone else will!"

Background and Qualifications

Married for 42 years with three children and five grandchildren, Ellen Kreidman says she lives and breathes what she teaches in her own wonderful marriage. She claims to offer a faster and more efficient alternative to traditional marriage counseling that can change the way you feel about your partner forever.

For the past 23 years, she has helped men and women put the fun, romance, communication, and excitement back into their relationship and create a long-lasting marriage.

Relationship Philosophy

Kreidman's motto is, that a man falls in love because of the way he feels when he is with that woman, and the same goes for a woman. Both have the right to feel that way their whole life. Therefore, a person should inquire how their mate feels when they are with them. Do they feel so good they would never even dream of being with someone else? It's all about how they feel when they are in their partner's presence. Each partner can find out what the *other* person needs, not just his or her *own* needs. If you discover how to make you mate feel important, special, attractive, sexy, intelligent, funny, wanted, and needed as often as possible, you will be amazed at what may befall you.

Kreidman is tired of hearing couples postpone their happiness until their kids are grown up or when they've got more time. Instead of saying, "When we're retired we'll work on us," they should be working on their relationship now, otherwise it could be too late! Someday may never come – all we really have is today and now. The most common problems that materialize in a relationship are demonstrated by a lack of the three T's:

The Three T's

1) Touching
2) Talking
3) Time

Talking is vital for a relationship, but often communication can go wrong because men and women talk and experience things in different ways. For example, to a man, sex is the most meaningful demonstration of love; whereas for a woman, she needs to feel emotionally fulfilled to respond to him sexually.

Kreidman believes it's never too early to start working on a relationship because love is not enough. Couples need solid help to show them how to either improve their relationship or to keep what they have now and future-proof their love for many years to come. A relationship not being filled with love is the prime reason why men and women go looking for it elsewhere.

The Therapy

Ellen Kreidman claims she can offer a technique that is so much faster and more effective than marriage counseling, and that can help couples to change their feelings, even if they've already heard the words, "I'm not in love with you anymore." If a couple were in love in the beginning of their relationship, then she believes they can feel like that again, no matter how disconnected they are now.

Her *"Light Your Fire"* program can be carried out as a couple or alone. Those that choose to start alone will still see positive results in their relationship because over time their partner will start to respond to the "new you" in a different way.

The Magical Formula for Passion, Pleasure and Playfulness

- ♥ The 10 second kiss
- ♥ The 5 second compliment
- ♥ The 30 minute talk
- ♥ The 26 second hug
- ♥ The 60 minute seduction
- ♥ The 2 hour fantasy
- ♥ The 3 minute quickie
- ♥ The 2 minute belly laugh
- ♥ The 24 hour day

An affair doesn't necessarily mean the end of a relationship, according to Kreidman. It is a chance to ask oneself, "What made my spouse want to connect with another person?" It is possible to use the pain of infidelity to make a marriage even better than before. A man doesn't fall in love with his mistress; he is in love with how he feels about himself when he is with that other woman. What she teaches through her program is how to make a partner feel so loved and needed all the time that they never go looking for it elsewhere.

Examples

Is this all There is to Life?

Dr. Kreidman became interested in relationship therapy and began to truly understand the nature of creating great relationships when her life changed completely. Her husband used to be "filthy rich" – they had a live-in maid, money was no object, and they travelled to Europe three or four times a year. Then he lost it all; just as Dr. Kreidman found out she was pregnant with their third son. To add to the stress, her father in-law died and her mother in-law came to live with them. "I cried for nine solid months – I sat in a corner feeling very sorry for myself. I was a victim. I asked, 'How did my life get to this?'"

Two months after her son was born, her husband was still out of work, and she was on her way home from the supermarket with her son in the back seat. Tears were rolling down her face and she was saying to herself, "Is this all there is to life? Will you just tell me, is this it?"

It was at this moment that she came to a self-realization – "Yes Ellen, this is all there is! For things to change, you have to change!" Over time, she has rephrased this statement as, "If this is to be, it's 'cos of me!"

Dr. Kreidman explains that you have to take responsibility for your life instead of blaming everything outside of yourself for what's happening to you. This has become the basis for her *"Light Your Fire"* program – looking inside yourself and asking, "What in me has caused my relationship to suffer?"

My Marriage was Crumbling

Kreidman has published various success stories on her website. This one is from Pamela Deputy, who tells of how her marriage was crumbling before her eyes. Her husband had shut down; he refused to talk about his emotional pain, until eventually he asked for a divorce. They stayed living together with their five-year-old son while he got everything in order. Meanwhile, Pamela began listening to Dr. Kreidman's tape series.

Pamela realized she had to put her self-pity aside, look at her own behavior, and make small improvements every day. She realized she could no longer play the victim. Gradually, over time, Pamela's husband began to open up, coming home for dinner earlier every evening, but still saying he wanted a

divorce. He complained, saying, "You are not making this easy for me!" That was the whole point, and over time he began to fall in love again with Pamela as she paid him compliments, became the sweet wife he first fell in love with, and changed her attitude. Within four months he decided he wanted to stay forever. Pamela says in her letter, "I can tell you that these tapes saved a marriage, my sanity, and us from having to tell a 5 year old that the Daddy she adored was leaving."

Ellen Kreidman Quotes

- *If you don't have a loving affair with your mate, someone else will!*
- *The meaning of life is to love somebody with all your heart and soul, and to have them love you.*
- *If this is to be, it's 'cos of me!*
- *It's exhausting to be in a bad relationship!*
- *Your marriage is the most precious gift you have. It deserves to be treated and protected in every way possible.*
- *Become your mate's biggest fan and you'll affair-proof your marriage, not for those brief youthful years, but for a lifetime.*
- *Physical pain alerts you to a problem in your body that needs attention. Emotional pain does the same thing. It tells you that there is a lesson that you need to learn so you can grow stronger.*

Books and Media

- ❑ Ellen Kreidman has been featured in countless articles, including *USA Today*, *New York Times*, *People*, *Family Circle*, and *Cosmopolitan*.
- ❑ She has also appeared on many TV programs, including *Oprah*, *The TODAY Show*, and *The View*.

Her books include:

- 📖 *Light His Fire* (New York Times best-seller)
- 📖 *Light Her Fire* (New York Times best-seller)
- 📖 *Is There Sex After Kids?*
- 📖 *The Ten Second Kiss*
- 📖 *Single No More – How and Where to Meet Your Perfect Mate*
- 📖 *Is There Sex After Kids?*

How to Find Out More

- 💻 Go to Ellen Kreidman's website: *www.lightyourfire.com*

45. Dr. Janis Abrahms Spring

"Infidelity can be a relationship wake up call."

Background and Qualifications

Dr. Janis Abrahms Spring, Ph.D., ABPP, is a nationally acclaimed expert on issues of trust, intimacy, and forgiveness. She received her B.A. from Brandeis University, her Ph.D. in clinical psychology from the University of Connecticut, and her post-graduate training from Aaron Beck, MD, at the Center for Cognitive Therapy at the University of Pennsylvania. Her books, *After the Affair* and *How Can I Forgive You?* were finalists in 3 categories of a Books for a Better Life Award – best first book, best relationship book, best psychology book, and she was the recipient of the Connecticut Psychological Association's Award for Distinguished Contribution to the Practice of Psychology. In private practice for more than 3 decades, she lives with her husband in Westport, CT, and has four sons.

Relationship Philosophy

Though infidelity is often the deathblow to a relationship, it can also be a wake-up call – challenging couples to confront the issues that led to the affair and to build a healthier, more intimate relationship than before. As a clinical psychologist who has been treating distressed couples for more than 30 years, Dr. Janis Abrahms Spring has found that couples can survive infidelity, provided that both partners are willing to look honestly at themselves and at each other, and acquire the skills they need to help themselves through such a shattering crisis. Her therapy is designed for those going through the pain, confusion, and anger of infidelity by helping them cope with their raging emotions, make a thoughtful decision about their future, and, if they choose to recommit, reclaim a life with their partner.

The Therapy

To move beyond the affair and grow, partners must address crucial questions, including the following:

Crucial Questions After an Affair

- ♥ Why did the affair happen?
- ♥ Once love and trust are gone, can they ever be rekindled?
- ♥ How can I – or should I – recommit when I feel so ambivalent?
- ♥ How do we get the lover out from between the two of us and become sexually intimate again?
- ♥ Is forgiveness possible? Is it healthy?

Those willing to do the work necessary to make sense out of the affair have a chance of creating a relationship that was stronger than ever before.

How to Forgive

In her book, *How Can I Forgive You?,* Dr. Spring addresses several critical questions:

- ♥ Is forgiveness good for us?
- ♥ How do we forgive someone who shows no remorse?
- ♥ How do we heal ourselves?
- ♥ How can we overcome our obsessive preoccupation with the offender and get on with our lives?
- ♥ Why should forgiveness be the job of the hurt party alone?
- ♥ Shouldn't the offender be asked to make good?
- ♥ When is forgiveness cheap? When is it genuine?
- ♥ What makes for a meaningful apology?
- ♥ Why is it so hard to apologize?
- ♥ Why is it so hard to forgive?
- ♥ Are some injuries simply unforgivable?

According to Dr. Spring, forgiveness is not the job of the hurt party alone. It is a transaction that takes place between the two people held together by the interpersonal violation. It must be earned. The offender (the unfaithful partner) must be willing to perform bold, humble, heartfelt acts of repair such as delivering a meaningful apology, taking responsibility for the harm caused, understanding why the affair happened, and working to make the relationship less vulnerable to further betrayals.

As the unfaithful partner makes meaningful repairs, the hurt party participates in the forgiveness process. The hurt party works to release their obsessive preoccupation with the injury and to create opportunities for the offender to make good. They also accept a fair share of responsibility for what went wrong in the relationship, learn to talk about the offense without alienating or demeaning the offender, and decide what kind of relationship with the offender serves their best interest.

4 Approaches to Forgiveness

1) **Cheap Forgiveness** – an inauthentic act of peacekeeping that resolves nothing.

2) **Refusing to Forgive** – a rigid response that keeps one entombed in hate.

3) **Acceptance** – a healing gift that asks nothing of the offender.

4) **Genuine Forgiveness** – a healing transaction and intimate dance that frees us from the corrosive effects of hate, and helps us make peace with the person who hurt us, and with ourselves.

If the offender isn't remorseful, the hurt party is not required to forgive, but they are required to heal themselves. Refusing to forgive – stewing in hostile juices – is not a healthy alternative; neither is Cheap Forgiveness. In her book, *How Can I Forgive You?*, Spring spells out a radical, ten-step process for healing the self, called Acceptance.

10 Steps of Acceptance

1) Honor the full sweep of your emotions
2) Give up the need for revenge
3) Stop obsessing about the injury
4) Protect yourself from further abuse
5) Frame the betrayal in terms of the others personal struggle
6) Look honestly at your own contribution to the injury
7) Challenge false assumptions about what happened
8) Weigh the good against the bad in the offender
9) Carefully decide what is best for you
10) Forgive yourself for your own failings

This alternative to Genuine Forgiveness is particularly relevant in cases of abuse, betrayal, or neglect, when the offender isn't able or willing to earn forgiveness. This is a generous, healing gift you give yourself. All it takes is you, and it asks nothing of the offender. This process honors the full force of the violation, ensures your own physical and emotional safety, and allows you to restore your own integrity and sense of self.

Examples
Does an Affair mean the End to a Marriage?

In an interview with the *New York Times*, Dr. Spring reveals that people often ask her, "What's your success rate?" in helping repair a marriage after an affair. Her response is that she doesn't base success on whether people stay together, but whether people make a thoughtful, self-interested decision about staying together. In some cases, there's no point to reconciling if a partner continues to be unfaithful or untrustworthy. "Trust and forgiveness are not cheap gifts."

Dr. Spring is also asked whether the unfaithful partner should confess to an affair or not. She believes there is no clear answer; some marriages are destroyed by the confession, while

others are deconstructed, rebuilt on firmer foundations, and made to last.

Janis warns, however, against one of the biggest dangers of not revealing the affair: the unfaithful partner gives up the affair person, returns to the marriage, but the couple never confronts the underlying problems in their relationship. They may stay together, but they never get close or resolve their conflicts as individuals or couples.

Two Types of Love

One of the classic mistakes people make when they have an affair is failing to distinguish between two types of love. In her book, *After the Affair*, Spring distinguishes romantic love from mature love. "Romantic love is an intense but unwarranted attachment to the lover that the unfaithful partner may feel." The unfaithful partner may think their love is real because, otherwise, they wouldn't be willing to sacrifice so much for this person. The blind spot, though, is that their so-called grand passion may have more to do with their unmet childhood needs and excitement than with who this other person really is.

What pumps romantic love is a chemical high; endorphins pour into the blood stream and lead the unfaithful partner to obsess over the lover. A perceptual distortion also takes place: the lover is idealized and seen as perfect; the marriage partner is trashed and seen as unlovable. Romantic love sends the message that the lover is their soul mate and that this relationship was made in heaven. But, in all love relationships, passion and romantic love fade, as the natural cycle of love takes over. Spring makes the point that to have a successful, intimate relationship, it will take work.

Dr. Janis Abrahms Spring Quotes

- *We enter intimate relationships blindly, often effortlessly, swept up with passion and an idealized perception of our partner, often cocky about our ability to keep things hot.*

- *Most of us are totally unprepared for what lies ahead and ignorant of what's required to last the course... the affair shocks us into reality. Fortunately, it also invites us to love again.*

- *Healing, like love, flourishes in the context of a healthy relationship. I would go so far as to say that we can't love alone, and we can't forgive alone.*

Books and Media

- *After the Affair: Healing the Pain and Rebuilding Trust When a Partner Has Been Unfaithful (With Michael Spring)*
- *How Can I Forgive You? The Courage to Forgive, The Freedom Not To*
- *Life with Pop: Lessons on Caring for an Aging Parent*

How to Find Out More

- For more information, go to Dr. Spring's website: *www.janisaspring.com*

329

46. Dr. Howard Markman

"An education in marriage"

Background and Qualifications

Howard J. Markman, Ph.D. is a professor of psychology, and for close to 30 years, has been the Director of the Center for Marital and Family Studies at the University of Denver.

He is the leading researcher in the prediction and prevention of marital distress, and based on his research, developed PREP (**P**reventative **R**elationship **E**nhancement **P**rogram), with Dr. Scott Stanley. PREP is used throughout the world, helping couples to create lasting and healthy marriages, and offering skills and techniques before problems start to arise. His books include the bestseller *Fighting for Your Marriage* and *12 Hours to a Great Marriage*. He offers couples retreats, and has appeared on *Oprah*, *The TODAY Show,* and *20/20.*

Relationship Philosophy

Dr. Markman and PREP inc., believe that most couples wait far too long to work on their relationship. Often, they've never been taught the skills required to have a healthy marriage that lasts a lifetime, and PREP offers them an education before problems arise, or for when they've reached a transition point, such as planning a first child, or when problems have started to bubble in the relationship.

Dr. Markman has conducted decades of research at the University of Denver and is funded by the National Institute of Mental Health. It is this research that forms the basis of PREP. Real couples are observed over many years and compared to couples who did not take part in PREP education. Through this work, Markman and his research team have been able to isolate risk factors that can make a real difference in whether a marriage will be happy or not. The PREP method is also being constantly refined and improved, as research is used to continually test the effectiveness of the PREP method. The research also shows that PREP couples have a lower rate of pre-marital break up and post-marital divorce.

The PREP method is based on the fact that success in a relationship is just as much about the things you DON'T do as the things you DO. Results have shown that the main ways couples can improve their odds of having a successful relationship is to eliminate negative styles of talking and fighting so they can handle disagreements as a team. They have to learn to avoid put-downs and the "silent treatment," overcome unrealistic beliefs about marriage, and to compromise when they have conflicting attitudes about important issues, particularly money worries.

Communication Danger Signs
- ✓ Escalation
- ✓ Invalidation
- ✓ Withdrawal and Avoidance
- ✓ Negative Interpretations

The Therapy
Dr. Markman's PREP approach shows couples how to get to the heart of problems, avoiding standoffs and pushing each other away, and learning to connect as a couple. They have discovered that it's not the differences between people in a relationship that can create problems, but how they handle those differences. This fact forms the basic principle of their educational program.

PREP is a research-based skills-building program. It is a designated to help people say what they need to say and get to the heart of problems while staying connected. PREP strategies and skills are divided into two sections: first ways to lower the risk factors of a relationship breaking down, and secondly, ways

to increase the protective factors which can help a marriage succeed.

5 Keys to a Great Marriage

- ♥ **Decide, don't slide** – Rather than slide through major transitions or life experiences, decide who you are and where you intend to go.

- ♥ **Do Your Part** – You have a lot of control over what you can do to help your relationship. Don't focus on your partner as the source of the problems. Do positive things for your partner. Decide to let negative comments bounce off you. Deal with ongoing concerns when both of you are calm and you can bring constructive attention.

- ♥ **Make it safe to connect** – The way you handle difference is more important that what those differences are

- ♥ **Open the doors to positive connection** – Conflict is inevitable, but doesn't have to rule your life. People want deep friendship, companionship, spiritual meaning, fun, passion, connection and the possibility of joint parenthood.

- ♥ **Nurture your commitment** – Build something meaningful and hold on to it for the long term. Commitment is knowing you can count on each other to be there, to support one another, and to help one another.

For example, most couples know their marriages are happier when they make time to have fun. But usually, it's the fun that tends to fall by the wayside first as everyday life takes over, demands and chores pile up, and work life becomes increasingly stressful. Yet, Dr. Markman and his research team have shown the vital importance of finding time to be together completely free from financial, family, or other stresses. It's not an indulgence to have fun together; it's a necessity. Although most couples know this, when finances are tight and life gets tough, all too often, fun is seen as an unnecessary luxury, but it could be what keeps a relationship together.

Communication is the lifeblood of a relationship; it removes the blockages that seem to arise, and keeps all the good feelings flowing. When talking about sensitive topics, such as loneliness, sensuality, sex, or money, the chance of escalation, defensiveness, and invalidation are high. It is important to bring a sense of emotional safety. When you feel safe enough to share something vulnerable, and your partner responds with love and acceptance, it builds a deep sense of intimacy. Dr. Markman has developed a structure to bring a sense of safety.

The Speaker-Listener Technique

♥ **The speaker has the floor** – Use a specific object to clearly indicate who is speaking.

♥ **Share the floor** – Switch roles after you have spoken

♥ **No problem solving** – This time is more about sharing what is important and your feelings. Trying to solve the problem tends to block listening as each person is thinking ahead and becoming positional.

Rules for the Speaker

♥ **Speak for yourself, don't mind read** – Talk only about your thoughts, feelings and concerns, not your perceptions of the other persons motives.

♥ **Keep it brief** – Don't go on and on. Pause to let your partner have time to digest

♥ **Stop and let the Listener paraphrase** – Stick to one thought so your partner can paraphrase what you just said. If they missed something, say, "Close, and" then gently restate what you meant to say.

Rules for the Listener

♥ **Paraphrase what you just heard** – This doesn't mean that you agree with what your partner just said. This is a way to let your partner feel that you have heard them. You will be

333

surprised how quickly a fight can de-escalate when an upset partner feels heard. Seek to understand how they feel. Ask for clarification only if you truly don't understand.

♥ **Don't rebut** – Stay focused on your partner's message. Do not offer your thoughts, or opinions to help them solve their problem. Just pay attention to what your partner is saying.

One of the most powerful parts of this technique is separating the problem discussion from the problem solution. Couples tend to get quite anxious when one person is upset with the other. Usual strategies to avoid this anxiety are to quickly convince the other it is not a problem, or that it is actually the speaker's fault, or to fix it right away. That old set of strategies misses the possibility to truly connect. By focusing only on the problem discussion, you get to hear what it is like for your partner. Most likely, you will need a break, and then re-engage to talk about how what they said affected *you*. Once both people have been heard, and you have taken time to let it all settle in, you are ready to focus on solving the problem.

Ground Rules for a Great Relationship

♥ Have a weekly couple meeting to bring up any issue before it becomes stagnant and results in an overblown fight.

♥ Either person can bring up an issue at anytime. The Listener can say, "This is not a good time," and then must take responsibility for setting up a time to talk in the near future.

♥ Use the Speaker-Listener Technique whenever you anticipate having trouble communicating

♥ When conflict is escalating, either partner can call a "Time Out" and agree to talk again at a defined time, using the Speaker-Listener Technique.

♥ Completely separate the *Problem Discussion* from the *Problem Solution.*

♥ Make time for fun, friendship, support, and sensuality. Protect these sacred times from conflict.

Examples
That's Not What I Said

Bob and Mary both work and are exhausted at the end of each day. One day, Bob gets home early and has a great idea: we are both wiped; it would be great to eat out and relax. When Mary comes home, he asks cheerily, "What should we do for dinner?" She retorts, "Why is it always my job to make dinner? I work as hard as you do." Hearing her response as an attack, Bob fires back, "You don't always make dinner; I made dinner once last week!" "Bringing back hamburgers and fries is not making dinner, Bob," Mary snorts. "Just forget it," says Bob with mounting frustration, "I didn't want to go out with you anyway." "Hold on a minute," says Mary, somewhat calmer now, "You never said anything about wanting to go out." "Yes I did!" insists Bob, still feeling angry, "I asked you where you wanted to go out to dinner and you got really nasty." "What do you mean?" asks Mary. "You never said anything about going out."

Does this sound familiar? Bob had a great idea but did not set the context, nor was he clear enough about what he wanted. He left room for interpretation. This kind of misunderstanding happens all the time. Dr. Markman explains that we all hear communication through filters. What you intend to say is not exactly what you say, and is certainly not what your partner hears. These filters are based on our focus, style, life experiences, background, how we are feeling, what we think, our mood, beliefs and expectations, and even self-protection.

Money Problems

Research conducted by Dr. Markman and his team has also shown that money, sex, and children are the three biggest issues for couples, and the subject of money is the number one argument starter. This is because money issues are not just about money. Money symbolizes so much more – from how we live our life, how we work together with our loved ones, and what we deem to be important. It represents independence and security. Our upbringing, culture, and gender, influence how we approach money. So many decisions also revolve around money – from the groceries to the car, going out to the movies and vacations; decisions about our career, retirement savings, and buying a new house. It's no wonder two people are unlikely to agree on what to do with it!

For Ellen and Gregg, money is a serious issue. Ellen came home one day, setting the checkbook on the counter as she went to the bedroom to get more comfortable. Gregg became livid when he saw an entry for $150 made out to a department store. Ellen came back into the kitchen, looking for a nice welcome and warm hug. Instead, she was accosted by Gregg: "What did you spend $150 dollars on?" "None of your business," retorts Ellen, very defensively. "Of course it's my business," replies Gregg, "we decided on a budget and you've gone and blown it." Ellen blasts back, "If you'd have the guts to ask for a raise, we wouldn't be having problems with money."

Because money is such a hot issue for Ellen and Gregg, it didn't take much to set off a huge argument over money. Almost any small event concerning money would ignite negative emotions. Their argument, fueled by emotions and their negative patterns, could easily erupt into a wildfire. Dr. Markman teaches that regulating negative emotions is one of the most important skills anyone can learn.

Dr. Howard Markman Quotes

- *Invest in the relationship in ways that are meaningful to your partner and, no matter what, you should express your appreciation and initiate positive connection – fun, friendship, and romance.*

- *Protect fun and friendship from the need to deal with issues and conflicts.*

- *Talk about the issues when you decide to, not in the heat of the moment or when you are celebrating.*

- *The correlation between fun and marital happiness is high, and significant.*

- *Money is such an integral part of our lives that it is bound to be mixed up in the interactions between partners.*

- *Money issues have the potential to ruin or define a marriage like nothing else we know.*

- *The simple reality is that most of us are the least honoring of those we love the most.*

- *We know that it's possible for couples to create relationships in which they feel both emotionally secure in the present and confident about the future.*

Books and Media

Dr. Markman has been published extensively in professional journals, and regularly appears as an expert on marriage in the media. He has co-authored 12 books, including:

- *Fighting for Your Marriage: A Deluxe Revised Edition of the Classic Best-seller for Enhancing Marriage and Preventing Divorce*

- *We Can Work It Out: How to Solve Conflicts, Save Your Marriage, and Strengthen Your Love for Each Other*

- *Fighting for Your Marriage: Positive Steps for Preventing Divorce and Preserving a Lasting Love*

337

- *12 Hours to a Great Marriage: A Step-by-Step Guide for Making Love Last*

- *You Paid How Much For That!   How to Win at Money Without Losing at Love*

- *Becoming Parents: How to Strengthen Your Marriage as Your Family Grows*

* Dr. Markman has also developed a weekend couples retreat based on PREP, called *Love Your Relationship*.

o He co-produced the *Fighting for Your Marriage* video and audio tapes. PREP also has research-based programs for military couples, individuals, foster parents, and high school students, among other groups.

How to Find Out More

- For more information on Dr. Howard Markman, PREP, and the Love Your Relationship program, go to *www.prepinc.com* and *www.loveyourrelationship.com*

47. Drs. Charles & Elizabeth Schmitz

"Being in love is easy... it's an accumulation of the little things every day!"

Background and Qualifications

Known as The Marriage Doctors, the Schmitz have been married for over 40 years and have been helping couples build loving relationships for the past 25 years.

Dr. Charles Schmitz has taught in higher education for over 38 years in counseling psychology and leadership development. He achieved his PhD from the University of Missouri, Columbia, and is now Dean of the College of Education and Professor of Counseling and Family Therapy at the University of Missouri.
Dr. Elizabeth Schmitz has lectured in counseling and leadership since also receiving her doctorate from the University of Missouri.

The Schmitz decided to put their research experience into practice with couples and set up their company, Successful Marriage Reflections, with the goal to help reduce the divorce rate.

Relationship Philosophy

They believe that having a great marriage is simple; however, so many couples are incapable or unwilling to do the simple things that are required to make a marriage work. They believe there are 7 core values of all loving relationships:

7 Core Values of Loving Relationships

♥ The couple in love is committed to always putting each other first in their relationship with each other. They recognize the relationship is about US, not about you and me.

339

♥ The couple in love is committed to democracy in their relationship – creating an egalitarian, shared partnership.

♥ The couple in love is committed to ensuring their mutual happiness.

♥ The couple in love values absolute trustworthiness and integrity in their relationship with each other.

♥ The couple in love is committed to caring and unconditional love for each other.

♥ The couple in love is committed to being mutually respectful towards each other.

♥ The couple in love values their mutual sense of responsibility for each other.

The Therapy

The Schmitz believe the key to a loving relationship is to master these core values. Far too many people focus on complicated explanations for relationship success, but instead all it takes is commitment to small gestures of love, which accumulate over time, and really show your partner how much you love, value, and respect them. It's not about complicated therapy and explanations about your unhappiness; it's about simply doing the small things that matter everyday.

Examples of those small things include: remembering birthdays and anniversaries, saying thank you and please, telling your lover "I love you" each morning and evening, clearing the dinner table together, calling if you're going to be late, helping carry the groceries, being more unselfish, sending your lover an email, text or call at least once a day to say you're thinking of them, or giving your lover at least a dozen hugs per day.

Being in love doesn't make us immune from apologizing for bad behavior either. Over time, in a relationship, we become so comfortable with the one we love, that we may often say things that are hurtful in the heat of the moment. This doesn't mean we don't have to say sorry, otherwise, that hurt can turn into resentment. In fact, it is curious that we are more likely to be hurtful to the people we love the most. Just because we are engaged or married, we are not exempt from saying I'm sorry when we've hurt our partner's feelings or disappointed them. In fact, it's even more important to say sorry to the person you love the most.

Examples
Lasting love

Drs. Schmitz have interviewed many couples over the past 25 years about the secrets of everlasting love, but the story of Sandy and Pris is one of the greatest stories of love they have ever come across. They have been married nearly 60 years. "Before we interviewed them we thought we knew a lot about love and relationships. That evening, however, we got an education for which we will be eternally grateful."

In their article, the Schmitz explain that Sandy has loved Pris since the first time he saw her. During the interview he looks at the woman he married and exclaims, with tears in his eyes, "She is still the same beautiful woman I married 60 years ago." She chokes back her tears declaring her love for him. "We have been married for more than 60 years and are more in love now than ever."

The Schmitz believe there are great lessons to be learned from this beautiful relationship. First, they have created a "mutual admiration society," always supporting and encouraging each other. Second, they love each other very much and tell each other many times every day. Third, they are always totally honest with each other, showing integrity in the way they interact, and demonstrate their character by their words and actions. Finally, they never go to bed mad at each other.

341

How will I Know I am in Love?

Throughout their research and interviews, the Schmitz have discovered what they believe are the secrets of everlasting, true love. However, one of the questions most commonly asked, especially by young people, is: "How do I know if I am in love?" The doctors Schmitz believe the answer to this question comes with 7 criteria.

7 Criteria for Being In Love

- ♥ The physical element – the goose bumps, sweaty palms, tears when you say goodbye. These positive physical reactions come when people think about or actually see the one they love.

- ♥ Emotional – the uncontrollable smile, the feelings of longing for the person whenever they leave a room; emotions one wouldn't routinely feel for anyone else.

- ♥ Positive worry – it's natural to develop a feeling of concern for that person's well-being.

- ♥ "I cannot live without her" mentality, when you begin to think about the future and the reality sets in that you'd like that person to be part of your future.

- ♥ Oneness of the relationship – you begin to factor them in when you make decisions, no longer just thinking about yourself and your needs.

- ♥ Pre-occupied feelings – whereby you think about them most of the time and can't get them out of your mind.

- ♥ Love itself and the ability to express it – You tell them you love them, you miss them, and care about them, and would shout about it from the rooftops!

Of course, these are the feelings that affect you when you are caught up in love. Deep love comes with the commitment to stay in love even when these feelings are no longer there.

Drs. Charles and Elizabeth Schmitz Quotes

- *A marriage, like the Tango, works best if partners move with great synergy and togetherness, learning to be a unit of one.*

- *In our humble opinion, no two people who profess to love each other can ever take the position that they don't have to apologize to each other for saying and doing hurtful things.*

- *One of the most egregious of all sins you can commit in your relationship with the one you love... is taking them for granted.*

- *If you cannot trust the one you love, then it is not true love.*

- *Respectfulness is at the heart of all great loving relationships.*

- *People in love care for each other in ways that they have never cared for another human being. They feel a sense of responsibility for another person that they have never felt before. It feels so good to put another's needs above your own. To do so is to love deeply.*

Books and Media

- *Simple Things Matter: In Love And Marriage*

- Their book, *Golden Anniversaries: The Seven Secrets of Successful Marriage*, won the INDIE book awards Gold Medal for Best 2008 Relationship Book, 2009 Mom's Choice Awards Gold Medal for Most Outstanding Relationships and Marriage Book, and 2009 Nautilus Book Awards Medal Winner for Relationship Books.

How to Find Out More

- For more information, go to the Schmitz website: *www.goldenanniversaries.com*

48. Dr. Gilda Carle

"Give up on Prince Charming... or you'll end up with a frog!"

Background and Qualifications

Dr. Gilda Carle started her career as a teacher in New York City's South Bronx, before working with large corporations to improve interpersonal relations and communications. She then turned her experience from the organizational level to personal relationships and has been described by *The New York Times* as "the busiest TV therapist in the business."

Holding a PhD in Educational Leadership from New York University with a concentration in psychology, sociology, and social psychology, Dr. Carle is also Associate Professor of business, psychology, and communications at New York's Mercy College.

She now runs a private practice helping couples and singles, as well as instructing women and teens to achieve their full potential. She offers straight-talking, no nonsense advice. She is not afraid to call it like it is, having spent years teaching in crime-ridden schools.

Relationship Philosophy

Dr. Carle believes to succeed in love, a woman must sharpen her personal power, project it, and attract a partner who can respect and reflect it. Couples must play to each other's strengths in this way rather than attack each other's differences.

She also urges women to give up the "prince charming" myth of a man or they'll keep attracting frogs! In order to have the best relationship, Dr. Carle's advice is to work on who you are first, being the best you can be to attract the best lover. If you exude a happy life, others will naturally want to be a part of it. The key objective therefore is to find someone who can enhance the wonderful life you're already living, so the starting point must be personal life enhancement. If you bet on yourself rather than the prince, you'll allow yourself to shine and attract someone who shines with you.

The Therapy

Once in a relationship, Dr. Carle believes that communication is the key. You have to make your man feel safe enough to express his true feelings and fears. If he won't open up to you, it's because he doesn't feel protected enough. You have to offer him a safe haven without judgment or criticism as well as being honest, truthful, and forthright yourself.

Self-care is also important in relationships. A person has to learn how to communicate their boundaries, which can be tough, as it doesn't necessarily make them the most popular person on the block. Yet, boundaries make a person clear as to where they stand and also to let others know if they are crossing the line. However, when a relationship becomes the only important thing in a person's life, their boundaries change to keep their partner interested.

It's important that every person sets individual boundaries from the start of every relationship and sticks to them in order to set the standard for the kind of treatment they will permit. Self-preservation in this way ensures you are with someone who's willing to treat you with the respect you deserve.

Examples
Let go of Other People's Issues

In her eBook, *Relationship Fix,* Gilda Carle describes one of the most difficult challenges she has faced in her own adult life – learning to keep quiet and let go of other people's issues. "It still takes restraint for me to keep my big mouth shut when I observe someone I love sabotaging his or her life. Like so many women

and men, I always considered fixing someone's dysfunctions to be an act of love. But I was wrong."

Dr. Carle realized that this attempt to help someone is actually an attempt to control him or her according to her own agenda. Unsolicited advice and attempts to save someone does not help them; it does not allow them to follow their own life's path and allows us to avoid the much-needed work we need to do on ourselves!

"Letting go does not mean to stop caring about someone. It's recognizing that people must traverse through their dark tunnel alone, where they learn to process the ebbs and flows of their life, as complicated as it may be."

Projecting a Power Image

One of the steps to help avoid relationship derailment is to feel one's own power. Dr. Carle describes this process as projecting a Power Image.

Firstly, this involves recognizing the difference between inner and outer control. Think of yourself and how life is going, and name the force that drives you. Are you driven internally, by your own thought processes and motivation, or externally, by the people around you, through their praise or criticism? In my experience, most people describe themselves as being in control; it takes courage to look at how you let others run your life. Where are you craving praise? What are you willing to do in order to earn praise? How has criticism changed your beliefs and your direction? What have you given up because you have been criticized or didn't get the support you thought you needed?

Dr. Carle advises against external control, because people can change their minds and attitudes about you, whereas with internal control, you own it. It's important to take hold of your internal control through understanding that, "Praise and blame are both the same." It's important to make your life positive regardless of the mindset of others.

We also need to recognize that we create our own destiny: through the choices we have over our actions, mistakes, and future. It's important to use the expression, "I choose to," rather than "I have to," because only we have the power to control what we do or say. Then, you really need to own that it truly is your choice.

Once you have understood your inner personal power, you can then project a Power Image: one that reflects the strength of your body language, voice, and words. It projects the fact that you are in charge of your life and enables people to respectfully treat you in that way. Remember, you teach other people how to treat you.

Dr. Gilda Carle Quotes

- *You'll never be loved if you can't risk being disliked!*
- *Boundaries don't close people out; they contain you so you don't disperse your energies where they are unappreciated.*
- *We attract not who we want, but who we are!*
- *We declare our destiny... so either choose to be a victim and remain stuck in the past, or choose to use your power and live your passions now.*
- *If you don't expect your man to be a savior, you won't get angry when he's not!*
- *The art of receiving begins by giving to yourself.*
- *The hardest thing about what I do is hearing the sad stories of people who have given away their power – and are suffering deeply as a result.*

Books and Media

Dr. Carle has written 3 best-sellers:

- 📖 *Don't Bet on the Prince! How to Have the Man You Want by Betting on Yourself.* She describes this not just as a woman's self-help book, but a guide to finding out who you are, where you want to go, and how.

- 📖 *He's Not All That! How to Attract the Good Guys!*

- 📖 *How to Win at Love*

- 📖 Dr. Carle has also written several mini-mags offering advice for couples, singles, and teenagers. Titles include: *How to Win at Love; 10 Questions Women Should Never Ask & the 10 They Should; Women's 10 Big Worries & How to Beat 'Em; He Says, She Says: When Love Gets Lost in the Translation; Your Guide to a Perfect Relationship;* and *Teen Talk with Dr. Gilda: A Girl's Guide to Dating.*

- 📺 She has also hosted her own show as the Love Doctor on *MTV online*, as well as appearing on *Larry King, Oprah, Montel Williams, The View, Sally Jessy Raphael*, and Ricki Lake.

How to Find Out More

- 💻 For more information, go to Dr. Gilda Carle's website: *www.drgilda.com*

49. Olivia Mellan

"Moving towards Money Harmony."

Background and Qualifications

Since 1982, Olivia Mellan has been a groundbreaker in the field of money psychology, couples communication, stress management, and conflict resolution. She has over 25 years experience of helping couples and individuals understand their attitudes and change their behavior towards money. She also speaks all over the country to businesses, professional groups, and to the general public about financial matters.

Mellan has seen hundreds of people in her private practice and is also author of five books, all of which deal with relationships and money: *Money Harmony: Resolving Money Conflicts in Your Life and Relationships, Overcoming Overspending: A Winning Plan for Spenders and Their Partners, Money Shy to Money Sure: A Woman's Road Map to Financial Well-being, The Advisor's Guide to Money Psychology,* and *The Client Connection: Helping Advisors Build Bridges That Last.* Her audio-CD set, *The Secret Language of Money,* explores couples dynamics and gender differences around money. She is a trained psychotherapist and money coach, as well as being a self-confessed recovering overspender herself.

Relationship Philosophy

Money is an extremely emotionally loaded issue. It is tied up with our deepest emotional needs – for power, security, independence, control, self worth, and security. Some people feel guilty for having too much money. Others feel ashamed for not having enough. Some are afraid to deal with it for fear it may corrupt them in some way. Meanwhile, others worry constantly about it, which affects their quality of life and their relationships.

Although we behave differently toward money, it affects almost everyone in some way. This emotional charge often prevents us from dealing with money issues rationally and constructively, which helps explain why money is a primary source of anxiety in relationships and life in general.

According to Mellan, there are many different money personality types. There are money hoarders and spenders, worriers and avoiders, planners and dreamers, risk-takers and risk-avoiders, money monks and money amassers, and money mergers and money separatists. Most people are a combination of money types, and each type has good qualities as well as shortcomings.

Opposite money types often meet in a relationship. For example, one partner may tend to save and worry while the other spends excessively. Planners are often married to dreamers, risk-takers to risk-avoiders, money monk (who believe that money is dirty) to money amassers (who believe he who dies with the most money wins). If they didn't start out as opposites, they often become more polarized as they try to balance out the habits of the other. The ways these different types communicate about money can cause hurt, misunderstanding, and chronic conflict within a relationship.

As the world economy goes through increasingly difficult times, anxieties about money can cause people to revert more strongly to type. Money hoarders will tend to save more, whereas spenders will increase their spending. Worriers will worry more, and avoiders will bury their head in the sand even more.

Overspending is a major problem, with 8% of Americans suffering from this addiction. It can jeopardize relationships and leave a person feeling emotionally empty and anxious about the pressure of extreme amounts of debt. Overspenders' spouses also suffer from financial and emotional stress. Mellan offers practical advice to help overspenders and their partners work through the problem as a team.

The Therapy

Mellan identifies seven ways that couples polarize around money issues, and outlines gender differences that affect couple relationships. These couple's polarization dynamics, where couples lock into oppositional modes and attack each other for their differences, are the norm, not the exception, for most couples. For the past 20 years, money has always been on the top two list of marital disharmony or causes for divorce. In our current financial climate, this is bound to get worse, unless couples work to depolarize and move toward what Mellan calls "Money Harmony."

The good news, according to Mellan, is that there are solutions to money problems in a relationship. The key is open, respectful, and loving communication. It's important to share your feelings of loss, disappointment, fears about money, as well as your hopes and dreams, in order to modify your goals together. She offers some key strategies for couples to work together on financial problems:

Key Strategies for Money

- ♥ **Begin by having regular money talks** at times when you are not stressed. At the start of a serious relationship, you should share your money history, what money means to you, and any money secrets – such as hidden debt. Each person should also share his or her vulnerabilities about money in order to understand each other's money personality type. Plan short-, mid-, and long-term goals for your finances, in order to be able to support each other and move forward feeling aligned with each other's hopes and dreams.

- ♥ **Never merge all your money together**. Women especially need some financial independence in order to retain a sense of self. It's important to be able to do things

or make small financial purchases without having to discuss it first with your partner or ask them for money.

♥ **Have a system for joint expenses**. List what each of you thinks should be a joint expense (joint savings, a joint emergency fund) and make contributions according to your income (and assets, if relevant).

♥ **Seek help when needed**. There's no point laying awake at night worrying about money, or about how to tell your partner you've racked up a huge credit card bill. Find expert help from a consumer credit specialist. You may also need to find a good money coach, or therapist who is trained to deal with money conflicts.

One of Mellan's pieces of advice for the spouse of an over spender is to separate some assets in order to give you the space to be supportive and help them through their addiction. Weekly money meetings can help you talk about a spending and saving plan, but it's advisable to never use the word "budget" with an overspender. They will hate it, and it will make them want to rebel and get off the program of financial moderation and balance. "Spending plan" or "financial plan" is usually a much better choice. Also, partners should also expect periodic relapses, which (as with any addiction) can require a great deal of patience and perseverance (from the spender), and love and support (from the partner).

Examples
Dealing with a Shopping Addict
Paul, an over-spender, came in with his very frugal wife Sally. The first thing Mellan taught them was empathetic communication skills. The second skill was the power of practicing the non-habitual. After a few months of working together, he went from being a shopping addict, who was rebellious and loath to talk about money with his wife, to being

openhearted, and willing to take a shopping buddy who wasn't an over-spender along with him, when he needed to shop for something. They got out of debt, and their intimacy deepened.

Many years later, they came back when the husband had slipped and became less vigilant about his tendency to overspend. Part of the ways he did this was to take all his colleagues out to lunch or being an excessively generous gift-giver; he gave his wife expensive gifts she didn't value.

They did another chapter of hard and serious work to deepen their empathetic listening skills and each recommitted to "walking a half-mile in each other's moccasins." She allowed herself to be more of a spender in moderate ways, and he began to save money and spend more responsibly. They kept a spending diary about what they spent and how they felt about it. They revisited their goals. The relationship deepened again, and they were back on the path of couple's marital harmony.

Olivia Mellan Quotes

- *Money Harmony is a process, not a final destination. It involves using money as a tool to accomplish some of life's goals in a way that reflects your values and your integrity. In a couple's relationship, money harmony can deepen and enhance intimacy.*

- *Most of us have powerful feelings about money. These feelings can make it hard for us to arrive at rational decisions about our money and to keep our relationships harmonious when dealing with money.*

- *Like an alcoholic trying to stay sober at a party with heavy drinkers, over-spenders find their resolve to "just say no" continually challenged by their environment – a society where spending is the norm.*

353

- *"Mellan's Law" of Couples' Polarization says that if opposites don't attract right off the bat – and they usually do – then they will become opposites eventually. Each member of the couple needs to acknowledge their secret envies and appreciations of their partner's style – and learn to "walk a half-mile in their partner's moccasins."*

- *There are gender differences around money. Men and women live in two different cultures, and though things are changing, they often change more slowly than we would like. Our task is to develop compassion and deep empathy for each other's burdens, hopes and fears, and to cherish and support each other's goals and dreams. Men and women need to build a bridge so they can move back and forth between each other's worlds.*

Books and Media

- 📖 Olivia Mellan's monthly column, The Psychology of Advice appears in *Investment Advisor*.

- ☐ Mellan has also featured on *Oprah, The TODAY Show*, and *ABC's 20/20*, as well as interviews in publications such as *Money* and *Working Women, US News & World Report, Psychology Today, Money,* and *The New York Times.*

She has published several books in the field of relationships and money, which include:

- 📖 *Money Harmony: Resolving Money Conflicts in Your Life and Relationships*

- 📖 *Money Shy to Money Sure: A Woman's Road Map to Financial Well-Being* (with Sherry Christie)

- 📖 *Overcoming Overspending: A Winning Plan for Spenders and Their Partners* (with Sherry Christie)

- 📖 *Your Money Style: The Nine Attitudes to Money and How They Affect Happiness, Love, Work and Family*

And two books for financial advisors, based on her columns in Investment Advisor Magazine:

📖 *The Advisor's Guide to Money Psychology: Taking the Fear Out of Financial Decision-making* (with Sherry Christie)

📖 *The Client Connection: Helping Advisors Build Bridges That Last* (with Sherry Christie)

📖 Olivia has a chapter in *Peak Vitality*, a 2008 book that includes work from Deepak Chopra, Wayne Dyer, Prince Charles, Alice Walker, Carolyn Myss, and many others. Olivia's chapter is titled *Money Harmony*.

○ Her Audio-CD set; *The Secret Language of Money*, includes CD 1; *Take Charge of Your Money: Mastering Your Money Style*; and CD 2; *Men, Women, and Money: Overcoming Money Conflicts*.

How to Find Out More

🖥 For more information, go to *www.moneyharmony.com*

50. Drs. Lana Holstein & David Taylor

"A mind-body-spirit approach to sexuality"

Background and Qualifications

An expert in sex therapy and women's health with over 30 years experience, Dr. Lana Holstein M.D., helps couples to improve their intimacy and have a fantastic sex life. Her husband of 35 years, David Taylor, M.D., also trained as a specialist in Family Medicine and is certified in the Feldenkrais® Method of somatic education.

After graduating from Stanford University, Dr. Holstein completed her medical training at Yale Medical School, where she met and married her Harvard trained classmate David Taylor. Holstein set up a successful family practice, and then specialized in women's health at Canyon Ranch, working especially with midlife and menopausal health problems. She found there was a void that needed filling in the provision of professional guidance and counseling for couples looking for help to improve their intimacy and sexual relationships.

She began running her successful workshops and retreats with David in the luxurious surroundings of first Canyon Ranch and then Miraval Resort. Their four-day retreat, *Partners, Pleasure, and Passion,* has been a great success for over the past decade with hundreds of couples being helped to achieve a magnificent sex life. The success caught the interests of the producers of the *Oprah Show*, and it became apparent there was a huge unmet need for competent guidance around intimacy and sexuality.

Dr. Taylor left his private practice to join Lana in their mission of bringing soulful, spiritual sexuality to the world, spreading their message through workshops and seminars as well as their books and numerous radio and TV appearances. They now run workshops in conjunction with Terry Real's Relational Life Institute and on their own through their new business, Intimacy Growth Associates.

Relationship Philosophy

Lana and David believe that enabling couples to have a great sex life can renew the sense of vitality and connection in a marriage, and bring back the joy of being together. When we first get together with someone, the electric chemistry and spark of passion is what keeps us excited and interested, but over the years, this can start to disappear. However, according to Dr. Holstein, this is recoverable and can be experienced and even enhanced for year after year.

Their experience is that couples, at whatever age, can increase the passion of lovemaking and depth of intimacy. In their books and workshops, they teach couples to reconnect and discover the pathways to divine sex, through sensual massage, connecting exercises, and sharing their feelings about sex, to create sexual electricity never felt before. Holstein and Taylor believe too many couples compartmentalize sex, seeing it just a small part of their being that involves simply their bodies. By thinking about sex in this way, they are missing out on the full mind, body, and spirit experience of lovemaking that enables couples to feel intimate and join together in a magnificent way.

The Therapy

Drs. Holstein and Taylor combine their years of medical expertise with a mind-body-spirit approach to sexuality within a committed relationship. They take couples through the seven dimensions of sexuality, each stage representing an integral part of our inherent energy and vitality as humans, from basic bodily functions to human emotions and our relationship with spirit. By learning to exchange energy through all seven of the dimensions, couples can achieve a life-long sex life that is fulfilling, spiritual, and intimately fabulous.

The 7 Dimensions of Sexuality

♥ **The Biological Dimension:** the physical and chemical functioning of our bodies through our sexual organs and functions. This dimension has the positive energy of health, whereas the negative energy is that of disease or dysfunction, such as erectile dysfunction.

♥ **The Sensual Dimension:** the energy of pleasure flows through our bodies because of our ability to feel. Stagnation of this energy can be caused when we're always living in our heads, spending too much time planning, evaluating, analyzing, judging, and generally forgetting we have bodies!

♥ **The Desire Dimension:** the feeling of being sexually empowered. Energy here is the power to attract a mate: the power of feeling desire and being desired. The flip side is rejection, which causes a massive energy drain.

♥ **The Heart Dimension:** the energy of committed love and devotion. All too often, we guard our hearts to protect ourselves from abandonment.

♥ **The Intimacy Dimension:** this is the energy of truth and trust. When you first meet a partner, how wonderful does it feel to stay up all night getting to know that new person? The flip side to this is betrayal, perhaps from an affair, or general apathy and disengagement.

♥ **The Aesthetic Dimension:** reveals the inner beauty and quality of the soul and evokes awe and gratitude in our partner. But the energy of this dimension is sucked out by judgment and criticism of our partners and ourselves. We fail to tap into this energy when we live life in routines, oblivious to our partner's beauty and the beauty of the world around us.

♥ **The Ecstatic Dimension:** the energy of the sacred contributes to our sexuality. It is the place where egos dissolve and we have oneness with our beloved. All too often, people think that sex has nothing to do with spirit or is from the world of the profane, but achieving the ecstatic dimension is the highest sexual goal, enabling us to be touched on every level of our existence.

Examples

The Pennies in the Jar!

Holstein and Taylor aim to dispel the myth that after you're together for a while, the romance has to fade. They use the story of the pennies in the jar – it is said that during the first year of marriage, if every time you have sex you put a penny in the jar and from the second year of marriage every time you have sex you take a penny out, you will never empty the jar!

That story is not only a common myth about marriage, but also a common problem as a couple gets used to each other. Often, they end up like roommates because they focus their energy outside the relationship and take each other for granted. However, this is not an inevitable process in marriage. Holstein and Taylor's success with their work demonstrates that couples can, in fact, acquire the skills to keep the passion alive, or restart it by managing sexual energy and passion.

Creating the Whole Relationship Package

On *CBS's Early Show*, Holstein and Taylor were invited to discuss the increasingly common and frustrating (for both men and women) phenomenon of the sexless marriage. CBS followed the story of one couple who attend a Holstein and Taylor workshop at the Miraval Resort in Arizona. Christine and Joe had been married for 8 years, but after having two children and a demanding work life to juggle, their sex life disappeared. It became a once yearly event, with blame passing between the couple as they began to drift apart. Eventually, with the future of their relationship in jeopardy, they spent a week at the retreat where they found an exciting new connection. Through intimate homework assignments and group counseling, they rediscovered that sex could be so much fun, and it brought a new intimacy into their relationship. Christine believes that if

they hadn't gone to the workshop, they wouldn't be together anymore, despite having two children together. They feel their relationship has the whole package now!

Dr. Holstein observes that women often say that they don't want sex because they don't have the energy for it; sex feels like a duty rather than a way to enjoy a deeper connection. She encourages women to turn this belief on its head: sex builds connection and intimacy, and actually gives you more energy!

In their book, *Your Long Erotic Weekend*, Dr. Taylor offers an incredible kissing lesson: the Feldenkrais® way. Of course, everybody already knows how to kiss. But, no matter how good a kisser you fancy yourself, this exercise will help you get a better sense of yourself and lead to a different kind of experience when you kiss. This new awareness will awaken you to incredible new possibilities.

Drs. Holstein and Taylor Quotes

- *Exceptional sex can and should be a repeatable reality for every committed couple.*

- *Great sex is one of the most powerful forces in life; a healing force, as well as a physical vehicle for love, and yet, for far too many, it's a birthright that we never claim.*

- *When two human beings connect their energies skillfully in a relationship, the flow of vitality is magical to experience.*

Books and Media

- ☐ Drs. Holstein and Taylor have appeared on many TV programs, including *NBC Today*, *CBS Early Show*, and *Oprah*.

- ☐ *Magnificent Lovemaking* is an hour-long program that was broadcast across the country as a *PBS* pledge special.

- ○ *Your Long Erotic Evening* is a set of two audio CD's (one for him, one for her) that guides a couple through the first and most crucial of their workshop's intimate "homework" assignments

Their books include:

📖 *Your Long Erotic Weekend – Four Days of Passion for a Lifetime of Magnificent Sex.* This course is based on Dr. Holstein and Dr. Taylor's 4-day workshop. It reveals the secrets of lasting passion and pleasure, shows you how to awaken your sexual self, as well as master the secrets of orgasm. The course includes numerous experiential exercises of guided imagery, breathing, and movement (including the kissing lesson mentioned above), which are available recorded in the authors' own voices on the companion CD of the same name.

📖 *How to Have Magnificent Sex: The Seven Dimensions of a Vital Sexual Connection*

How to Find Out More

💻 Go to Drs. Holstein and Taylor's website: *www.holsteinandtaylor.com*

51. Dr. Jonathan Rich

"How to resolve your financial differences"

Background and Qualifications

Dr. Jon Rich is the author of the book, *The Couple's Guide to Love and Money*, which helps couples resolve one of the primary causes of arguments and divorce – money.

Dr. Rich received a BA from the University of California, San Diego, his M.A. from San Diego State University, and his Ph.D. from the California School of Professional Psychology. He has worked as a licensed psychologist for over 20 years, including working for the Texas Department of Corrections and lecturing in the Counseling Department at California State University, Fullerton from 1990 to 1997.

He has a private practice specializing in psychological testing and works for the Quality Improvement and Program Compliance Division of the Orange County Health Care Agency. It was during his private practice, that Dr. Rich began to see that economic factors were increasingly taking their toll on relationships. A downturn in the economy tends to heat up disagreements about money, and so, Dr. Rich decided to write his book to help couples overcome the number one relationship destroyer and help them to recession-proof their relationship.

Relationship Philosophy

Money is always a volatile topic for couples, according to Dr. Rich, even more so in the current financial climate, with dwindling retirement funds, a beleaguered stock market, and skyrocketing real-estate prices. It's no wonder couples hit crisis points over how to manage their finances.

Yet, while economic volatility at home can intensify arguments about money, at the core of financial relationship disputes is the conflict of financial personalities. Dr. Rich believes that everyone has a particular financial personality which influences their choice of lifestyle, financial risk tolerance, and willingness to accept financial help from outside sources. When different financial personalities get together, sparks can fly.

The 6 Financial Personalities

1) **Spartan** – this group will spend hours comparing prices or making any purchase over $50. They will pay off their credit card every month, and may be described as frugal. They will only take on smart debt, such as mortgages, and have a tendency to scrimp on important purchases that may have financial consequences long term.

2) **Monarch** – this group will treat themselves to special luxuries such as expensive coffee and manicures. They will always choose the upgraded version and have a tendency to get into debt.

3) **Banker** – this group tends to keep all their savings in a bank account, and is conservative and careful with cash.

4) **Gambler** – they will take risks for a better future and think nothing of investing retirement money in stocks.

5) **Homesteader** – it has usually been years since they looked at a bank statement, because they like to let someone else worry about their bills and investments.

6) **Pioneer** – they are incredibly good at creating an income and wealth, but often make money decisions without consulting their partners. They tend to find it difficult to share financial decisions and usually handle the bills and checkbooks.

Past experiences can help determine financial personalities. These ghosts from the financial past can dictate how a person manages their money and communicates with their partner about finances.

The Therapy

The way to resolve money disputes is to understand how money personalities clash and create these conflicts. It's important for each person in a relationship to identify their financial personality and aim to merge them together. This can be done through effective communication about money, learning to negotiate difficult financial topics, and achieving joint financial goals to create a secure financial future free from excessive debt.

6 Reasons Couples Fight About Money

- ✓ **How** to spend money
- ✓ **Where** money should come from. This could be which person should earn the most, whether they should accept help from parents, or the government.
- ✓ **Security versus taking risks** – people have a different tolerance for risk
- ✓ **The importance of careers** – where and how we work can have a major impact on the quality and happiness of our lives, yet, changing careers could put a financial burden on our families
- ✓ **Family roles** – problems arise when couples disagree about the male/female roles
- ✓ **Trust** – if one person has made bad decisions about money in the past, this affects the trust in a relationship. Or trust can be affected by one person's own bad experiences with money

The key area in Dr. Rich's therapy is learning to focus on long-term goals you have in common. For example, this may be agreeing that you want to buy a house in a year. You would then plan day-to-day finances and realistically work together as a team. Deciding on a future financial path together and how you want to get there, allows you to share a common dream. Will you be frugal now so that you can afford luxury later? Will you have a moderate life now and later? This shared vision allows a team effort towards a common goal.

Another important step is to understand that your partner's behavior with money is not always about you or your relationship. For example, if your partner is frugal, this doesn't mean they don't care about you. Likewise, if they are frivolous with money, this doesn't mean they don't care about your future. They probably developed their financial style long before they met you. Understanding this will help to prevent you from reacting with needless anger.

Examples
Thinking her way to a Better Life

Stella was raised in a large family, and the only way for her to get attention was when she had a problem. Her dysfunctional belief was "If I look pitiful, and I have problems, people will help me." As an adult, Stella was always complaining to anyone who would listen. People would play social worker for her, helping her out, offering her advice, and trying to fix her life.

She had many advantages from acting weak, but was blinded to the long-term costs of acting this way. Once Stella saw that her acting weak cost her $500 per month in lost income, her self-respect, and some good friends, she was ready to adopt new, more functional thoughts. From these new thoughts, she came up with small, concrete actions that she could do to bring her changes into reality. Although acting with more responsibility initially threatened those around her who were used to helping her, she was able to stick with her changes, and the positive ways it made her feel.

I Deserve the Best Lifestyle

Keith was born lucky. His parents were both professionals and he was never wanting for anything. His father often said to him, "Don't be cheap. You get what you pay for." Keith's

dysfunctional belief was "I deserve a certain lifestyle, and I will spend money to maintain that lifestyle, even if I don't have it." When Keith finished law school at 25, he was living in a penthouse overlooking the city, had impeccable clothes, drove a nice car, and had a stunningly attractive girlfriend. His parents boasted about their successful son. However, he soon maxed out his credit cards and was having sleepless nights about making the rent and car payments. When he didn't pass the bar exam on the first try, he became desperate.

Keith's girlfriend had $10,000 put away to finish college. When Keith saw the money, he cajoled her into letting him invest in a "hot stock tip." The $10,000 turned into $12,000, and he was elated. Then, they watched as the stock went to $9,000, $5,000, $2,000, and eventually to nothing. His girlfriend left him; he was devastated; he had no money and no prospect.

Keith loved the benefits of this dysfunctional belief: people loved being around him, he felt successful, and more confident. However, the disadvantages ultimately outweighed the advantages: it costs $4000 more per month than his friends spent, the kind of people who are attracted to his money didn't necessarily value Keith as a person, and he felt like a fraud. He found ways to look successful professionally, without spending so much money personally. He got a roommate and traded in his car for something much less expensive. He even paid back the money he lost in the stock market.

Dr. Jonathan Rich Quotes

- *Nothing is more personal than money.*
- *Put two people together with different ideas about money, and you have a sure formula for disagreement.*
- *Working out the financial differences between you and your partner is not easy. It takes the skill of an attorney, psychologist, and salesperson rolled into one.*

- *Keep in mind that you and your partner function as a team. Even if you win an argument, you've still lost, because you've chipped away at the relationship.*
- *Big, surprising, and exciting things can happen when you work together with someone else.*

Books and Media

- He has been quoted and featured in many major publications, including Publishers Weekly, Self-Help Psychology Magazine, Cosmopolitan, New York Daily News, Men's Health, and More Magazine.
- Dr. Rich's book, *The Couple's Guide to Love and Money*, was released in 2003.

How to Find Out More

- For more information, go to *www.moneyworkbook.com*

About the Author

The Relationship Doctor, Scott Braxton, Ph.D. MBA

Co-founder of Excellent Communications, LLC, a company dedicated to providing leading edge communication technology. Scott has a Ph.D. in Biochemistry and an MBA in leadership. He has held scientific and leadership positions in some of the most well-known biotechnology companies in the San Francisco Bay Area for the last 20 years, companies such as Genentech, Incyte, Synteni, ACLARA, Gorilla Genomics, Gene Logic, GeneGo, and Thompson Reuters. He helped take two companies public for $100+ million dollars each, and one to be sold for $83 million dollars. He has taught at or consults for universities and biotechnology and pharmaceutical companies.

"I was married for 10 years and have two beautiful daughters. When the marriage ended, I was bitter and resentful. I played the blame and shame game and basically cut my ex-wife off from the children and me. I thought it was much better that way.

"When I started dating again, I was exposed transformational workshops, and began to realize I was responsible for how I acted and the meanings I interpreted in my marriage. After taking a few of these courses, I reconciled with my ex-wife. We are not together as a couple, but we communicate easily and work together to bring up our two children.

"As I grew older, I was having more and more trouble in my intimate relationships. I had been giving up more and more of myself to try to get the love I wanted. When my second long-term relationship ended, I was devastated and felt like a failure. Fortunately, I sought coaching, and was introduced to the teaching of David Deida. I learned to own my manhood, find my purpose, and live it. I started understanding how essential polarity is in a relationship and how to stay myself if my partner was angry or testing me to see if I could be trusted. I also had to resolve my own shame about having desires, and had to deal with self-esteem issues.

Once I got my life back on track, I became a coach and began studying everything I could about communication and relationships. I became a certified hypnotherapist, certified NLP Practitioner and Master Practitioner, Master Results Coach and a Performance Consultant certified to practice Neurological Re-Patterning®, Advanced Neurological Re-Patterning®, and started helping others to live the life they always wanted.

As I worked with couples and singles, I would be introduced to experts I had never heard about before. I realized that it would be essential to study these experts in depth, since I wanted to provide maximum value to my clients. The study evolved into this book. However, this is not the end of the quest for knowledge, but only a new beginning.

A brief chapter can only say so much about an expert. After all, it took them several books to say what they had to say. One could probably spend three years studying just one expert. My hope is that you have gotten a flavor for what these experts have to say and how it applies to you, or how you can use this information to help others. You may have noticed certain patterns that emerge and are common. You will want to take your time and study the experts who most speak to you.

Namaste,
Scott Braxton

Dr. Scott Braxton

"Experience and express the love you have"

We all need love and each other. We all want to be loved as we are, *and* we have a desire to grow and evolve. For most of us, we tend to gauge how valuable and lovable we are by how loved ones treat us. This instinct started in childhood, when we felt loved when we were paid attention to, and when we blamed ourselves for our parent's bad mood or anger. Children of divorced parents often think they are at fault, no matter how much they are told otherwise.

In love, we are often attracted to someone who reminds us of our family of origin, so we feel safe and "at home." If we had a cold and distant father, someone who is cold and distant will seem comfortable. If your mother was caring and attentive, you will think caring and attentive is love. If one of your parents was strict and verbally abusive, then verbal abuse will seem like an expression of love. Some people are *definitely* not interested in someone like their parent, and look for opposite traits.

What was it that first attracted you to a lover? Was it just that they paid attention to you, or was there something more about them that fascinated you?

Think back to when you romanced someone. Who did you think you had to be in order to 'win' that other person? What were you willing to do and what did you think you had to keep hidden? Sure, it was fun, but at what cost?

Once you were in relationship, were you afraid to show parts of yourself at certain times? Did you feel cut-off from your 'real self' in certain situations? Did you worry that they may not love you if they really knew who you were? Did the habits that initially attracted you, subsequently cause you to become annoyed as the relationship developed?

In this type of relationship, we become aware that our partner pays attention to us, and loves us best, when we are attending to their needs, wants, and desires. Perhaps we get better at this, for a while. But, have you ever noticed that we tend to not trust the love we receive if we have to work hard for it? We also seem to love our partner best when they are fulfilling our needs, and so our love is conditional. This type of love is great for romantics, but lacks a certain depth of intimacy and authenticity.

Romantic love is this feeling of intense, but unwarranted attachment to a lover. It is often fueled by hormones and is not what real love is all about. This grand passion may have more to do with patterns laid down in early childhood and unmet childhood needs, than who the other person is. It has been said that early-stage romantic love is one of the greatest barriers to mature love, because it feels so good.

So what happens when the other person fails to meet some of your needs? Many of the people I work with complain that their partner no longer does the things they used to do, when the relationship just started. Much like the song, "You don't bring me flowers, anymore," we get attached to "the way things used to be." When someone notices a lack of attentiveness, they usually decide something's wrong – either with themselves or with the other person. Typical reactions are to withdraw or attack. Women tend to want to "talk about it" which can be seen as a sort of attack, and men tend to withdraw, not knowing what else to do. A vicious cycle often ensues where the man seems distant, and the woman's desire to talk about it causes the man to withdraw, which drives the woman crazy, which causes her to demand to talk about it, which causes…

Many people believe their relationship would be happier if their partner would change. If only she didn't complain so much; if only he would pay more attention; if only she was as interested in sex as she was in the beginning; if he would just show his emotions; the list goes on and on.

371

However, this is true only from a 'victim' viewpoint. People are programmed to replay past hurt or disappointment. We unconsciously transfer old pain onto new relationships. By learning to take care of yourself, you can avoid power struggles and be open to the learning your partner offers you. Then you will actually be 'in relationship' with what is, and with the other person. If you think about it, we are rarely really in relationship with another person, but rather, we relate to a projection we have of the other person. We either pretend they are perfect and have some qualities we admire, or we notice all their flaws, that if only they would change those characteristics, they would make us happier.

A great question to ask is, "Am I getting enough in this relationship to make it worthwhile to let go of what I am not getting?" Really answer this question yes or no. Everyone has needs that do not get met in marriage. This is not tragic unless one focuses on the unmet needs and begins building a path of resentment based on entitlement and victim mentality. If you focus on what you are not getting in your relationship, your mate will give you even less, and thereby 'justify' your bitterness, and eventual desertion. The greatest relationship killer is the way one thinks about one's partner. Toxic thinking patterns kill trust, erode intimacy, and cripple communication.

If your relationship is suffering, look inside first and ask, "What in me has caused my relationship to suffer?" Also ask, "Why am I viewing my relationship as difficult?" Often, you will find that the meaning you add to your partner's communication or action is causing you to feel tight and constricted. What are you assuming about their motives that would have you be suspicious, and withdraw love? Are you viewing their comments as an attack on your character or ability? Have you already made decisions about them that have you retreat and keep yourself separate? Conflict often comes either from not getting your needs met, or from a 'mental con' where you tell yourself things that aren't true, and these distorted thoughts become a self-fulfilling prophecy. Humans tend to filter, distort, over-generalize, dwell on the negative, label, blame, and jump to conclusions. Realize that your ego's job is to defend yourself, and it will look for attacks where none really exist.

You can eradicate the sting of any painful thought or point of view by asking Byron Katie's four simple questions: Is it true? Can you know for certain it's true? Who are you when you believe that thought? Who would you be without that thought?

If you feel you *are* getting enough in this relationship to make it worthwhile, make a list of the things you get in this relationship and who you get to be when the relationship is working. Then, stop whining, complaining, criticizing, and acting like a victim, and start embracing the other person. Have an actual relationship. You will be amazed at the transformation in your relating when you stop talking with your friends about what's wrong, and only talk about what you are enjoying. Start focusing on the details of your partner, in the here and now. How are they standing, breathing, talking? What are they really saying and feeling? Really pay attention and accept your partner so you can appreciate and cherish them. What you focus on expands.

Couples benefit by focusing on their relationship as a priority. If you let the relationship drift, you will be lost at sea, and eventually abandon ship, only to repeat the process with someone else. Couples need to be intentional, committed, and to take responsibility to make things better. Find things to do that make you feel great, and do those things together. Create shared experiences and memories together because these are the things that create loving bonds. Build up your emotional love bank of fun and connection.

Most couples wait until it seems that the relationship is lost before they seek help. Instead, it would benefit couples immensely to discover communication skills before they are needed. Enlist professional help. Invest as much in learning

about relating as you do in golf or tennis lessons, cable TV, gadgets, clothes, or a vacation.

What if you discovered the treasure of feeling all your feelings – facing what you have previously been afraid to look at, and speaking your truth from a place of responsibility and creativity? Could you become aware of the negative, critical, or demanding comments you make to your partner, and the impact on the energy of your relationship? Are you prepared to uncover your own personal Demon Dialog, and be able to instantly halt the negative pattern and re-establish a deeper connection? Are you willing to become skilled at really listening to your partner in such a way that they will feel validated and understood? That way, there is a possibility of moving smoothly through the suspicion and conflict that seems to pervade human existence, and into a space of commitment and share communication we all desire.

You probably know that men and women communicate differently and have different needs and desires in relationship. Neither point of view is 'wrong' and failure to acknowledge and validate these differences will lead to great difficulty and a lot of unnecessary stress. For some women, fear of isolation and abandonment is the greatest dread. For many men, the shame of failure and the loss of status cause the greatest anxiety. Many women want more affection and intimacy in their relationship, and some men have a desire for more sexual expression and fulfillment. However, both partners need to feel connected and important to the other, and for things to be easy.

Men thrive on praise. Let him do things for you, and praise him for it and he will shine. On the other hand, if you are miserable, he feels like a failure. This is nearly intolerable for a man, and he will do anything to avoid this feeling, including blaming you. He may even put the relationship in jeopardy by having an affair to avoid those feelings. You must know that a man does not fall in love with his mistress, but rather with the way he feels about himself when he is with her. If you provide that feeling to your man, he will never look for it elsewhere.

Women need to feel safe, secure, protected, nurtured, and adored. A woman can flow in radiance and abundance when she feels taken care of. When a woman doesn't feel safe, she drops out of her feminine and starts to take care of herself. It is important for the man to make his partner feel important, special, attractive, intelligent, wanted, and needed as often as possible. Provide this for your woman, and she will be happy and fulfilled.

Gary Chapman talks about the five languages of love: quality time, affirmations, gifts, acts of service, and physical touch. Each of us has a dominant language we speak when expressing love and receiving love. Imagine if you became determined to provide love in your partner's language. Your partner might be able to fully feel the love you have for them.

Transitioning from romantic or conditional love to mature love takes real effort: effort that you need to know is worthwhile. You may be curious what is on the other side to be willing to do the work this takes. This transition could involve significant conflict. These places of conflict are actually points to grow and heal. Without these challenges, one would not be able to develop and evolve. Intimate relationships offer the greatest challenges and are the most powerful arena for emotional and spiritual growth. It is not conflict, per se, that destroys relationships, but rather how one handles that conflict. When negative emotions run high, intelligence is low. When we become angry or enraged, we lose perspective, and often, the intent becomes to hurt the other person as much as we are hurting.

When this happens, safety and connection are lost, and both people move into survival mode – the lowest level of the Maslow's hierarchy of needs. There is no possibility of feeling safe or comfortable, much less having your psychological needs met. Self-actualization, one of the higher levels on the hierarchy

of needs, and one of the promises of a healthy relationship, is completely lost in these moments.

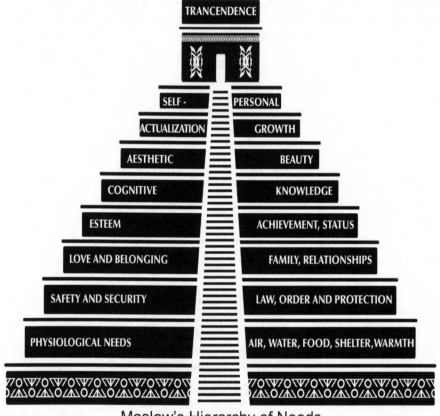

Maslow's Hierarchy of Needs

Granted that some unfortunate people live in a war-torn area where their safety is literally at stake every day. Some people have lost their livelihood and are unwillingly homeless. Some people have lived with severe physical and emotional abuse their whole lives, and do not know anything else. These people are stuck in survival mode.

However, for most people, true freedom and happiness come as you realize that peace, love, and security are an inside job. These feelings come from a mindset, rather than any particular outside circumstances. When you discover how to take care of yourself, when you give up the focus on what you don't have, you can become grateful for what you do have.

One of the best ways to take care of yourself, and your relationship, is to stop destructive arguments as soon as possible. This does not mean to avoid conflict; conflict is inevitable. It also does not mean to block feeling fear, pain, or anger. These are legitimate signals that something is going on for you, and should definitely be paid attention to and learned from, just not acted out. It does mean to avoid the heavy negative emotions of blame and shame. Use pattern interrupts to change the emotional state to something more productive. Take a walk outside, dance with your partner, or use a pre-arranged comical phrase to pull you both out of the emotional gutter. Talk about something that is unarguable – your own internal state and feelings. This can be vulnerable, and you may find that this vulnerability leads to deeper connection.

Use authentic conflict as a point to get curious about the other person and their world. Use the conflict to examine your long-held beliefs or behavior patterns that may no longer be serving you. Using Margaret Paul's Inner Bonding process, you can feel the pain this conflict causes, and have the intention to learn from it. Really have a conversation with your wounded and core self to discover what is causing your pain. When you ask for guidance from your Higher Self, you move beyond your false beliefs, and can take loving actions towards yourself and others, healing your pain, anger, and shame.

You could actually use your relationship as a path to spiritual freedom. This is one of the promises of mature love. Another, often overlooked dimension is the potential for sacred sexual union that is a truly transformative force; a force that can yield radical intimacy, bursting open our hearts and penetrating the boundaries of our individual ego to reveal the Mystery of Existence itself. Sacred sex can be a path and an expression of spiritual enlightenment. If you exude a happy and fulfilled life,

others will naturally want to be part of that. The only price you have to pay: you get to be happy, as a conscious, creative act.

If you have a shared goal of creating happiness for yourself, and providing the space for happiness and growth to flourish in your partner, you will have something greater to live into than your day-to-day problems. This goal will call you into being the greater self you always suspected you could be. This gives you a future worth living into. You will find yourself putting this into practice by creating daily rituals of connection and coming from a sense of fondness and admiration. You will naturally want to show your love in unique ways, keeping the spark of intimacy and desire alive.

Perhaps the greatest paradox of relationship is this: you cannot experience deep spiritual connection with another until you love yourself, AND you cannot love yourself until you experience the love of a deep spiritual connection. As you ponder this situation, notice if you can see a spiral of loving yourself enough to risk a spiritual connection, which can feed your self-love to allow deeper spiritual connection. How deep can you go?

Acknowledgements

Thousands of hours of research and writing went into the preparation of this manuscript. I want to thank my assistant, Catherine Jeans. She is a freelance writer, journalist, and TV producer from the UK. Specializing in self-help, nutrition, and natural well-being, she has written for the national and international press, as well as editing and producing many network TV programs in the UK. She has interviewed and worked with many high profile experts, particularly in the field of relationships. Her connections and intimate knowledge in this field were immensely helpful.

I would like to thank all of the people I have ever been in relationship with, because you have taught me about love and about myself. Anytime I felt wounded, it was an opportunity for me to look inside and heal a part of myself. Most of the time, I was not mature enough to do that. Instead I would argue and blame, and for that, I apologize. Although I wish I did better, I would not trade a single event.

To Lyn, my ex-wife, I am sorry for the pain I caused you unknowingly, and the pain I caused you because I was too unaware of my own wounded inner child. I strived to be perfect for you because I thought that was the only way to get the love I wanted. Instead, I was inauthentic and demanding. I am so grateful that we have mended our relationship, and I know that we will be in partnership as long as we both shall live. I can count on you in so many ways. Thank you.

To my daughters, Cara and Charlotte; know that you have taught me to slow down, to be present, and to have patience. I love you both and want the world for you. In my haste to teach you all I have learned, I sometimes do not listen as well as you would like. I am a work in progress; I am constantly learning and growing with your needs. I hope you do not have to learn all of your lessons first hand, and that books like this one will

give you the best possible foundation for an incredibly happy life.

To my amazing Sweetheart Lavender, thank you for your joyful commitment to growth and communication. We constantly find areas for challenge and healing, I am delighted to find comfort and security in your persistent dedication to loyalty, love and connection. As Jack Nicholson said in the movie *As Good as It Gets*, "You make me want to be a better man."

My mother often quoted Nietzsche, "That which doesn't kill you, makes you stronger." Thanks Mom! I have so enjoyed the conversations about love and relationships we have had over the years. Your constant learning has inspired me to keep learning. You taught me to take responsibility for what happens to me and for my own feelings. It is a lesson that has taken a lifetime to sink in. Please know that it was worth it. My father taught me about integrity: staying true to myself, and always doing my best, no matter if the external reward is lacking.

Finally, I would like to thank the Spirit that moves within all of us. If we ever want to experience true, unconditional love, all we have to do is really reach inside and be in touch with this Source. Whether it is externalized as God, Jesus, Allah, Divine Spirit, guardian angel, spirit animal, Universal Source, or internalized as soul, spirit, higher self, or Buddha nature; whether through prayer, meditation, journaling, or dreaming; access to unconditional love is only a thought away. I have had many moments when I (as an ego) disappeared, and Source was allowed to flow through me. I am awestruck during these moments. I know that you have had these moments as well, and I hope you are learning to trust them.

Namaste,

Scott Braxton

BONUS TOOLKIT

FREE - From the Experts Themselves

Visit:

http://www.ExcellentRelationships.com/LoveBookBonuses.html

Free Bonus by Byron Katie
- ☺ Judge Your Neighbor Workbook
- ☺ The One Belief at a Time Workbook

Free Bonus by Dr. John Gray
- ☺ Romance Planner

Free Bonus by Dr. Barry McCarthy
- ☺ Is There Sex After Marriage?
- ☺ What is the Right Couple Sexual Style for You?

Free Bonus by Dr. Gary Chapman
- ☺ What is Your Love Language?

Free Bonus by Drs. Gay and Kathlyn Hendricks
- ☺ Seven Magic Moves for Relationship Harmony
- ☺ How to Get Free of Jealousy in Your Close Relationships

Free Bonus by Michael Webb, "Mr. Romantic"
- ☺ 101 Romantic Ideas

Free Bonus by Dr. Margaret Paul
- ☺ Inner Bonding Program – 7 day eCourse

Free Bonus by Drs. Charles and Elizabeth Schmitz
- ☺ The Marriage Quiz

Free Bonus by Dr. David Richo
- ☺ Human Becoming eBook

Free Bonus by Dr. Sue Johnson
- ☺ Hold Me Tight (Excerpt)

Free Bonus by Dr. Jeffrey Bernstein
- ☺ Why Can't You Read My Mind (Preview)

Free Bonus by Ellen Kreidman
- ☺ 10 Ways to Light His Fire
- ☺ 10 Ways to Light Her Fire

Free Bonus by Dr. Willard Harley
- ☺ The Most Important Emotional Needs
- ☺ How to Survive Infidelity

...Plus Dozens More!

49390547R00233

Made in the USA
Charleston, SC
24 November 2015